Michigan's Story

by David B. McConnell

a condensed version
based on the award-winning
Forging the Peninsulas
those wishing more details please read the original text

selected art by

T. L. Deeter
David B. McConnell
Tim M. Pickell
George L. Rasmussen

cover design by
David B. McConnell

digital preparation of the cover by
T. L. Deeter

We dedicate this edition in memory of
Martha Powers
for her assistance in preparing
the teacher's guide

Hillsdale Educational Publishers

Made In Michigan

> *Forging the Peninsulas*
> by David B. McConnell was the winner of the
> Award of Merit by the Historical Society of Michigan

© 1996, 2002 David B. McConnell

Hillsdale Educational Publishers, Inc.
39 North Street
P.O. Box 245
Hillsdale, Michigan
517-437-3179

08 07 06 05 04 03 02 — 9 8 7 6 5 4

Library of Congress Cataloging in Publication Data

McConnell, David B. (David Barry), 1949-
    Michigan's story / by David B. McConnell ; a condensed version based on the award-winning "Forging the Peninsulas" ; selected art by Theresa L. Deeter, David B. McConnell, Tim M. Pickell, George L. Rasmussen.
        p.   cm.
    Includes bibliographical references and index.
    ISBN 0-910726-85-X (hardcover).
    1. Michigan--History--Juvenile literature.   I. Title.
F566.3.M35   1995
977.4--dc20
                                                                95-493
                                                                 CIP
                                                                 AC

2002 edition ISBN 0-910726-48-5 hardcover only

Acknowledgments

No book is the work of a single person. It is the product of many hands, both directly and indirectly. First, I thank my mother who has worked with me for many years and on many projects. Without her patient support and ability, I doubt this book or many of my others would ever have been completed.

Next, I thank those who work in the archives, libraries, and museums I have visited. You certainly helped to make this book possible. Special thanks to: Nancy Bartlett, Bentley Historical Library University of Michigan and to John Curry, Michigan State Archives.

Thanks to the helpful staff of the Mitchell Public Library in Hillsdale.
Appreciation to Terri Carr for her assistance in condensing the original material.

Without the many teachers throughout the state who tirelessly promote Michigan and its history there would be no need for *Michigan's Story*. I am grateful for the many helpful comments and ideas they have so willingly shared.

Very special thanks to Ed Bonne and Eric Keiber for taking time from busy schedules to provide valuable advice.

◻

On the Cover ....

Michigan's Story is really about the millions of men and women who built this state and made it what it is today. A few of these people are pictured on the cover.

top row: Rebecca Shelly- peace activist, Major Henry Gladwin- British commander at
    Detroit, Charlotte Kawbawgam- Native American
middle row: a hunter of the Huron tribe, Sojourner Truth, Father Frederick Baraga
bottom row: Kinchen Artis- Civil War soldier, James McDivitt- astronaut, unknown
    pilot from the Women's Airforce Service Pilots– World War II
(for photo credits refer to the index and see the same photos in the book)

◻

About the Author

Each of us has fond memories of our very young days. I can remember joining my parents at educational exhibits when I was barely taller than the top of the table. This was my introduction to educational materials and meeting thousands of teachers over the years that followed. Intertwined were the smiles and handshakes from various authors I met. In my youth I had no thoughts of becoming a writer myself. My inclinations took me into the wonders of science and even a brief career in medical research. But history has always been a delight for me and for the last 25 years I have worked to write and develop books which help a new generation to feel the excitement of the past- in particular the excitement of a very interesting part of the world- Michigan! I hope I can blow a spark into the minds of young readers so their imaginations will glow with all the possibilities of Michigan's thrilling past, present, and future!

Writings: *Explore Michigan A to Z* 1993. *Forging the Peninsulas: Michigan is Made* 1989, 1994, & 2001. *A Little People's Beginning on Michigan* 1982, 2002. *Michigan Activity Masters* 1985 & 1999. *A Puzzle Book for Young Michiganians* 1982. *Discover Michigan* 1981. *A Little People's Beginning on Michigan* 1980. *Our Michigan Adventure* 1998, 2001, 2002 and the questions used in *Computer Games on Michigan* 1996, 2002.

Awards: Award of Merit from the Historical Society of Michigan for *Forging the Peninsulas*, 1990. Michigan Product of the Year, Greater Michigan Foundation, non-consumer division, for *Discover Michigan,* 1982. Listed in *Michigan Authors* 1993 and the 2002 on-line edition.

Contents

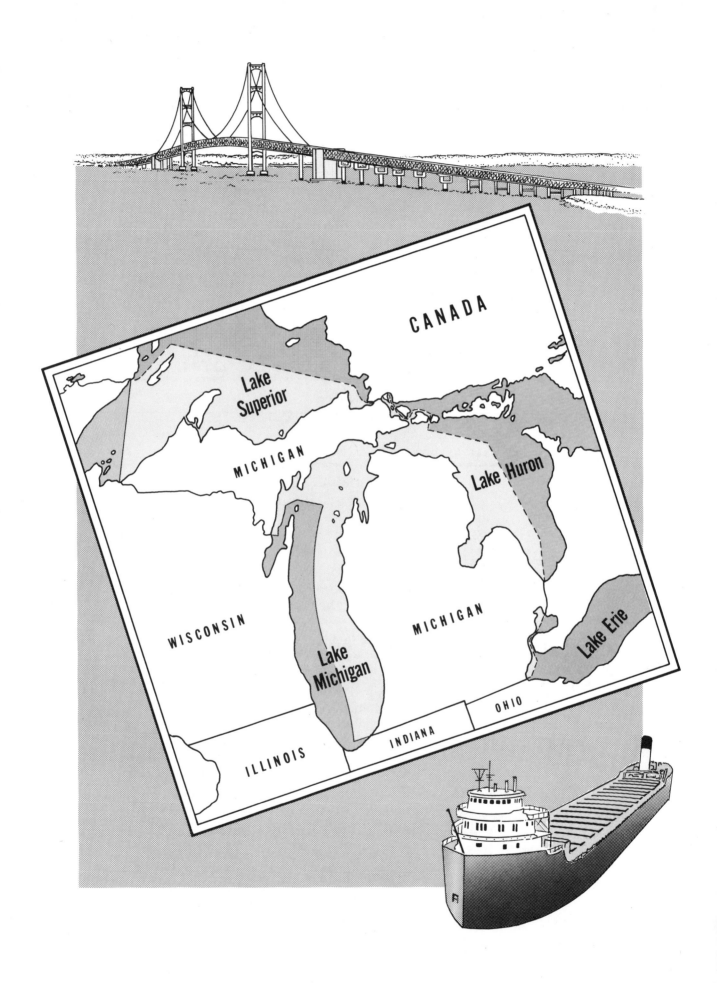

CANADA

Lake
Superior

MICHIGAN

Lake Huron

WISCONSIN

Lake
Michigan

MICHIGAN

Lake Erie

OHIO

ILLINOIS

INDIANA

Meet Michigan!

Chapter 1 Section 1

The Basics

Learn about the size and location of Michigan, its people and major cities.

We Are Unique!

A quick glance at any map shows Michigan is unique. Why? Because it is the only state made of two *peninsulas. A peninsula is a portion of land nearly surrounded by water.* This is the only state on the mainland of the United States which is divided by water. The water of the Straits of Mackinac (MAC in aw) once kept the people apart. The Mackinac Bridge now connects the Upper and Lower Peninsulas.

What else is unusual about Michigan? Take another look at the map. This state is in the center of several large freshwater lakes known as the Great Lakes.

The Great Lakes & Us

These huge lakes are tied to our past, present, and future. They cradle Michigan and give it a unique shape. Michigan has the longest coastline of any state except Alaska! Michigan's 3,000 miles of coastline borders on four of the five Great Lakes. They are Lakes Huron, Michigan, Erie, and Superior. Which Great Lake does not touch Michigan? It is Lake Ontario. An easy way to remember the names of all five Great Lakes is to take the first letter of each and spell HOMES. The Great Lakes are quite important because they hold one-fifth of the world's supply of fresh water.

Even the name Michigan relates to the Great Lakes. It comes from the Native American words for great or big lake. Michi, or mishi, means great quantity. Gami is one word for lake. Over the years these different words were combined and the spelling changed until, finally, the word Michigan was officially used in 1805.

The Great Lakes even affect Michigan's climate. Winds from the west are warmed as they pass over the Lakes in the winter and are cooled by them in the summer. Moisture is picked up by the winds as they pass over the water and this gives extra rain and snow to some areas.

The St. Lawrence River (St. stands for Saint) carries water from the Great Lakes downhill to the Atlantic Ocean. This is the only way for water to leave the Great Lakes! The St. Lawrence River also allows ships from the ocean to reach Michigan. Michigan has ports (cities next to the water) which receive ships from many foreign countries.

Michigan- How Big? How High?

The land of Michigan covers over 58,000 square miles. Michigan spans quite a distance corner to corner. The western tip of the Upper Peninsula is as far west as St. Louis, Missouri. The eastern edge of the Lower Peninsula is directly north of Tampa, Florida. Michigan is even larger than several foreign countries including Greece and Nicaragua. On the other hand, it is smaller than England or France.

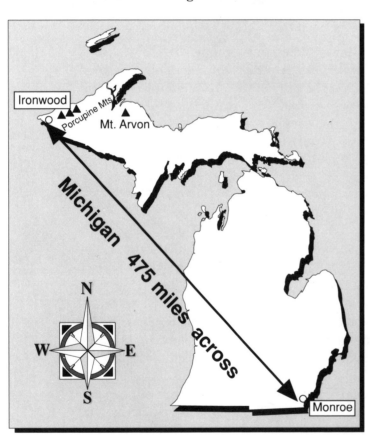

Which peninsula is larger? The Lower Peninsula is. It has about three-fourths of the land area. Much of the land there is gently rolling hills.

The Upper Peninsula has higher places, especially in the west. Mt. Curwood and nearby Mt. Arvon are both nearly 1,980 feet above sea level. The Porcupine Mountains are another high point. But Michigan has nothing as high as the Rocky Mountains. Most of the state is between 500 and 1,000 feet above sea level.

Finding Michigan- Where Are We?

Where exactly is Michigan? It can be spotted easily on a map by looking for the Great Lakes. But, let's be more precise. There is a sign north of Traverse City which shows where 45 degrees north *latitude* crosses Michigan. This spot is exactly halfway between the equator and the North Pole. *Latitude is a measurement going north and south from the equator. If you*

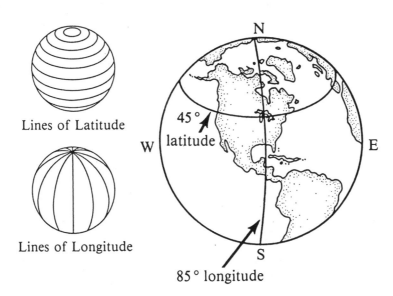

Lines of Latitude

Lines of Longitude

45° latitude

85° longitude

look on a globe or map of the world you will see lines of latitude. In a sense, they are like the rungs of a ladder, going across the globe or map.

Another line, 83 degrees west *longitude*, passes near Detroit. *Longitude is a measurement going east or west from a city in England. This city has been given the location zero (0) degrees longitude and everything else is measured from there. You can see these lines which connect the North and South Poles on the globe.*

Compare the latitude and longitude of Detroit with other places in the world. Detroit is at about 43 degrees north latitude. An imaginary trip to the east, along the line 43 degrees north latitude goes a bit north of Rome, Italy, and eventually crosses northern Japan. If you follow the 83 degrees west longitude line to the south, you pass through Central America, finally ending in the Pacific Ocean off the coast of Peru!

Michigan's Big Neighbor

People often forget Michigan is next to another country, Canada. Bridges and a highway tunnel con-

The Canadian flag

nect Michigan to Canada since all of the boundary between us is water. Three rivers form this border at the nearest crossings. The Detroit River is between Detroit, Michigan and Windsor, Ontario; the St. Clair River is between Port Huron, Michigan, and Sarnia, Ontario; and the St. Mary's River is between Sault Ste. Marie, (Soo Saint ma REE) Michigan, and Sault Ste. Marie, Ontario. Ontario is the Canadian *province* next to Michigan. *A province is much like a state in the United States.*

There is considerable trade between Michigan and Canada. Products made on either side of the border are often sold on the other side. Canada and the United States have more trade between them than any other two countries in the world.

Michigan's People

One of the most exciting things concerning a state is learning about its people. Each of us and the things we do are a little part of Michigan's history. In the beginning this was the land of the Native Americans, the first Michiganians.

Today, Michigan is a mixture of over 20 ethnic groups. As a matter of fact, Michigan has more *ethnic groups* than almost any other state! *An ethnic group is one based on race or place of origin. People in the same ethnic group have similar customs.* These people have come from the far corners of the world.

How has this affected the makeup of our people? If a survey were made of everyone living in the state, it would show the largest ethnic group is German. The second largest group has ancestors from England. Those from Africa come in third with about 13 percent of the population. The Polish are

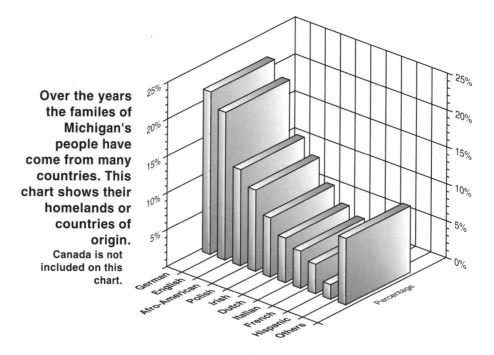

Over the years the familes of Michigan's people have come from many countries. This chart shows their homelands or countries of origin. Canada is not included on this chart.

the next largest group and there are many more groups as well. Each has brought its own special culture with it.

Michigan is the eighth largest state in population with over 9,900,000. The people, however, are not evenly distributed. Most live in the southern third of the Lower Peninsula. In fact, just three counties have 41 percent of the whole population! They are Wayne, Oakland, and Macomb. Comparing the combined population of these three counties to the number of people living in some states is interesting. Thirty-six states have smaller populations than this three county area! Obviously, these counties influence much of what happens in Michigan.

Eighty Three Counties

Michigan has 83 counties. Each is an area of land, usually shaped like a square. Keweenaw County is farthest north. Marquette County has the most land. Benzie County is the smallest in size and is about one-sixth the

© 1989 Hillsdale Educational Publishers

Michigan's 83 counties

size of Marquette County. It is a good idea to know in which county you live and the counties next to it.

Just what is a *county? It is a unit of state government.* Having counties is one of the ideas brought to this country by the early pioneers. A state is usually a large area and it is hard to be in touch with all the people. Counties make it easier to govern.

Each county has its own county seat, almost like a state capital. A courthouse is at the county seat. The courthouse has a court and several offices to keep county records. Each of you will have information about yourself kept at the courthouse! Birth and death records are kept there. When real estate (a home, a farm, an office building, etc.) is sold, records known as deeds are filed in the courthouse. These records are used to see who will pay property taxes and how much they owe. When you decide to marry, you must go to the courthouse to get a marriage license.

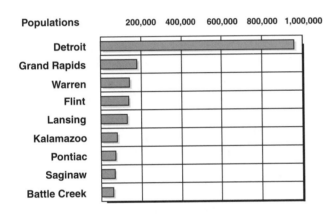

The Largest Cities

Detroit is by far the largest city in the state. In the last census, it had 965,000 people. Grand Rapids is the second largest, but it is not nearly as big as Detroit. It has over 185,000 people. Warren and Flint are next in size with Warren having 145,000 people and Flint 130,900. Lansing is fifth with roughly 128,000 people. Of course, populations change all the time. These figures are based on the U.S. census (an official count of the population) which is taken every 10 years. Recently, most Michigan cities have lost people who have moved to smaller towns and to other states which have more jobs. The number of jobs in Michigan industry seems to be shrinking.

What Are the Facts?

1. Name the four Great Lakes touching Michigan. Explain how the Lakes affect Michigan's climate.
2. Explain what the line 45 degrees north latitude has to do with Michigan.
3. Using the graph in the book, tell which are the four largest ethnic groups in Michigan.
4. Which three counties have the largest populations? What percentage of Michigan's people live in the three counties combined?
5. Name Michigan's five largest cities in order of their size.

Express yourself:
Study a map of Michigan and find the name of a place which interests you. Tell where it is and why you think it is interesting.

Michigan's Cities
larger selected cities shown
the size of the dot gives a rough
idea of how many people live there

Houghton

Ironwood

Iron River

Marquette

Sault Ste. Marie

Iron Mountain

Escanaba

St. Ignace

Mackinaw City

Cheboygan

Menominee

Petoskey

Gaylord

Alpena

N

Grayling

W E

Traverse City

Cadillac

S

Manistee

Ludington

Mt. Pleasant

Midland

Bay City

Saginaw

Muskegon

South Haven

Grand Rapids

Flint

Port Huron

Holland

Lansing

Pontiac

Warren

Kalamazoo

Battle Creek

Livonia

Detroit

Benton Harbor

Ann Arbor

Dearborn

Jackson

Hillsdale

Chapter 1 Section 2

What's Underfoot

**Learn how valuable minerals were formed here
and how fossils give us clues about life long ago.**

Many Changes Over Time

Michigan has not always been as it is today. Since the time the earth formed, this land has gone through some really radical changes! *Geologists* tell us a very long time ago saltwater seas covered Michigan and much of the area around it. *A geologist is a scientist who studies rocks and the formation of the land.* The Great Lakes and most of Michigan is still lower

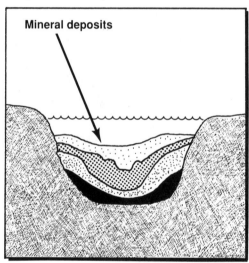

Mineral deposits

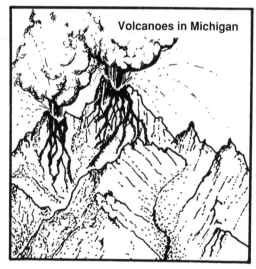

Volcanoes in Michigan

than much of the nearby land. That is why the Great Lakes fill with water.

When one of the great seas covered the Upper Peninsula an unusual thing happened. Material containing iron began to settle to the bottom. It continued to collect until it was 300 to 750 feet thick in some places. This became the iron ore which is mined today.

About 1.2 billion years ago the earth began to tear apart in the western Upper Peninsula. A weak spot had developed there. Molten rock or lava pushed through to the surface and volcanoes formed. This would have been exciting to see, but there were no people in Michigan to watch. As far as scientists know, the only living things at that time were algae and bacteria. Copper and silver metal are now found in the area of the volcanic activity.

8

Useful Minerals from the Great Seas

Can you think of any ways to prove that great seas once covered Michigan? In the Upper Peninsula, there is sandstone which was once sand under one of these seas. During millions of years the pressure and weight from the earth above turned the sand to sandstone. Nature's process of *erosion* has removed the earth and rock which was once above the sandstone and now it is on the surface! *Erosion is the wearing away of soil or rock by wind and water.*

About 500 million years ago the sea shrank until it only covered the Lower Peninsula. Because the sea no longer covered the Upper Peninsula, the underground rocks of the two peninsulas are quite different now. Eventually the smaller sea could not hold all of the minerals dissolved in its water. They began to collect on the bottom. Lime, salt, and gypsum were deposited from the sea. These minerals became valuable deposits in Michigan, mostly under the Lower Peninsula. The minerals left behind are another way to prove that there were once great seas which covered Michigan.

During the time of the great seas, fish and other sea creatures lived in the water. Some of the earliest had shells and we can find these shells as fossils.

Another kind of fossil is common. It is of a sea *coral*. Similar corals still live in the oceans of the world. After much time, this coral turned into a rock which is the Michigan state stone, the *Petoskey stone!* It has this name because it is often found on the shores of Lake Michigan near Petoskey. If you find a Petoskey stone, you are holding something in your hands which is about 350 million years old!

Petoskey stones are fossils of sea coral polished by the waves of Lake Michigan.

Coral is the hard limestone-like deposit left by certain tiny sea animals which live in large groups.

Many plants grew along the shore of the sea as it dried up. As they died and fell to the ground, great quantities piled up and decayed. Over a very long time, these shore plants became coal. Some Michigan coal has been mined but it doesn't have the quality of coal from other states and the deposits are smaller.

Our Dirt & Rocks Have History!

The rocks of Michigan tell a story of the past. They hold clues about what took place millions of years ago. Newer rock is always on top of the older rock unless an unusual event caused the rock layers to fold over. If you were to drill an oil well in the center of the Lower Peninsula and look at the drilling core, you could actually see many layers of rock. The oldest would be at the bottom.

Why?
Why is any of this important today? Michigan is unique among states because the two peninsulas are geologically different. Understanding rock formations is necessary to find the valuable mineral resources in Michigan. Knowing what is underground helps geologists discover oil, gas, limestone, gypsum, salt, copper, silver, gold, and iron. All in Michigan! It has been said that Michigan has a wider variety of minerals than most places of its size on earth!

All of these minerals have been an important part of Michigan's economy and history. Where people live and what they do to earn a living depends upon what natural resources are found in the area. The minerals in our state have affected the lives of many people over the years and will continue to be important to us in the future.

What Are the Facts ?

1. List four minerals which are in Michigan because the land was once covered by great seas.
2. List two valuable metals left here because of ancient volcanoes in Michigan.
3. What actually is a Petoskey stone? Why does the Michigan state stone have this name?

Geography research:
Discover which mineral resources are found where you live. For example, does your area produce salt, iron ore, limestone, or oil? How are these minerals used? Get a sample if you can.

Chapter 1　Section 3

Time at the Edge of the Ice

Believe it or not! Thick sheets of ice called glaciers once moved over Michigan from the north and made many changes to the land.

Every City, Every Town Covered By Ice.

This land was once covered with ice. Every place where any city or town is today was under this ice. Not ice from a cold winter but hundreds to thousands of feet of ice. Billions of tons of ice. It all started 1.6 million years ago.

This kind of ice is called a *glacier. A glacier is a very thick ice sheet which slowly covers a wide area of land because more snow falls in the*

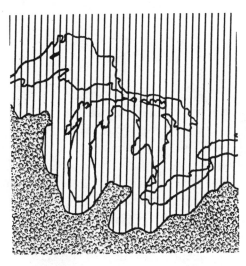

This map shows how far south the last glacier went as it covered Michigan. This was about 14,800 years ago.

winter than can melt in summer. The ice began to form around the North Pole and it moved inch by inch to the south. Michigan has been covered by four glaciers over a very long period of time. The last one melted away about 12,000 to 13,000 years ago.

You may not believe it, but there are still clues left behind for the doubtful. The whole surface of the land shows signs of what the ice did. If you know how to look, clues are everywhere- like skid marks from a highway accident!

The glaciers came down over Michigan just like a bulldozer. Tremendous amounts of gravel, rock, and dirt were pushed south by the ice. When the ice finally melted, much of this material was left behind. This rock and gravel often formed hills. Studying the shapes of the hills helps you to see the "footprints" the glaciers left behind. The hills are one of the clues that show glaciers were really here. If you visit a gravel pit in Michigan, you will probably see many kinds of rock. Each type was made in a different place and perhaps at a different time. It was all pushed south by the bulldozer action of the glaciers. When geologists see so many kinds of rock in one place, they realize it is further proof that a glacier once passed over the area.

What Did the Glaciers Do?

The mass of ice which came over Michigan was truly great. The ice weighed so much it actually pushed the land down! Careful studies by scientists show that Michigan is still slowly rising because weight of the ice has been lifted.

Glaciers did much to form the Great Lakes. The ice scraped away softer rock making low places which became Lakes Michigan and Huron. As the last glacier melted, a tremendous amount of water filled up the low places and created the Great Lakes. They may be one of the most valuable gifts left by the glaciers.

The first people who lived in Michigan probably came here 12,000 to 13,000 years ago. (Art by David McConnell)

Melting ice was also responsible for making many smaller lakes in Michigan. Often huge chunks of ice fell away from the glacier as it slowly returned north. The ice chunks made depressions in the ground and as the ice melted, the depressions were filled with water. In some places, this kind of lake still exists. Just imagine, the first water in these lakes arrived well over 10,000 years ago!

Besides bringing gravel and rock to Michigan, glaciers pushed dirt to the south. Much of the dirt found in the Lower Peninsula originally came from the Upper Peninsula or even Canada. This is why the southern Lower Peninsula has better soil for farming than most of the Upper Peninsula and the northern Lower Peninsula. The better soil of this part of Michigan is another gift from the glaciers. Our dirt and rocks do have history!

Were There Any Witnesses?

Did anyone ever see these four glaciers? Maybe the last one. *Archaeologists* believe the first people moved to Michigan at about the same time it was melting-

12,000 to 13,000 years ago. *An archaeologist is a scientist who studies about past human life and activities. They often study remains found buried in the ground. Fossils, bones, lost tools and ruins are some of the clues they use to help them form their ideas.*

We don't know too much about the first people. They must have moved here from the south. The last glacier probably still covered the land to the north. Archaeologists have found bits of animal bone and stone spear points which led them to think these people moved from place to place to follow animals which they hunted.

What Are the Facts?

1. What is a glacier?
2. Give examples of two clues which help to prove Michigan was once covered by a glacier.
3. Name two important and useful things the ancient glaciers formed in or around Michigan.
4. How many years ago do archaeologists believe the first people lived in Michigan?

Use a map today!
Find out where the edge of the North Pole ice is today. How many miles would the ice need to travel to form a new glacier which would cover Michigan?

Consider the Big Picture
The Great Lakes affect Michigan in many ways.
Michigan's people have come from many lands around the world.
Most of Michigan's people live in a small part of the state.
Natural processes from the distant past provided Michigan with valuable mineral resources and helped shape the land.

Building Your Michigan Word Power
Number a sheet of paper from 1 to 5 and beside each number write the word listed below which best matches the definition. There are extra words.

coral, county, glacier, Isle Royale green stone, isthmus, latitude, limestone, longitude, peninsula, Petoskey stone, province, township

1.   A unit of government in Canada which is like a state.

2.   A very thick ice sheet which slowly covers a wide area of land because more snow falls in the winter than can melt in the summer.

3.   Michigan's state stone. It is a fossil of sea coral which goes back to the time the state was covered by an ocean.

4.   The largest unit of local government within a state. Each one contains cities, villages, and townships. In Michigan, many are shown on maps as square boxes.

5.   The rock-like skeletons of various saltwater forms of life which live in large groups.

Talking About It
Get together in a small group and talk about-

How does the large concentration of people in the southeast Lower Peninsula affect Michigan?

Should the Great Lakes region share water from the Lakes with dry parts of the country like Arizona?

If all of Michigan's people had first come from the same country or part of the world, would our culture be better or worse today?

Put It To Use
Use a Michigan map and an almanac, census report, or U.S. atlas to find how many people live in the largest city in your county and in the largest city in each of two counties which touch yours. Make a graph to show this information in a creative way.

2

The First Michiganians
- Native Americans -
A Long History

Learn about the major tribes of Native Americans living in Michigan when the Europeans arrived.

From the Beginning

The Native Americans or Indians were the first citizens of Michigan. Michigan has been their home for 12,000 to 13,000 years. These first people did not leave a written history of themselves. They used picture writing and we can see a few examples of their history painted on cliffs, carved in stone, or on birch bark.

Besides picture writing, the tribes had a strong tradition of telling their history through stories. In that way, information of great events was passed from one person to another and from one generation to the next. Sometimes the stories were fictional and made into legends. The tribes had legends about how the Sleeping Bear Dunes were created and why rabbits have short tails, etc.

Grouped by Tribes

At first the Europeans lumped all the native people together as one group with the name Indians, but the native people did not see themselves that way. They lived in groups of related people which were similar to small nations. We call their groups tribes. Each had different customs and beliefs.

In most Indian marriages, a young man offered gifts to the mother and father of the young woman he wished to marry. If the gifts were returned, the proposal was rejected, and the gifts would be offered to a different family. (Art by George Rasmussen)

15

Tribes moved, or *migrated*, from time to time. *A migration happens when an entire group of people leave one area and move to another. Usually such moves are caused by disease, war, a change in climate, lack of food, or other serious problems.* Since the tribes moved their locations, they should be considered as tribes of the Great Lakes region, not just the tribes of Michigan.

Where Did the Tribes Come From?

It is believed Native Americans are relatives of people who reached North America from Asia many thousands of years ago. At this time the water level was lower in the oceans. Alaska and Siberia were connected by land.

Most historians feel the more recent tribes migrated into Michigan from other parts of North America. Ojibwa oral history says their tribe once lived by the Atlantic Ocean.

Certain historians have suggested that the Native Americans caught European diseases when they first met white people. Since they had no resistance to those diseases, the results could have been terrible. The Ojibwa might have moved because of diseases caught from the early French explorers or even from Viking explorers who visited the East Coast before the French and English.

War was another reason for migrating. Parts of the Huron tribe moved to Michigan because they were attacked by the Iroquois (EAR a quoy) tribes and forced out of their home in Ontario.

Indian Tribes

This map shows where the main Indian tribes lived in Michigan about the year 1760.

Names of the Tribes

How many tribes lived in Michigan and what were their names? About 1750 there were three major tribes and three or four slightly less important tribes who lived here. As we go back in history, it is harder to know which tribes lived where.

The first three tribes were part of a loosely organized group known as the "Three Fires." They had common traditions and thought of themselves as belonging to the same family.

Three main tribes living in Michigan:

Ojibwa (Also called Chippewa or Ojibway) [o JIB wa. CHIP eh wah, O JIB way]
Ottawa [OT ah wa]
Potawatomi [POT a WAT o me]

Smaller tribes living in Michigan:

Menominee [meh NOM eh nee]
Huron (Also called the Wyandotte) [HYOUR on, Wy n dot]
Miami [my AM ee]

You Called Me a Snake or Who Made These Names?

A careful study of tribal names will show they are not necessarily the names used by the tribes themselves. Some of the names are not flattering at all. They might be the name an enemy tribe used. Sioux came from an Ojibwa word for snake, which was shortened by the French. Several names were changed by the French or English. Some are nothing like the name the tribe used for themselves. For example, the Ojibwa or Chippewa actually called themselves the *Anishinabe* (ah nish in A bey). *This means "original people."*

Wigwams were used by tribes in the Michigan area. The shelters, covered with birchbark could easily be taken down and moved as the Indians traveled and hunted. (Art by David B. McConnell)

The Ojibwa

Let's look more closely at each tribe. The Ojibwa was the largest tribe in Michigan and has the most members still living here. They were one of the larger tribes north of Mexico and their area ranged from Ontario to North Dakota. The Ojibwa mainly hunted and fished for their food. They were experts in using birchbark canoes and often fished from them.

17

What did the Ojibwa look like? Indian agent Henry Schoolcraft said about half of the men were over six feet tall. They tattooed their faces and foreheads with blue or black lines.

The Ottawa

The Ottawa tribe's name came from the word *adawa* or *adawe* (ah da wah) which means to trade. They traveled hundreds of miles to trade woven mats and furs for pottery and sea shells. Corn, sunflower oil, tobacco, and medicinal herbs were also traded with other tribes. Their many travels helped the Ottawa to become expert in the use of their canoes. Since they were related to the Ojibwa, many of the Ottawa customs were similar. By the 1700s they lived in the western part of Michigan.

The Potawatomi

This tribe finally settled in southern Michigan, northern Indiana and Illinois, parts of Ohio, and Wisconsin. Their name is from an Ojibwa phrase which has to do with fire. It has two possible origins. It may mean "keepers of the fire" because they always carried some of their fire from place to place. Another meaning for their name is "people of the place of the fire" because they used fire to clear the grassland for farming. They planted corn, squash, beans, tobacco, melons, and sunflowers. The Potawatomi could depend more on farming as they lived in a warmer part of the state than the other two main tribes.

Menominee—Wild Rice in the U.P.

The Menominee tribe lived in the central Upper Peninsula and along the Menominee River. Their name is an Ojibwa word for "wild rice people." They used the wild rice which they gathered from swampy areas as a major source of food. Their customs were much like those of the Ojibwa people who also lived in the Upper Peninsula. Little is known of the history of the Menominee.

Miami—
They Walked along the Rivers

In 1673, French missionaries found the Miami tribe living along the St. Joseph River in southern Michigan. Their main village was in northern Indiana on the Kankakee River. Even though the Miami lived along these two important waterways, they usually traveled on foot! The Miami farmed and stayed in permanent villages unless attacks from nearby tribes forced them to move.

Huron—The People with a Different Hair Style!

One of the first tribes contacted by the French along the St. Lawrence River was the Huron Tribe. The tribe called itself Wendat, but the French used the word Huron because the men of the tribe had a haircut which reminded the French of the hair on a wild pig. All of the hair was cut off except for a ridge down the middle of the head which stuck straight up. Huron is like a French word for wild pig. The Iroquois men wore their hair the same way.

For some reason, the Iroquois tribes became bitter enemies of the Huron. In 1649, the Iroquois began an all-out war against the French and the Huron. Many of the surviving Huron escaped to Michigan. Some moved near Detroit where they were known as the Wyandotte.

The Iroquois— Warriors of the Lakes

The Iroquois did not live in Michigan, but they had a powerful effect on those who did. They were not just a single tribe but rather a group of five tribes. They were sometimes known as the Iroquois League. They lived in the land south of Lake Ontario in what is now New York state. The Iroquois had a more organized form of government than other tribes.

A man of the Huron tribe. Note the haircut used by the Huron and their related Iroquois tribes. (Art by George Rasmussen.)

The Iroquois became very warlike and powerful. They were among the first tribes to have guns which they received in trade from the Dutch. They attacked neighboring tribes, often forcing them to move.

Many Indian Names

Any time you look at a map, you will discover Native American names are everywhere in Michigan! Remember, even the name of our state comes from Native American words for big lake.

Thirty-three Michigan counties use Indian names or the county name is made from several Indian words. One meaning for Saginaw is "place of the river's outlet." Lenawee (len AH way) is a Shawnee word for people. In the Upper Peninsula, Keweenaw means "place to carry a canoe from place to place." One meaning for Kalamazoo is "churning water." Look on the map to check if your county has an Indian name.

Michigan cities use many Indian names too. Some are named for proud chiefs. Pontiac, Tecumseh, Okemos and Tawas are examples. Petoskey is the last name of an Indian family.

The Michigan counties selected on this map have Indian names. Names of some of the other counties sound like Indian words, but actually have other origins.

Where Are They Now?

The United States government acquired control of Indian land in Michigan through treaties between 1807 and 1842. In time, Indians were often forced to leave the state. After the 1840s, many were taken to government reservations in the Southwest. The Sauk tribe who once lived in the Saginaw Valley were moved to Iowa and then to Kansas. Later, they were forced on to Oklahoma where they live today. Other tribes fled to Canada.

Many of the Native Americans who stayed in Michigan had to live on reservations. There are four main federal government reservations in Michigan and some other very small ones including two state reservations. Three are in the Upper Peninsula while one is in the Lower Peninsula. Michigan's largest reservation is the Isabella Reservation near Mt. Pleasant. These reservations are similar to small towns. Tribal Councils govern each one. The Bureau of Indian Affairs, through the United States government, holds this land in trust.

Since these reservations are considered to be land which is not governed by the state, some reservations have opened gambling casinos. These casinos can bring in much extra money for the tribal members.

L'Anse Reservation
(sounds like lay ahnce)

Bay Mills Reservation

Hannahville
Reservation

Michigan's four main Indian reservations

Isabella Reservation

21

Today most Native Americans no longer live on reservations. They live and work like anyone else; some are farmers; some work in factories. The largest Native American population in Michigan is in Wayne county. The first Michiganians remain proud of their heritage. Many prefer not to be called Indians, but by their proper tribal names.

Indians continue to live in Michigan today. These tribal members are at a meeting concerning fishing rights. (Courtesy Michigan State Archives)

What Are the Facts?

1. List the three main tribes living in Michigan about 1760 and tell about where each one lived.
2. Give two reasons why tribes may have migrated to Michigan. Name a tribe and its reason for moving.
3. Write down four new facts you have learned about the Native Americans in Michigan from studying this unit.

Use a map today!
On a map look for Native American names used in Michigan. Write down the name of 1 county, city, river and lake which appears to have a tribal name. Use a geographical dictionary or the book *Indian Names in Michigan* by Virgil J. Vogel to find the meaning for these Native American names.

Consider the Big Picture

Native Americans have lived in Michigan since the time when the last glacier melted 12,000 to 13,000 years ago.

Michigan's Native Americans are grouped into tribes and each has its own language and customs. The tribes moved from place to place over the years.

Today most Native Americans live and work like anyone else, but some do live on the four main reservations in Michigan.

Today many Native American names are still used for places in Michigan.

Building Your Michigan Word Power

Use each of these four words in its own sentence to show you know what it means: Anishinabe, migration, Ojibwa, tribes. Have your sentences say something about Michigan.

Talking About It

Get together in a small group and talk about-
Many tribes are building gambling casinos on their land. In which ways do you believe this will help them. In which ways might this be harmful.

Is it right or wrong to dig up the ancient burial grounds of Native Americans to learn more about how they lived long ago?

What major things do you think caused the Native American culture to fade away during the last 300 years? What things might cause today's culture to fade away in the future?

Think of the places talked about in the world news today where people are migrating. Compare their reasons for moving with why the tribes migrated long ago.

How did the extinction of some animals in Europe lead to the near extinction of the Native Americans in Michigan?

Put It To Use

Look at the map on page 16 and tell which major tribe lived in each general area listed here: the Upper Peninsula, along Lake Michigan, along Lake Erie, along the border with Ohio.

Make a crossword puzzle using the names of eight Michigan counties which are Indian words.

3

FRANCE COMES to NORTH AMERICA

The Pathway To Michigan!

The St. Lawrence River was the pathway which finally brought the first Europeans to Michigan. They were the French. Michigan became a part of the French empire.

If you stop thinking of America as highways and start thinking of it as rivers, you get closer to the country. Charles Kuralt, *Reader's Digest.*

Pathway to Michigan

Life in Europe had been much the same for hundreds of years. With the discovery of America, there was an excitement to visit this new land! People left their old European castles and sailed across the Atlantic Ocean. Some found the *St. Lawrence River* to be a pathway toward the heart of North America. *The St. Lawrence River is what drains water from the Great Lakes to the Atlantic Ocean. It flows between the United States and Canada part of the way then goes north through Canada until it reaches the ocean.* It allowed Europeans reach the Great Lakes and Michigan.

Today it is hard for people to realize how important rivers were to travelers in North America then. Imagine the worst dirt road you have ever seen and realize there was nothing as good as that to use! Also imagine the thickest forest or woods you have ever seen and realize such forests covered most of the land!

Much of our early history is tied to the St. Lawrence River and the people who used it. It brought the Europeans here and the Europeans changed forever the land now called Michigan.

Rivals in a New World

The conquest of this part of North America was a contest between two European countries- England and France. The king of France sent explorers to find a route to China and Japan. The king wanted to be the first to find a way through North America. He wished to reach those lands by sailing west. No one at that time had any idea how large North America was, or how far it was; so it seemed to be a reasonable idea.

24

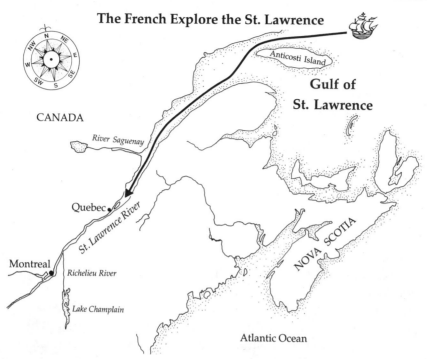

The French Explore the St. Lawrence

The St. Lawrence River was a major route for the French. They used this river to reach Michigan. Each year they brought supplies to trade; then went back to France with furs. Look at this map and the color map on M3 to see their complete route. (Map by David McConnell)

Their Motives

Why did Europeans want to go to China and Japan? These places had spices and silk which attracted their attention. Silk made very nice clothes and spices helped European food to taste better, especially if the food had not been kept cool or wasn't very fresh!

Another reason to come to North America was to get furs. In Europe, furs had been used in expensive clothing for a long time. But by the 1500s, many fur-bearing animals were hard to find in Europe. The last beaver was seen in England in the 1520s.

About 1600, the king of France decided to begin a settlement in North America but didn't want to pay for it himself. So, he offered to give fur trading rights to any company willing to start the settlement.

A Great Frenchman Challenges the Wilderness

Samuel de Champlain (duh sham PLANE) was sent from France and began to search for a good place to start a settlement. In the spring of 1608, after much exploring, Champlain had chosen a place. It was about 375 miles up the St. Lawrence River. The Native Americans called the place *Kebec* which means narrow place in the river. The French changed the name to Quebec (kay BECK) and a great city was born.

More Exploring

Champlain kept looking for a way to reach China and Japan in his "spare" time. Indians told him of a salt sea to the west. But how far away was it and how could he get there? He also heard of a great sea to the north. He wanted to try to find it but the Native Americans were not interested in giving away all of their secrets. He could not find any one who would guide him there.

A young man with Champlain was Etienne (ay TYEN). He spent much time with the Indians and easily learned their customs. Etienne, to whom historians gave the last name of Brule´ (broo LAY), eagerly went on several canoe trips. On one of them he traveled west using the Ottawa River finally reaching Lake Huron. He was the first European to see Lake Huron and probably several of the other Great Lakes.

The trouble with Brule´ was he never bothered to write anything down about his travels. Sometimes even Champlain didn't know where he was! Brule´ would be gone for long periods of time, living with the Indians, practically disappearing, and then coming back to Quebec. Brule´ and a companion named Grenoble helped find the way to Michigan. They probably reached the Upper Peninsula about 1622. The French kept sending explorers west through the Great Lakes. They hoped to find a way through to the Pacific Ocean, but they never did.

At that time, the land which became Michigan was a part of "New France". The French were exploring the land and trading with the tribes. We know what life was like then because Champlain wrote four books about his adventures.

What Are the Facts?

1. Why did Europeans, like the French, need to come to North America to find fur bearing animals?
2. About which year did the first French person reach Michigan and what part of the state did he see?
3. Why did the French keep exploring rivers and lakes going toward the west?

Express yourself:
Write your opinion on what kind of knowledge the Native Americans had about the geography of North America. Back up your ideas with as many facts as possible.

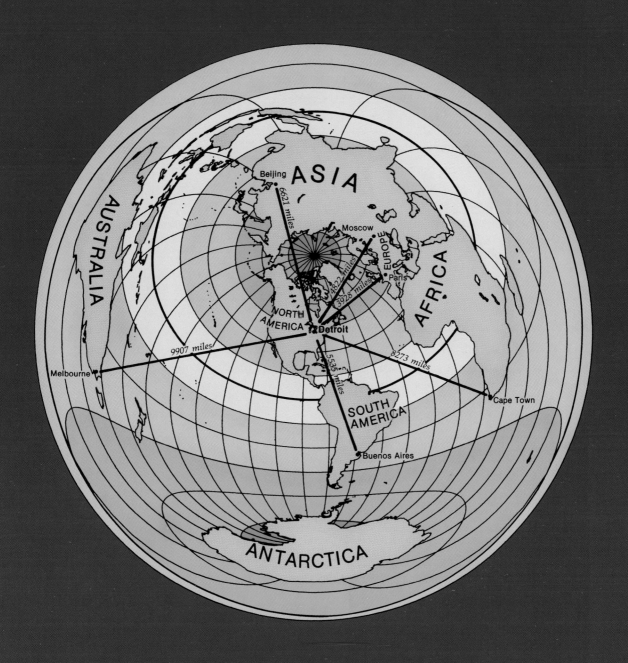

A View of the World from Michigan

This is a special map of the world. A straight line from the center to anywhere else will show the distance and direction to the place. Only straight lines starting at Detroit are accurate. Do not use this map to compare sizes. The greater the distance from Michigan, the more the shapes and sizes of continents have been stretched.

93°W
48°N

90°W

87°W

Ontario

84°W

Minnesota

Grand Portage

Lake Superior

C A

Duluth

Superior

M i c h i g a n

Sault Ste. Marie

Sault Ste. Marie

Menominee River

Manitoulin Island

St. Croix River

Wisconsin

Lake

Huron

Manistee River

St. Paul
45°N

Mississippi River

Green Bay

River

Fox River

Muskegon

Saginaw River

Iowa

Wisconsin River

Madison ☆

Grand

River

Lansing ☆

Lake
St.
Clair

Tha

Milwaukee

Lake

Dubuque

Michigan

Detroit

42°N

Chicago

Fox River

Gary

Toledo

Lak

Des Moines River

Kankakee River

Maumee River

Fort Wayne

Cle

Ohio

Illinois River

Illinois

River

☆ Columbus

39°N

Mississippi River

☆Springfield

Indianapolis
☆

Indiana

Cincinnati

Missouri River

River

St. Louis

Wabash River

Vincennes

☆
Jefferson City

Frankfort
☆

Missouri

Ohio

Louisville • Lexington

M2

Kentucky

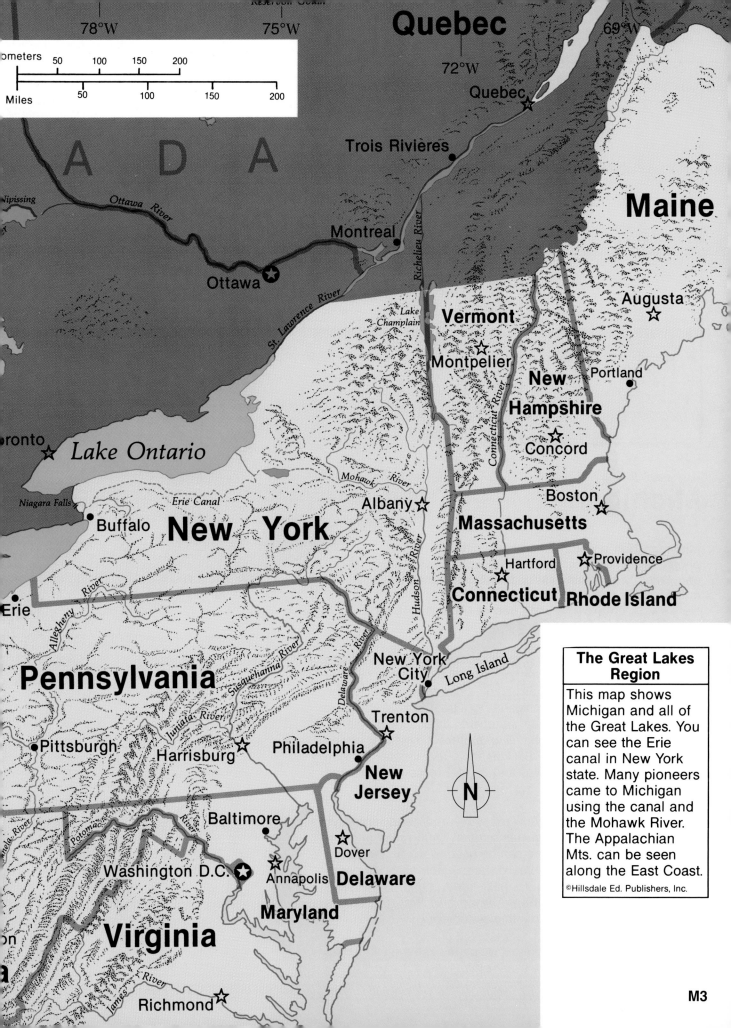

78°W 75°W 72°W 69°W

Quebec

ometers
50 100 150 200

Miles
50 100 150 200

A D A

Ottawa River

Nipissing

Trois Rivières

Maine

Montreal

Ottawa

St. Lawrence River

Richelieu River

Augusta

Lake Champlain

Vermont

Montpelier

New Hampshire

Portland

Concord

ronto

Lake Ontario

Mohawk River

Albany

Boston

Connecticut River

Niagara Falls

Erie Canal

Buffalo

New York

Massachusetts

Hartford

Providence

Erie

Allegheny River

Hudson River

Connecticut

Rhode Island

Pennsylvania

Susquehanna River

Delaware River

New York City

Long Island

Juniata River

Trenton

Pittsburgh

Harrisburg

Philadelphia

New Jersey

N

The Great Lakes Region

This map shows Michigan and all of the Great Lakes. You can see the Erie canal in New York state. Many pioneers came to Michigan using the canal and the Mohawk River. The Appalachian Mts. can be seen along the East Coast.

©Hillsdale Ed. Publishers, Inc.

Potomac River

Baltimore

Dover

Washington D.C.

Annapolis

Delaware

monia River

Maryland

Virginia

James River

a

Richmond

M3

Michigan

Michigan has a population of roughly 9.8 million people, which ranks it 8th among the 50 states. The population is not evenly divided. Wayne County has more people than any other and over 41% of the state's residents live in just three of Michigan's 83 counties, Wayne, Oakland and Macomb!

Michigan is 23rd in size among the states with 58,216 square miles of total land area. There are also 38,575 square miles of Great Lakes water within Michigan's boundaries. Four of the five Great Lakes touch Michigan. Our Great Lakes' shoreline of 3,200 miles is longer than the entire Unites States Atlantic Seaboard. The Michigan shoreline is greater than that of any single state except Alaska. Besides the Great lakes, Michigan has over 11,000 inland lakes and 36,000 miles of rivers and streams.

Michigan has nearly 120,000 miles of roads and highways within its borders. This includes almost 1,400 miles of interstate highways. These roads can be used to reach Michigan's 90 plus state parks and recreation areas. Ten of the larger of these parks are shown on the next three pages. Isle Royale National Park, Sleeping Bear Dunes and Pictured Rocks National Lakeshore are also within our borders.

Note: Maps on this, and the next two pages use the same map legend and are drawn at the same scale.

90°W   89°W   88°W

CANADA
UNITED STATES

MINNESOTA

ISLE ROYALE NATIONAL PARK

MICHIGAN'S UPPER

Manitou Island

Eagle River   Keweenaw Point
Keweenaw Peninsula
Calumet   Laurium
Hancock   Lake Linden
Houghton
Portage Lake   Keweenaw Bay   Lak

41   Pt. Abbaye

Ontonagon   26   L'ANSE RESERVATION
Porcupine Mts.   38   Baraga   Mt. Arvon
64   L'Anse   Elevation 1979 feet
Presque Isle River   Sturgeon River   Mt. Curwood

Montreal River   Bessemer   Wakefield   Lake Gogebic   28   Negaunee   Marqu
Ironwood   45   Ishpeming   Lac
141   Michigamme
2   95
Michigamme Res.   35

Iron River   Crystal Falls
Caspian   Stambaugh   69   Ford River
Brule River

Iron Mountain   Norway   Glac
Kingsford   2   Escana
HANNAHVILLE RESERVATION

41   35
Menominee River   Wa

Menominee

Green Bay   Door Peninsula

WISCONSIN   Lu

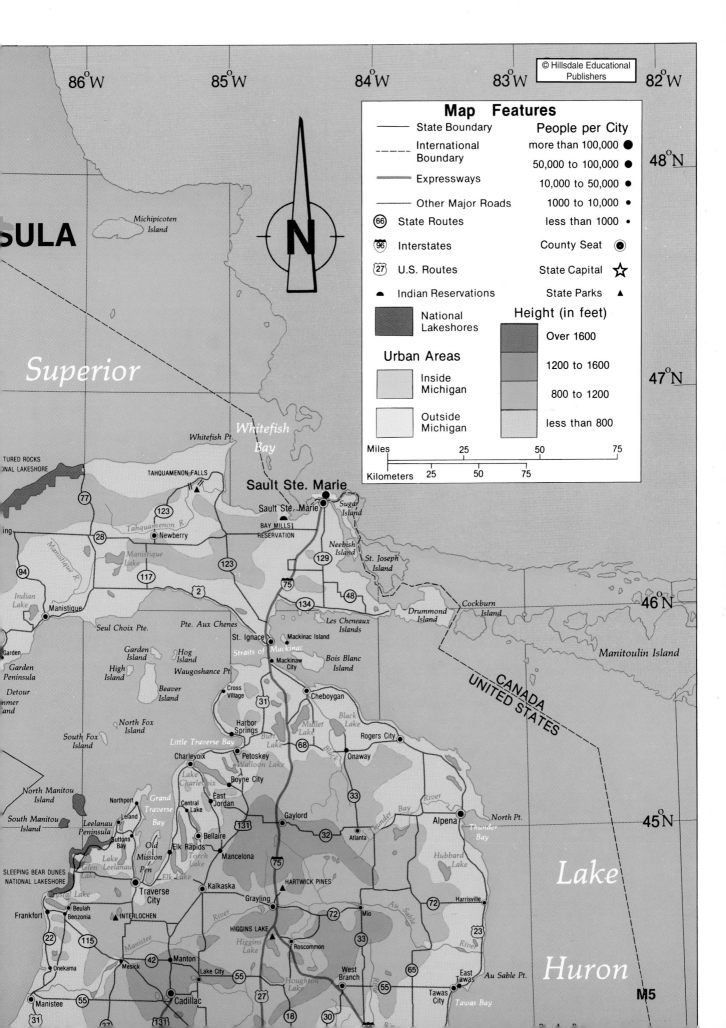

86°W 85°W 84°W 83°W 82°W

© Hillsdale Educational Publishers

Map Features

——	State Boundary
- - - -	International Boundary
▬▬▬	Expressways
——	Other Major Roads
(66)	State Routes
(96)	Interstates
(27)	U.S. Routes
⬤	Indian Reservations

People per City

more than 100,000	●
50,000 to 100,000	●
10,000 to 50,000	●
1000 to 10,000	•
less than 1000	·
County Seat	◉
State Capital	☆
State Parks	▲

National Lakeshores

Urban Areas

Inside Michigan

Outside Michigan

Height (in feet)

Over 1600
1200 to 1600
800 to 1200
less than 800

Miles 25 50 75

Kilometers 25 50 75

48°N

47°N

46°N

45°N

SULA

Michipicoten Island

Superior

TURED ROCKS
ONAL LAKESHORE

Whitefish Pt.

Whitefish Bay

TAHQUAMENON FALLS

Sault Ste. Marie

Sault Ste. Marie

Sugar Island

(77)

(123)

Tahquamenon R.

BAY MILLS RESERVATION

Neebish Island

(28)

● Newberry

Manistique Lake

(123)

(129)

St. Joseph Island

ing

Manistique R.

(117)

(75)

(134)

(48)

Les Cheneaux Islands

Drummond Island

Cockburn Island

(94)

(2)

Indian Lake

● Manistique

Seul Choix Pte.

Pte. Aux Chenes

St. Ignace ◉

Mackinac Island

Manitoulin Island

CANADA
UNITED STATES

Garden

Garden Peninsula

Garden Island

Hog Island

Straits of Mackinac

Bois Blanc Island

Detour
nmer
and

High Island

Waugoshance Pt.

Mackinaw City

Beaver Island

Cross Village

(31)

● Cheboygan

North Fox Island

Harbor Springs

Mullet Lake

Black Lake

South Fox Island

Little Traverse Bay

Bur Lake

Rogers City

North Manitou Island

Charlevoix

Petoskey

Walloon Lake

(68)

Black River

Onaway

South Manitou Island

Northport

Grand Traverse Bay

Central Lake

East Jordan

Boyne City

Lake Charlevoix

(33)

Leelanau Peninsula

Leland

Bellaire

Gaylord

Thunder Bay

Alpena

North Pt.

SLEEPING BEAR DUNES
NATIONAL LAKESHORE

Suttons Bay

Old Mission Pen.

Elk Rapids

Torch Lake

Mancelona

(131)

(32)

Atlanta

Thunder Bay

Glen Leelanau

Glen Lake

Elk Lake

(75)

Hubbard Lake

Lake

Frankfort

Crystal Lake

Traverse City

Kalkaska

HARTWICK PINES

Grayling

▲ INTERLOCHEN

Manistee River

(72)

Harrisville

(72)

Beulah

Benzonia

Au Sable River

Huron

(22)

(115)

HIGGINS LAKE

Higgins Lake

(33)

(23)

● Onekama

(42)

Manton

Mio

Au Sable River

Mesick

Lake City

(55)

Roscommon

(65)

Au Sable Pt.

Manistee

(55)

Cadillac

(27)

Houghton Lake

West Branch

East Tawas

Tawas City

Tawas Bay

(31)

(27)

(131)

(18)

(30)

(55)

M5

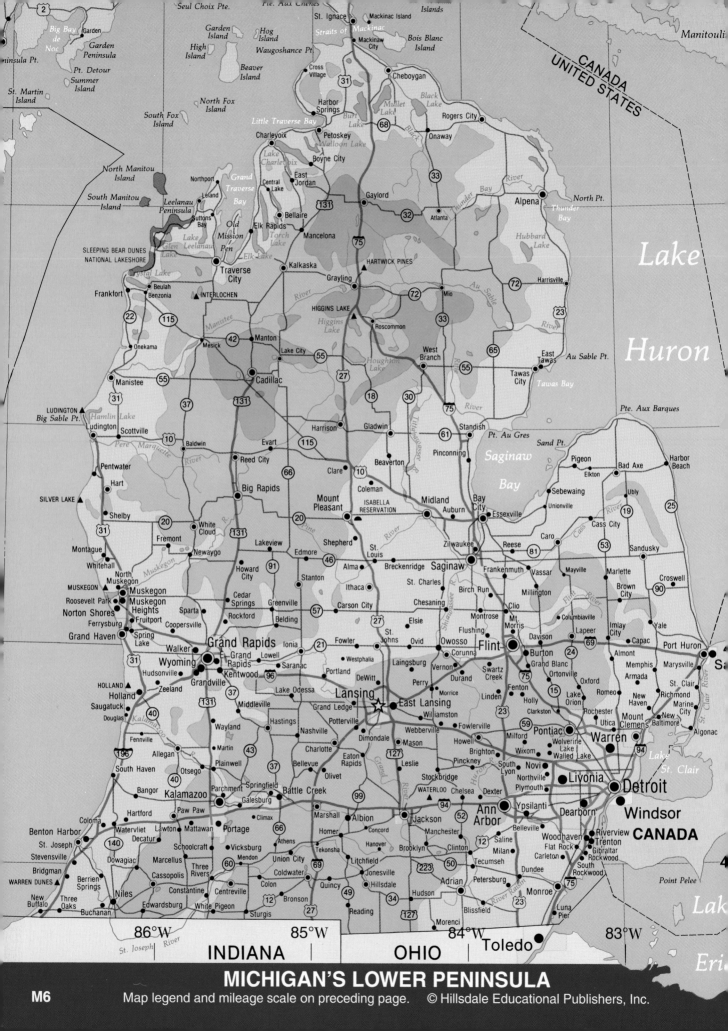

MICHIGAN'S LOWER PENINSULA

Map legend and mileage scale on preceding page. © Hillsdale Educational Publishers, Inc.

THE DETROIT AREA

This map also shows current and historic points of interest.
Windsor, Ontario and Canada are colored gray.

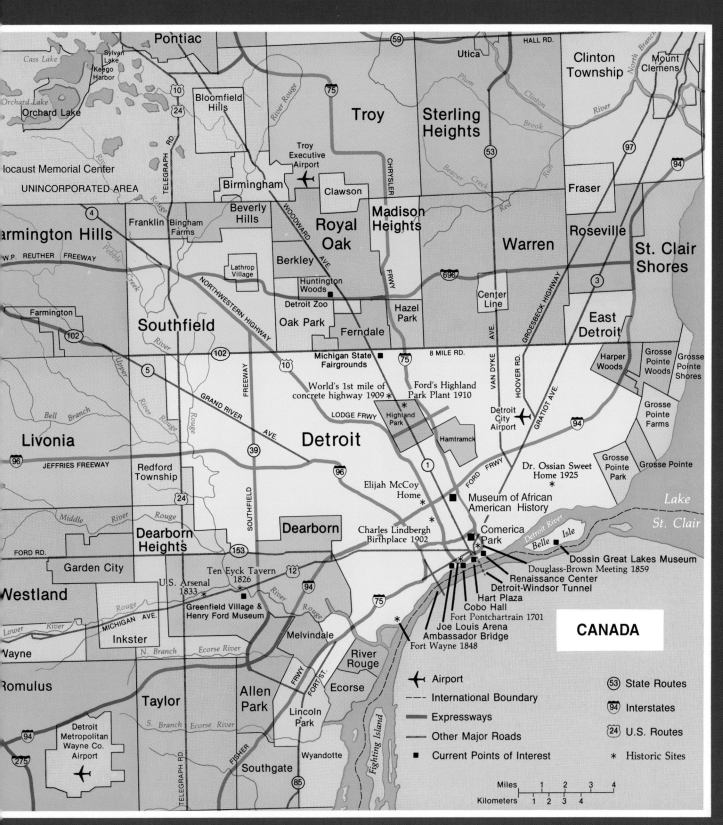

Cass Lake · Sylvan Lake · Keego Harbor · Orchard Lake · Pontiac · Bloomfield Hills

Orchard Lake · Holocaust Memorial Center · UNINCORPORATED AREA · Birmingham · Troy Executive Airport · Clawson · Troy · Sterling Heights · Utica · HALL RD. · Clinton Township · Mount Clemens

Farmington Hills · Franklin · Bingham Farms · Beverly Hills · Madison Heights · Fraser · Roseville

W.P. REUTHER FREEWAY · Lathrop Village · Royal Oak · Berkley · Huntington Woods · Warren · Center Line · St. Clair Shores

Farmington · Southfield · Detroit Zoo · Oak Park · Ferndale · Hazel Park · East Detroit

Livonia · Michigan State Fairgrounds · 8 MILE RD. · Harper Woods · Grosse Pointe Woods · Grosse Pointe Shores

World's 1st mile of concrete highway 1909 · Ford's Highland Park Plant 1910 · Highland Park · Detroit City Airport · Grosse Pointe Farms

JEFFRIES FREEWAY · Redford Township · LODGE FRWY. · Detroit · Hamtramck · Dr. Ossian Sweet Home 1925 · Grosse Pointe Park · Grosse Pointe

Elijah McCoy Home · Museum of African American History · Lake St. Clair

Dearborn Heights · Dearborn · Charles Lindbergh Birthplace 1902 · Comerica Park · Belle Isle · Dossin Great Lakes Museum

Garden City · Ten Eyck Tavern 1826 · Douglass-Brown Meeting 1859 · Renaissance Center · Detroit-Windsor Tunnel

Westland · U.S. Arsenal 1833 · Greenfield Village & Henry Ford Museum · Hart Plaza · Cobo Hall · Fort Pontchartrain 1701

Wayne · Inkster · Melvindale · Joe Louis Arena · Ambassador Bridge · Fort Wayne 1848

Romulus · River Rouge · Ecorse · CANADA

Taylor · Allen Park · Lincoln Park · Fighting Island

Detroit Metropolitan Wayne Co. Airport · Wyandotte · Southgate

Legend

- ✈ Airport
- --- International Boundary
- Expressways
- Other Major Roads
- ■ Current Points of Interest
- 53 State Routes
- 94 Interstates
- 24 U.S. Routes
- ✳ Historic Sites

Miles 1 2 3 4
Kilometers 1 2 3 4

THE LAND AND ITS USES

Key to Colors

 Forests

 Fruit

 Industry

  Grains & Dairy

  Beans & Sugar Beets

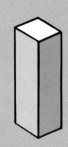 1 inch equals 500 people per square mile

Wayne County
3,430 persons
per square mile

WHERE PEOPLE LIVE IN MICHIGAN

Keweenaw County
3.6 persons per square mile

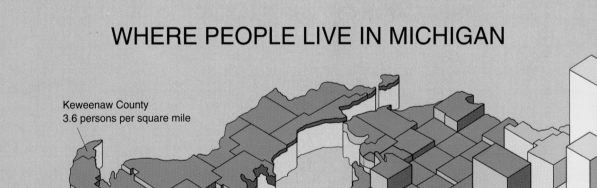

Designed by the Center for Cartographic Research and Spatial Analysis,
Michigan State University. ©Copyright Hillsdale Educational Publishers.

M8

Chapter 3 Section 2

Search for Souls: Missionaries & Priests

Priests spread French influence throughout the region and kept the only written records of many historical events. *(In this case priests are the ministers and leaders in the Catholic church.)*

Priests On the Way to Michigan

In the 1600s the people of France had an increased interest in religion. Almost as soon as the first attempt was made to start a settlement in North America, French men and women were ready to come as *missionaries. They wanted to make Christians of the Native Americans in the new land.*

The missionaries had an impact on what happened in New France. Their desire to reach the tribes meant they traveled far from French settlements. By doing that, the area under French control expanded. They studied the tribal languages and customs which made it easier for the French to know how to work with the Native Americans.

Not Easy Work!

Early missionary work was not for the weak or lazy! The historian Francis Parkman writes what it was like for a missionary spending the winter with Indians in a wigwam. The fellow shared a wigwam about 13 feet by 13 feet.

"Put aside the bear skin and enter the hut. Here were packed 19 men, women, and children with their dogs....... While the fire in the midst...... scorched me on one side, on the other I had much ado to keep myself from freezing........ During snow storms, and often at other times, the wigwam was filled with fumes so dense that all were forced to lie flat on our faces, breathing through mouths in contact with the cold earth......... The dogs were not an unmixed evil, for by sleeping on and around me they kept me warm at night; but, as an offset to this good service, they walked, ran and jumped over me as I lay,

snatched food from my birch dish or, in a mad rush at some discarded morsel, now and then knocked over both dish and missionary!"
"Father Le Jeune and the Hunters" in Parkman's *The Jesuits in North America.*

The early missionaries worked with the Huron tribe who lived north of Lake Ontario. The priests' work was going well until a serious problem developed. The Iroquois tribes decided to attack the Huron and others living in that area. A large part of the Huron tribe was killed and many of its members driven far away. The Iroquois also tortured and killed many of the priests. Their attacks made the late 1640s a time of terror in New France! Even much of the fur trade came to a halt.

The Father Marquette Story

In 1668 a young man, who became one of the best-known missionaries, made his way to Michigan. He was Jacques Marquette (JHAHK mar KETT). Marquette was a member of a Catholic religious group called the Jesuits (JEZH wits). The Jesuits did much of the missionary work in North America. Marquette once said he wanted to be a missionary from his earliest boyhood.

Probably the desire to be a missionary in those days is similar to someone in today's world thinking about being an astronaut. Either career would be challenging and exciting, taking a person to the edge of the unknown.

Before long, Marquette was in a canoe and on his way to the place which would become Sault Ste. Marie (Soo Saint ma REE). His group paddled up the Ottawa River and then west to Lake Nipissing. Their route was the one most often used by the French to reach the Great Lakes. It had 18 *portages*, and some of them were six miles long. *A portage is a place where the canoes must be carried because the water is too swift or between rivers.* The Sault (Soo) was a good place to preach to the Indians. Many visited there each summer to catch fish in the rapids.

Father Marquette was the founder of Sault Ste. Marie, the first permanent city in Michigan. (Courtesy Michigan State Archives)

Marquette started a permanent mission and spent one winter there. Sault Ste. Marie, Michigan's oldest city, began from that mission post in 1668. The next spring Marquette was sent to a place just west of the Upper Peninsula into what is now Wisconsin.

Learning About a Great River

During the first winter at his new post, Father Marquette helped nurse a sick Ottawa warrior back to health. Because of this he learned about a great river flowing from north to south. It was probably the same river he had heard called the "Mesippi." Could it be a passage to the Western Sea?

Marquette was ready to explore the river right away, but he had to wait for permission. In 1671 Marquette started a mission he called St. Ignace at the Straits of Mackinac. St. Ignace is the second oldest city in Michigan.

Voyage To Find the Mississippi River

In 1672 Louis Jolliet (LOO ee zhol ee AY) arrived at the St.Ignace mission. The news he brought Marquette was very exciting. The government had approved an expedition to find the great river Mesippi. They could leave in the spring!

On May 17, 1673, Jolliet, Marquette, and five other Frenchmen were on their way! Their two canoes followed the southern shore of the Upper Peninsula. Along the way they stopped at a Menominee village.

When they told the Menominee people their reason for going down the Mississippi River, the Indians gave them a stern lecture on the dangers they would face:

"There are Nations who never show any mercy to strangers, but break their heads without any cause....The great river is full of horrible monsters, which devour men and canoes together; there is even a demon, who is heard from a great distance, and who bars the way and would swallow up all who venture to approach him."

Father Marquette in *Jesuit Relations*, volume 59, translated by Reuben G. Thwaites.

Marquette told the Indians he could not take their advice "...because the salvation of souls was at stake, for which I would be delighted to give my life...."

They took their canoes up the Fox River across Wisconsin. Later they found two native guides to help them reach the Wisconsin River. They canoed 118 miles down the Wisconsin. On June 17 Marquette wrote "...at 42.5 degrees of latitude, we safely entered the Mississippi...with a joy I cannot express."

They went into uncharted land filled with tribes who spoke unknown languages. After much traveling, they were quite certain the Mississippi did not go to the Western Sea (Pacific Ocean) but went instead into the South Sea (Gulf of Mexico). When they reached what they figured was the latitude of 33 degrees, they felt they might be at risk of falling into the hands of the Spanish. If that happened, they knew all knowledge of their voyage would be lost while they rotted in prison- or worse! It was time to head the canoes north and fight the mighty Mississippi's current and paddle home.

Marquette's travels to find the Mississippi River in 1673 and return.

Back Home—Almost!

Near the end of September the explorers dragged into a Jesuit mission on the Fox River but no one was there. Jolliet and his crew left for Sault Ste. Marie with Marquette staying behind. In the spring when everyone returned, they found Marquette was not the healthy young man they remembered. He had chills and fever and could not eat much. He remained sick and very weak all summer.

Marquette's illness continued over the next several months. In a desperate attempt to get Marquette back to St. Ignace at the Straits of Mackinac, two friends decided to take a new route and follow the east shore of Lake Michigan. No Frenchman had ever seen that side of the Lower Peninsula. The priest was now only semi-conscious and he prayed often. On May 18, 1675 they came to a river and Marquette told the men it would be a good place for him to be buried. They took him ashore, probably near Ludington, and he died late in the evening as his companions prayed and wept.

Meanwhile, Louis Jolliet had almost made it back to Montreal when both his canoes turned over in a rapids on the St. Lawrence River. Some of the men drowned and he lost all of his notes and papers. To add humiliation on top of the disaster, his sister-in-law sued him for rent on one of the canoes which he had borrowed from her!

Remember to Take Notes!

Much of the history presented in this chapter would be unknown except for the journals the priests kept while in New France. The Jesuits recorded everything they possibly could. In France they published 70 books about what happened to the priests.

What Are the Facts?

1. Besides fur trading, what activity brought the French to America?
2. Tell some of the difficulties of being a French missionary in Michigan.
3. What is Michigan's oldest non-Indian settlement and who started it?
4. What did the Native Americans Marquette met on the way to the Mississippi River think about his trip?
5. Who died on the beach near Ludington in 1675?

Use a map today!
On a map of the United States, show the approximate route Marquette took on his voyage to and down the Mississippi River. The latitude measurements Marquette put in his diary may help you, though they are not always correct.

Express yourself
Imagine what Michigan was like for the early French explorers and missionaries. What did they think about the geography, the people they met, the climate, the food, the bugs, the joys, and the surprises?

Chapter 3 Section 3

The Explorers:
Through Woods and Over Waters

Learn about the king of France claiming Michigan and all of the Great Lakes in a ceremony at Sault Ste. Marie and how Detroit was started as a fort to keep the British out of the Great Lakes.

Claiming Michigan and Much More!

In 1670 the government of New France heard rumors about a British group called the Hudson's Bay Company which planned to trade furs in the land to the north. Furs were the economy of New France and such news was upsetting!

To protect French interests, a plan was developed. They would officially claim the land for France and hopefully impress the tribes to continue their trade with them and not the British.

Sault Ste. Marie was chosen as the site to make the claim because it was a regular meeting place for many tribes. The French put on a really big show, and the event was called the Pageant of the Sault. It was a June day in 1671. A tremendous gathering of about 2,000 Indians from tribes as far away as Green Bay, Wisconsin, came to witness the ceremony. Chiefs from 14 tribes were present or represented.

A high official, named St. Lusson (loo SOwn), had been sent by the king of France to take a leading part. He and all the French officers wore their finest uniforms to impress the Native Americans. Priests along with dozens of fur traders were also there.

The French marched to a small hill where a large wooden cross was set in the ground. After a song and prayers for the king, St. Lusson held his sword in one hand and some sod in another, proclaiming in a loud voice:

Listen!

" We take possession of the said place of Sault Ste. Marie, as well as of Lakes Huron, and Superior, ... and of all other countries, rivers, lakes and tributaries, contiguous and adjacent there unto, as well as those discovered and to be discovered, which are bounded on one side by the Northern and Western Seas, and on the other side by the South Sea including all its length and breadth." *Jesuit Relations*, volume 50

This is an impressive piece of land!

A Man With Grand Plans- La Salle

La Salle

Another Frenchman was La Salle (la SAL). He was ambitious and adventuresome. During a short time of peace between the Iroquois and the French, La Salle had several Iroquois stay with him. They told him about a river which began in their land and which was so long it took eight or nine months to reach the great sea. What great sea? Could it be a way to reach the Pacific Ocean?

This set La Salle's imagination on fire and changed his life forever! Later LaSalle discovered this was the Mississippi River. Even though he knew this river did not reach the Pacific Ocean, he still felt this could be his big chance. In 1677 La Salle sailed to France and was given broad powers by the King to explore and build forts along the Mississippi River. However, the king told him he could not trade furs with the tribes who came to Montreal. (This way the existing fur business would not be upset.) Also, LaSalle would not get any money or help from the government!

Henri de Tonty— A Friend!

On the voyage from France, La Salle met Henri de Tonty, an Italian. He would become La Salle's trusted friend- one of the few he would ever have. Both Henri and his brother Alphonse eventually came to Michigan.

Henri had been in the army and lost one of his hands in battle. It had been replaced with an iron hand covered by a leather glove. Once or twice Tonty used his hand in fights with Native Americans. They didn't know the secret of his knockout blows and thought he had "powerful magic."

The First Sailing Ship on the Great Lakes Around Michigan

La Salle not only had grand plans, but he was also a hard worker. He expected to trade furs in the west- in spite of his promise to the king. A vessel larger than a canoe would be needed to do the job. He would build a full-sized sailing ship on the Niagara River, above the falls.

After much difficulty and concern about Iroquois attacks, the ship was finished and named the *Griffon*. There was nothing like this ship on the Upper Great Lakes.

Meanwhile his enemies had spread many rumors about La Salle going off on a crazy voyage. The people who loaned him money were afraid he would never come back to pay his bills so they seized all of his property!

Detroit, then Mackinac

The stubborn La Salle continued his plans, and in August 1679 the *Griffon* set sail heading west. After three or four days they reached the narrow straits, or as the French would say *detroit* (day TRWA), between the Lower Peninsula and Canada. Today, Michigan's largest city, Detroit, is located along those straits. As they travelled up the river, they were impressed by the large number of animals they saw. Many apple and plum trees along with grape vines grew on the land along the river.

They sailed north through Lake Huron toward the Upper Peninsula. The next stop was St. Ignace. It was the second oldest French settlement in Michigan, having been started eight years earlier. When they arrived, they found a busy community with a mission house, homes of French traders and Huron and Ottawa villages. Crowds of Indians were awed by the *Griffon* and they gave La Salle a warm greeting.

La Salle's Griffon was greeted by the Indians when it arrived at Michilimackinac. (Courtesy American Museum of Natural History, oil sketch by George Catlin)

The Furs Were Waiting

The *Griffon* continued and picked up furs as it went. At Green Bay in Wisconsin, La Salle felt he must make a daring choice. The furs had to go back to Montreal and be sold to pay his bills, but was the captain trustworthy? On the one hand, La Salle wanted to go back on the ship, but on the other hand, he felt the need to supervise the next stage of his plan. The decision was made; the *Griffon* would have to go back without him.

Danger In the Air!

The furs were loaded on the *Griffon*, and the captain told to sail quickly to Niagara, unload the furs, and return to the southern end of Lake Michigan. Near the St. Joseph River, La Salle would be waiting and counting on him to bring supplies to finish a second ship.

As they prepared the *Griffon* to sail, some of the Indians told the captain a storm was coming, but he didn't see any sign of it and left anyway. Before the ship was out of sight, the storm hit, and the ship was tossed violently. For five days the storm raged.

On November 1, 1679, after a long and very difficult journey, La Salle's group arrived on the east side of Lake Michigan. It was there they followed their plan and built the first non-Indian outpost in the Lower Peninsula. They called it Fort Miami after the tribe living in the area. The men hoped the *Griffon* would return, but it did not. No one ever saw the *Griffon* again and what happened to it is still a mystery!

Crossing the Peninsula

La Salle's group then had no choice except to travel over 600 miles to Montreal. In March they began their journey. It was decided to walk rather than use the St. Joseph River. It would not be easy because there were no paths and the forests were thick. La Salle said, "...in two days and a half our clothes were all torn, and our faces so covered with blood that we hardly knew each other." Fortunately on the third day, the forest was no longer as thick and it was easier for them.

Indians did not hunt in the southern part of Michigan at that time because it was claimed by five or six rival tribes. The only ones in the area were war parties who traveled in secrecy.

At one point, La Salle and his men had to cross a very large swamp which took three days! They didn't dare make a fire as hostile Indians might see the smoke. At night they took off their wet clothes and slept in blankets. One morning when they awakened, it was so cold their clothes were frozen "stiff as sticks." In their rather delicate condition, they had to build a fire to thaw out the clothes. But there were Indians watching and when they saw the fire, they ran up to attack! Luckily by the time they came close, the Indians could see La Salle and his men were French. The Indians called out in the Illinois language to La Salle and said they had mistaken them for Iroquois. A sigh of relief went through the shivering men.

La Salle did not leave behind enough information for us to know the

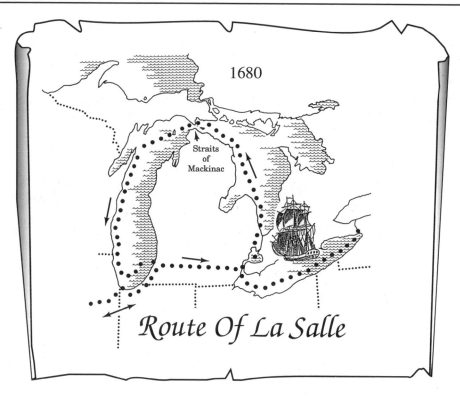

1680

Straits
of
Mackinac

Route Of La Salle

In 1680, LaSalle and his men were the first non-Native Americans to cross the Lower Peninsula.

exact route they took across the Lower Peninsula, but they were the first Europeans to see that part of our state. When they reached the Detroit River they crossed it on a raft. Finally they arrived at the place where the *Griffon* was built. No one had seen the *Griffon* there either and La Salle went on to Montreal with a heavy heart. He never returned to Michigan.

The Man Called Cadillac
Soon after La Salle, came another man with great ambitions. This was Antoine de Lamothe Cadillac (On twON day la MOT KAD el ak). Nova Scotia was Cadillac's first home in New France. He and his wife, Marie-Therese (ma REE TEH rez), had some land there.

For a time, Cadillac was a pirate, attacking English ships. Through his voyages Cadillac became an expert on the British colonies. In 1692 he provided the French government with maps of the American coastline and harbors. The government was pleased and gave Cadillac command of the first vacant military post in New France.

Reward For A Good Job
Cadillac's new post was at Fort de Baude (duh BODE) near St. Ignace, at *Michilimackinac (MISH ill ih mack in naw). The entire area around the Straits of Mackinac was often called Michilimackinac and was the center of*

fur trading in the west. He arrived in 1694. While at Michilimackinac, Cadillac traded in furs to make money for himself. He sent the furs he traded to his wife in Quebec where they could be sold.

The fur trade was important to Cadillac and he did not mind doing whatever was needed to get furs, including trading brandy to the tribes. That caused the priests to become violently upset with him.

An Idea For A New Fort & More

While at Fort de Baude, he began to see the possibilities for a fort which could keep the British traders out of the Great Lakes. Using his knowledge of sailing and maps, he decided the straits between the Lower Peninsula and Canada would be an ideal spot.

Such a fort could only be built with the permission of the king. Off Cadillac went to Paris. He had long talks with the man who helped him get the post at Michilimackinac. The official's name was Pontchartrain (PON cher train) and he had become Cadillac's friend. With Pontchartrain's help, he was able to convince the government he should build his new fort at Detroit. This is how Cadillac started what became Michigan's largest city.

Not Just A Fort

Cadillac's plan had several new twists. He wanted to move all the Indians from the Michilimackinac area to Detroit. There they would be trained in French schools. He also wanted to use them as soldiers! Many French families would be brought to live at Detroit where they could start farms. His ideas were radical! Very few French families lived outside the cities of Quebec and Montreal.

Just as La Salle's plans had upset many people, so did the plans of Cadillac. Can you think why? Fur traders were afraid his western location would allow Cadillac to take control by having all the Indians trade with him. The Jesuit missionaries were very upset with the idea of having Indians move away from their headquarters at St. Ignace. They also worried about brandy being traded to the tribes.

Detroit Is Born!

On June 4, 1701, Cadillac left Montreal in a convoy of 25 canoes. The canoes carried 50 soldiers and 50 *voyageurs (VOY uh zhahs)* along with many Indians and supplies to build the new fort. *Voyageurs were men hired by fur companies to transport goods and people.* His second in command was Alphonse de Tonty, the second Italian to visit Michigan. By July 23 the group had reached the Detroit River. They camped there looking for the best location for building the fort. The next day work began. It would be called Fort Pontchartrain in honor of Cadillac's government friend.

Cadillac was just barely in time because the British made a treaty with the Iroquois to build a fort on the Detroit River that very same month!

When they learned about the French fort, the British gave up their plans-
for the time being.

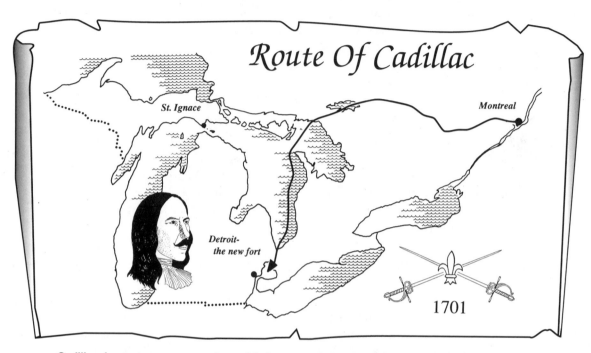

Cadillac began as a spy and provided maps of the American coastline to the French
government. Later, he planned and settled Detroit. (Art by David B. McConnell)

Women Actually Came!

The next event in Detroit's history was a first for Michigan. Mrs.
Cadillac and Mrs. de Tonty arrived with their families! Cadillac's goal was
to build a real settlement of French people in Michigan. He brought his wife
as an example. It had all the Native Americans excited and they felt it
meant the French were there to stay and would protect them when needed.

The ladies traveled in canoes with some of their children and several
Indians and soldiers. The trip was 600 to 700 miles. They arrived to a
chorus of shouts and firing of guns. Some of the local Indians fell on their
knees and said, "Now we know our French brothers mean to stay and be our
friends. Never before have French women been seen willingly to come to
these parts."

Marie-Therese Cadillac

Find out what life was like for Madame Cadillac before she arrived at
Detroit. Her school days were spent side by side with Indian girls at the
convent school in Quebec. There she must have learned about Indian ways

Madame Cadillac, accompanied by her son Jacques and Madame Tonty arrived in Detroit in October 1701. The arrival of French women showed Cadillac's intention to stay on at Detroit permanently. (Courtesy Michigan Bell an Ameritech Company)

and language. Her father was a fur trader and she saw how the business was run. Later, she helped sell furs for her husband as he shipped them to her at Quebec from Michilimackinac and Detroit.

Once, while they were living in Nova Scotia and her husband was on a voyage, the British attacked their town and both the town and her home were burned. She and her children were left stranded on the beach. As if things could not be worse, Spanish pirates saw them and kidnapped them. They were held for ransom, which her family in Quebec paid.

The Cadillacs were at Detroit for 10 years. Though Marie-Therese Cadillac went back to France and lived her last years there, she was a pioneer woman in every sense of the word!

Cadillac Leaves Michigan

Antoine Cadillac and Alphonse de Tonty had many troubles with the fur traders at Montreal and with the priests. By 1711, those in power decided to give him a promotion to get him out of Detroit. So he was made governor of Louisiana.

Fortunately for Detroit, the next 40 years were quiet times on the frontier and the outpost slowly grew. Eventually it had about 900 people or roughly 90 percent of the European population in Michigan.

What Are the Facts?
1. Give a reason the king of France felt he needed to make an official claim to Michigan and the Great Lakes.
2. Why was the *Griffon* built and what happened to it?
3. On his way across the Lower Peninsula, did La Salle find many Indian villages? Why or why not?
4. What was special about Detroit that would make it more than just another fort?
5. Who were the first European women known to come to Michigan?

Express yourself:
Write a paragraph in your own words explaining which person from this chapter you think did the most to develop Michigan. Give reasons for your choice.

Chapter 3 Section 4

Fur Is King !

Fur trading was the main business activity in Michigan for 200 years- longer than any other kind of business! The Straits of Mackinac area was a center for fur trading in the Great Lakes region.

Furs Are the Economy!
By this time it was very hard to find furbearing animals in Europe. It was big business to bring furs from America to Europe for hats and coats. For about 200 years fur was THE business of Michigan! The whole economy was based on the fur trade. Not farming. Not lumbering. Not making cars. From the 1640s to the 1820s fur was king! The search for good animal skins was what brought French traders to Michigan. Furs were what most Indians spent their time collecting.

Michilimackinac, Center of the Fur Trade
Michilimackinac was the center of the fur trade for an area much larger than Michigan. It was in the middle of the Great Lakes region. Traders came by canoe from Montreal and Indians from far to the north and west. It is true Cadillac got many traders and Indians to come to Detroit, but after about 10 years, everything shifted north once more.

Mackinac was a good place to meet. If traders went much further west, they risked winter weather before they could return to Montreal. In the early days the tribes did bring furs right to Montreal, but as more animals were hunted, they became scarce and the Indians had to move west to find enough. To protect the fur trade, Fort Michilimackinac was built by the French where Mackinac City is today.

Who Did the Work?

Most of the work in the fur trade system was done by Indians and voyageurs. With metal traps which the Indians got from the traders, an average of six beavers could be collected in a day. Trapping could be done in summer or winter, but the animals had better furs in the winter. The voyageurs paddled the canoes for the traders. In those canoes, furs were taken to Montreal and Quebec City. When the voyageurs returned in the spring they brought items to trade with the tribes.

Beaver is the One!

They were looking for all sorts of fur-bearing animals, but beaver was the focus of the fur-trade. Beaver skins became a kind of money. Everything was measured as being worth so many beavers.

Beaver pelts were used as money and traded for other items. (From Michigan State University Museum)

41

The value of beaver skins traded at Mackinac Island

Large blanket-=	*3 beaver skins or 4 buckskins*
One pound of gunpowder =	*1 beaver skin*
6 feet of calico cloth =	*2 beaver skins*
Earbobs (earrings) =	*1 small beaver skin or 1 doeskin*

Regulations for the Trade at Michilimackinac From *Michilimackinac- A Guide to the Site*

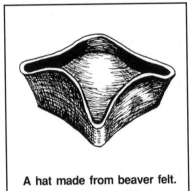

A hat made from beaver felt.

The big market for beaver was for hats. Beaver hats do not really look like fur hats because the fur is not used directly. Only the short hairs next to the skin were used. These short hairs were made into a kind of felt and it was the felt which was used to make the hat. Beaver hats came in many styles.

Let's Make a Deal!

Trading in furs was quite profitable to those in charge. Some historians believe profits reached up to seven times the costs. Such big profits lured traders and explorers farther and farther into North America.

The king of France controlled the fur trade by granting licenses to friends. The high profits attracted many to trade illegally. Those men traded without a license. The illegal traders were known as *coureur de bois* (koo ER deh BWAH). This translates as "woods runner." They often bribed officials to look the other way.

In exchange for furs, the tribes received useful items which made their life easier; however, these things were habit forming. Once a young Native American began to hunt with a gun, he needed to trap more animals to have a supply of gunpowder, lead balls, gun flints, spare parts, and tools for his weapon.

They also traded for items which weren't useful and liquor was one example. Trading liquor (brandy, rum, and wine) was almost always discouraged by the government and missionaries. But it happened anyway. It was easy to trade anything you wanted when you were hundreds of miles in the wilderness. There was little law enforcement.

The following list shows what was carried to Michilimackinac to trade for the year of 1775. Liquor was a large part of the merchandise.

 Look!

1,150	*barrels of rum and wine*
38,000	*pounds of gunpowder.*
44,000	*pounds of musket balls and shot (bullets)*
1,051	*muskets (guns similar to rifles)*
6	*bags of flour*
38	*cases of axes and ironware*
73	*bales of copper, brass and tin kettles*
200	*bales of tobacco*
130	*kegs of pork and lard*
16	*barrels of salt*

A bale is usually a 90 pound package. The materials listed were all carried by about 80 or so large canoes. From *At the Crossroads* by the Mackinac Island Park Commission.

What Are the Facts?

1. Between which years was fur trading the most important economic activity in Michigan? During that time, was the business center of Michigan in the northern or southern part of the state?

2. What was considered the most important fur-bearing animal? What was usually made from its fur?

3. Look at the list of trade goods brought to Michilimackinac in 1775. Make two columns on your paper. In the first column list all of the things the Indians got in their trading which were used up. In the second column write those things which would last for a long time.

4. What were the advantages and disadvantages of the fur trade for the Indians?

Use a map today!

Use a world map to show where furs were taken on the way to market in Europe from Michigan. Label Mackinac Island, Montreal, Quebec, the Great Lakes, the St. Lawrence River, and Atlantic Ocean. See if you can find out how long such a trip might take.

KEY ✼ DATES

1608- First French settlement in North America at Quebec
1620- Pilgrims arrive at Plymouth Rock
1622- Brulé goes to Lake Superior. First European to see Michigan
1649- Iroquois destroy French missions in Ontario. Huron tribe flees area
1668- Marquette at Sault Ste. Marie - Michigan's first European settlement
1671- St. Lusson claims the region for the king of France
1673- Marquette and Jolliet go down the Mississippi
1679- The *Griffon* is launched at Niagara Falls
1690- Fort de Buade is built at St. Ignace
1691- Fort St. Joseph is built at Niles
1701- Cadillac lands at Detroit to start building Fort Pontchartrain
1711- Cadillac sent to govern Louisiana
1715- Fort Michilimackinac is built at Mackinaw City

Consider the Big Picture

The French were the first Europeans to reach Michigan. They arrived over 350 years ago.

They came to trade for furs, to find a way to China and Japan, and to bring their religion to the people. Fur trading became the major business in this area for a long time.

The French reached Michigan by using the St. Lawrence River and the Great Lakes.

The French started Michigan's first cities as missions and forts.

Building Your Michigan Word Power

Write a short Michigan story which includes each of these words used correctly: coureur de bois, Jesuit, Michilimackinac, portage, priests, voyageurs.

Talking About It

Get together in a small group and talk about-

How do you think the members of Michigan's tribes felt when they met the first French people? Do you think their feelings changed over time?

Give examples of how the French and Indians worked together. Did they seem to get along well with each other? Why do you supposed this was so?

Why did the French priests go to so much trouble to tell the tribes about their religion? Would people today be willing to go through so much hardship to do the same thing? In what ways has our society changed?

What does Michigan's location on the Great Lakes have to do with the first European settlements here bearing French names?

What do you think happened to the *Griffon?*

Put It To Use

Plan a search to find the *Griffon* and decide where its wreck is located. Use exact longitude and latitude coordinates.

Do research on living in a frontier town like Detroit or St. Ignace in the early 1700s. Put yourself in the shoes of a woman at that time. Write a diary entry for a day in your life.

Compare values during the fur trading days and today. On a piece of paper write the list of items from the top of page 42. Find the price of similar things today.

The British-

A NEW FLAG ON THE FRONTIER

Chapter 4   Section 1

War In The Woods: French, British, & Indians

Learn how in the 1750s England and France began to squabble over land in North America. A war started and the British won in 1760 and took control of much land, including Michigan.

New France Meets New England

Over the years New France grew slowly, perhaps too slowly. By the 1750s New France had about 80,000 Europeans while New England had nearly 1,250,000! Why such a difference?

The focus of life in New France was the fur trade. The traders spent their time in the woods and on the rivers collecting furs. They were not really interested in having cities. Cities meant less land for animals.

While the French were roaming all over the Great Lakes region, the British were busy building towns and starting farms. The farms fed the growing population. The British allowed many people to come to America who wanted religious freedom. The French did not.

Even worse, the British were beating the French at fur trading. They offered better goods and at lower prices to the Indians! The British kept moving farther west. A struggle over North America was building.

Spats, Arguments, and Fights

The French put Charles Langlade in charge of protecting their interests. Langlade was born at Michilimackinac. His mother was Ottawa and his father was French. He knew much about the Indians' way of fighting in the woods.

In 1754, leading 250 Ottawa and Ojibwa warriors, Langlade went east to assert French control. The French and British fought at Pittsburgh. A young George Washington led the British soldiers. But Washington had to surrender and admit he was trespassing. The fireworks of the French and Indian War had begun! The war spread like a fire to all British and French territories around the world. Either side could lose its empire. At first, the French could not be beaten. They won battle after battle. The French woodsmen and Native Americans were a big help.

Everyone Wants the Indians

Both sides were tugging at the different tribes to join them. The French used warriors from western tribes; many of them came from Michigan. The Native Americans were often willing to attack the British because the British were starting farms and towns, and taking away Indian land in the process.

Later, French began to lose the battles. To get more support, Charles Langlade met with a grand council of the Michigan tribes across the river from Detroit. It was March, 1759. A famous chief named Pontiac was at the meeting listening. It was reported that Langlade's speech went something like this:

Listen!

"My Brothers, I will not try to tell you that the French are still winning the war. But do not make the mistake of thinking that because there have been setbacks, the French are lost.

Now I... ask again that you raise up your tomahawks in the French cause, which is and must be your cause as well.... you know in your hearts the French are your friends.... They

The French and British worked hard to gain the support of the Indians. The Indians fought for both sides during the French and Indian War. (Courtesy Mackinac State Historic Parks)

love the land as you love it and know that it belongs not to individuals, but to all, to share equally. The English may ply you with great gifts.... but the gifts disappear when you have won and your land disappears as well. If you do not fight him with the French, then mark what I say, the time will come when you will have to fight him alone...."

Wilderness Empire by Allan W. Eckert.

Trouble On the St. Lawrence

The St. Lawrence River was the supply line into New France. In 1758 the British sailed up the river and took control. The St Lawrence became the pathway for British victory. Soon the French could not get supplies to trade with the tribes.

In 1759, it came down to a battle outside the gates of Quebec, the capital of New France. The French fort was strong and it sat on a steep hill looking over the river. Charles Langlade, Chief Pontiac, and about 400 Indians from the Michigan area were there.

The two sides had been fighting for 80 days. The French were having problems but it looked as though the British would have to leave soon. Their supplies were very low and the river would freeze soon. The British commander took one last gamble.

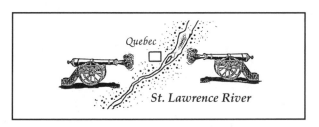

Quebec City- Will They See Us Coming?

On a rainy and moonless night, British soldiers quietly crossed the St. Lawrence River. The soldiers pulled themselves slowly up the great cliff. During the night more and more men scrambled to the top. The boats went back and forth across the river all night. It was amazing, but the French did not see them!

At six in the morning the French general got on his horse and rode outside the fort where he saw about 4,000 British soldiers lined up. He gasped, "This is serious!" The British had done what seemed impossible.

The alarm was given and thousands of French troops ran out of the fort. An intense battle began. The generals from both sides were killed and the French lost the battle. Once the British controlled Quebec, they controlled the St. Lawrence River. No supplies could reach French soldiers in the west- including Michigan.

An Empire Dies!

That night Charles Langlade met with Pontiac and then the Indians headed back to the Great Lakes country. By 1760 all of New France had been surrendered to the British.

What Are the Facts?

1. Why was New France weaker than New England at the time of the French and Indian War?
2. What was the French and Indian War about?
3. What argument did Charles Langlade use to convince Indians from the Michigan area to fight against the British?

4. Why was the St. Lawrence River important in the French and Indian War?

Express yourself:
If the British had lost the French and Indian War, give your opinion about how Michigan would be different today.

Chapter 4   Section 2

Chief Pontiac Rebels

The British made mistakes in dealing with the tribes. The Indians became quite upset. Chief Pontiac finally attacked and tried to drive the British out.

The British Take Over Michigan

The British came to Detroit to take charge of Fort Pontchartrain. Its new name would be Fort Detroit. Though the French soldiers left, many of the fur traders and those with small farms stayed behind. The French continued to be the largest non-Indian group in Michigan for another 60 years! Even though the French seemed friendly, some of them hoped their soldiers would come back some day. They told this to the Native Americans too.

What one artist thought Pontiac looked like. (Art by Dirk Gringhuis)

Bad Policies

The British government was not wise in dealing with the tribes. There were new orders not to give them presents or to trade any gunpowder to them. By now the tribes were used to using guns, and they needed gunpowder for hunting. Also the British demanded more furs for everything the tribes needed. Some traders cheated the Indians too. Meanwhile, the British wanted land for farms and settlers.

Major Gladwin, British commander at Detroit in 1763. (Courtesy Michigan State Archives)

The tribes were growing restless. They knew the French and British were still at war in Europe. There were rumors the French army would return. At Detroit, Major Gladwin was given command and he was not friendly to the Indians. The Potawatomi, Ottawa, and Huron all had villages near Detroit. Chief Pontiac lived in the Ottawa village where Windsor, Canada is today.

Trouble Is Brewing

On April 27, 1763 Pontiac invited many tribes to come to a meeting along the Ecorse River. He talked about a way to get rid of the British. He would ask to meet with Major Gladwin in the fort. Pontiac would bring many warriors in with him. Each man would be wearing a large blanket.

Over the next few days Indians began to show up at the French blacksmith asking for metal files. Did he ask why they wanted so many files? Did he provide the files with a curious look or just a little smile? Pontiac's warriors were cutting the barrels of their muskets short with the files! The guns would be under their blankets when they walked into the fort!

Mid-morning on May 7, 1763, 11 chiefs and 60 warriors solemnly walked into the fort– their fingers close to gun triggers. But they soon realized something was wrong. The soldiers were not going about business as usual. They were armed and ready. Every move of the Indians was tensely watched by the Englishmen. How did they know? There are many stories explaining how the British learned about Pontiac's plan. One says a young French woman heard about the plan and wanted to warn her boyfriend who was a British trader.

A grim Pontiac told Major Gladwin this was not the way to hold a council and he left. The next day Pontiac asked if all of his warriors could come and smoke a pipe of peace with the British. Gladwin told him only chiefs could come.

The next day all the Ottawa came to the fort anyway. They were not allowed to go in. Pontiac was furious that his plans had not worked. The 120 or so British soldiers knew they were in real danger because Pontiac had about 800 warriors.

Pontiac's men leave the fort after Major Gladwin discovered their plan to attack the British at Detroit. (Frederic Remington, Harper's Magazine April, 1897)

Pontiac Attacks Detroit

Suddenly yells and war cries came from the woods. The British soldiers tensed. They were far from any help. Warriors rushed up to the fort and furiously tried to hack a hole in the wooden wall with their *tomahawks. Tomahawks are small metal hatchets used in fighting*. After many warriors were killed, the Native Americans became convinced they could not cut their way into the fort.

That night the Indians started fires against the wooden walls. British soldiers raced back and forth with buckets of water to stop the flames. Officers expected the Indians would try to do the same thing the next night so they took precautions. A hole was cut through the wall from the inside and a cannon placed to fire on anyone coming close to the wall! In the darkness that night many more Indians died.

For days the battle continued. The British were becoming desperate. They had only three bullets left for each soldier and very little food. Major Gladwin clung to the hope that supplies and reinforcements would come by the end of the month...just a few more days. On May 30, the soldiers could see the supply canoes in the distance on the river. As the boats came closer, those in the fort were horrified as they realized the canoes had Indians in them. Pontiac and his men had already captured the food and ammunition. The fight went on. All of June and most of July passed with the British closed up in Fort Detroit. Finally the British reached Detroit by water with another 280 men and supplies.

Time Runs Out

The Indians did not give up. They were sure the soldiers would run low on ammunition again. But time was also going against them. It was fall and they needed to hunt and gather food for the winter. Warriors, with their families, began to drift away. Some of the Indian groups made peace. Near the end of October, Pontiac received a letter from the French telling him France and England had finally made peace. The French would not send soldiers to help take Detroit. Finally, Pontiac decided to stop the attack. The Indian siege of 153 days was the longest in American history and showed Pontiac's skill as an organizer and warrior.

Secret Plans For Michilimackinac

Detroit was not the only British fort the Native Americans attacked. At Fort Michilimackinac, the Chief of the Ojibwa tribe had become friends

Fort Michilimackinac was attacked by the Ojibwa during a lacrosse game. Many British soldiers were killed. (Courtesy Michigan Bell an Ameritech Company)

51

with the British commander. The chief suggested the Ojibwa and Sauk tribes play a game of baggataway or *lacrosse* in honor of the British king's birthday. The commander agreed it was a fine idea. The Indians could play just outside the fort. *Lacrosse is an Indian game with two teams having many players. The players have small rackets and try to move a ball across the other team's goal.*

Alexander Henry was one of the British fur traders at the Fort. He was adopted as a brother by Wawatam, another Ojibwa chief. It was Chief Wawatam who invited Henry to come on a hunt with him and his wife. Wawatam said he was "worried by the noise of evil birds." That was a tribal expression meaning there might be trouble. Since Henry was waiting for his canoes of supplies, he turned the chief down. He was touched when Wawatam and his wife left with tears in their eyes. That same day many Indians came into the fort to trade. Henry was puzzled when the only goods they bought were tomahawks!

The Lacrosse Game

Many of the soldiers came out to watch the game. It was a great sight! The British commander made a large bet on the Ojibwa side. Even though it was a warm day, Native American women wrapped in blankets sat near the gate. Suddenly the ball went over the wall and into the fort. The players rushed inside after it. As they ran they snatched weapons from under the women's blankets. One officer held off several Indians with his sword until he was killed, but few of the soldiers had time to defend themselves.

The Frenchman Charles Langlade and his family were watching the fighting from their house. Alexander Henry ran up to the Langlades and begged them to help him. Langlade said,

"What do you expect me to do?"

Amazingly, a Native American woman who worked in their house took Henry up the back stairs and hid him in the attic.

War Spreads Far and Wide

During that long summer of 1763 the British soldiers learned of other disasters. Many tribes all along the western frontier had risen up to throw out the British. By July, nine of the 12 forts west of the Ohio River had been captured. Only Fort Detroit, Fort Niagara on the Niagara River, and Fort Pitt at Pittsburgh held out against the tribes. It was part of the greatest Native American *uprising* against the Europeans in American history and became known as Pontiac's War or Pontiac's *Rebellion. A rebellion is an armed attack against those in control. It could be an attack against a king, a government, or the military.* Pontiac was a courageous leader who was trying to keep his people's land the best way he knew.

Pontiac's Rebellion greatly upset the British. They certainly did not want this sort of trouble to happen again so they decided to stop any more settlers from moving west onto tribal land. Maybe this would keep the tribes from attacking the forts. The British made the Proclamation of 1763 which said it was illegal for any settler to go west of the Appalachian Mountains.

It is always hard to please two groups at the same time. Settlers in the American colonies had long counted on the right to be able to move west and start farms and villages in "new" areas. The Proclamation of 1763 was a real aggravation to them. It became one of many problems between American colonists and the British government which finally led to the War for Independence.

Pontiac's Rebellion, which started to push the British out of the tribal lands, did succeed in a way. The British were pushed out after the War for Independence, but this did not help Pontiac and his people. The American colonists started the United States and more settlers swarmed west than ever before!

The African American Trader

In the mid-1760s Jean de Sable (JHAN duh SAW bul) came to Michigan. De Sable, born on the island of Haiti, was an African American with a French background .

It is said de Sable became good friends with Chief Pontiac and lived near his camp, trading with the tribes. This African American moved west when Pontiac left Michigan. In 1779 he became the first non-Native American to have a permanent settlement at the portage of Chicago.

De Sable was well-educated and spoke English, French and several tribal languages. He had a good reputation among both the English and Native Americans. Jean de Sable was a unique person and one of the first African Americans in the land of Michigan.

by
Aaron
Zenz

What Are the Facts?

1. Which things made the tribes angry once the British took over Michigan?

2. Who made the plan to take over the fort at Detroit in 1763? Did the French encourage or help with this plan?

3. How did the tribes plan to surprise the British soldiers at Fort Michilimackinac?

4. Chief Wawatam acted as an individual and had different feelings from those who attacked Fort Michilimackinac. What did Chief Wawatam do? Give an example to show his feelings were different.

5. How did Pontiac's Rebellion help lead to the American War for Independence from the British?

53

Chapter 4   Section 3

Michigan While Our Nation Is Born: 1774 - 1783

Did you know Detroit was a base for British raids during the Revolutionary War and that American frontier settlers planned to capture Detroit?

British Policies Lead To A Revolution

In spite of Chief Pontiac's uprising, the British kept control of all of North America east of the Mississippi River. But the Indian revolt made them change their policies in North America. For many years Britain had let the colonies do much as they wanted. After Pontiac's Rebellion the British tried to please the Indians by keeping settlers from going west onto Indian land. That angered the American colonies. The colonists believed they had a right to live wherever they wanted.

In addition, the British taxed people in the colonies to pay for the expensive French and Indian War. The Americans felt those taxes were too high and unfair. Next, the British government tried to keep the many French people living in Canada *and* Michigan happy by passing the *Quebec Act* in 1774. *This act allowed the use of French laws among other things.*

The Quebec Act and other new British laws helped push the colonies into the Revolutionary War. In that war the colonies declared their independence and freedom from England and the British government. It was the beginning of the United States.

Michigan During The Revolution

The French people living in Michigan did not see what all the fuss was about. The Quebec Act passed by the British let them have a government and religious system much like they were used to. So the people in Michigan were not interested in fighting the British during the Revolutionary War.

While the French people were not active in the Revolution, the British sol-

A French trader and an Indian woman (Art by Dirk Gringhuis)

54

diers were! Detroit became a base to send out raids against the colonies and against the American settlers who had moved into Ohio and Kentucky.

British Raids From Detroit

The British convinced many Indians to help fight on their side in the Revolutionary War. The Native American's concern for the land and their way of life was the reason they changed sides so quickly. The Indians did not mind attacking settlers because they wanted to keep them off their land. In return, the tribes received gunpowder and supplies from the British. Detroit served as the supply center for the entire area.

To encourage the Indians to attack American settlers, the British offered money whenever the Indians could prove an American had been killed. How could the Indians show such proof? Scalps taken from the dead was one way!

Henry Hamilton was the commander at Fort Detroit and the British lieutenant governor. He was given the nickname of "the Hair Buyer" because it was reported he paid the Indians for American *scalps*.

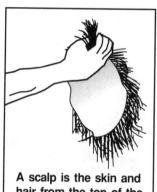

A scalp is the skin and hair from the top of the head.

The pioneer settlers who lived in Kentucky were living in terror of Indian attacks. The situation got so bad that 1777 was known as "the year of the bloody sevens." Many settlers were taken prisoner and brought to Detroit to be held for ransom. Even the great Daniel Boone was captured! The Indians were so proud of catching him they adopted him into their tribe.

Capture Detroit!

George Rogers Clark was an American settler attacked by the Indians. He was the kind of pioneer to take action. In the summer of 1778, after much effort, about 175 men agreed to leave their families and join Clark. Clark decided to attack the British fort at Kaskaskia (ka SKAS kee uh) first. It was across the river from St. Louis, Missouri. Clark's march against Kaskaskia was a total surprise. One night he walked through the open gate and into the commander's bedroom, forcing him to give up.

Next, the Americans marched across Illinois and captured Fort Sackville at the village of Vincennes (ven SENZ).

The British Go After Clark

When news of those events reached Detroit, "Hair Buyer" Hamilton was appalled. He left Detroit with soldiers to stop Clark. They took rafts and followed the Maumee and Wabash rivers. Hamilton easily took back Vincennes from the small American army left there.

A Grueling Winter March

George Rogers Clark was a very determined person. He turned around and led a larger group of soldiers back to Vincennes. It was an awful winter march across flooded fields. It took much more fighting to take Vincennes the second time. But Henry Hamilton finally surrendered.

Hamilton's hands and feet were bound with chains and he was taken to Virginia as a prisoner of war. He was hated by many and not treated very well, even though he denied that he personally paid for scalps. Daniel Boone, however, had been impressed by Hamilton while he was a prisoner at Detroit. To show his respect, Boone visited him. Perhaps Hamilton was not as bad as his reputation.

George Rogers Clark and his men marched through the swamps of Illinois to make their second surprise attack on Fort Sackville at Vincennes. (Photo courtesy of Illinois Bell)

Detroit Stays Out Of Reach

Clark waited and tried to raise enough men to attack Detroit. But he could not get men or supplies from Virginia. Everything was needed to fight the British in the East. In the end he gave up his plan of taking Detroit.

Spain Comes To Michigan!

Late in the war, Spain and France decided to try to help the colonies in the revolution against England. Spain did not do much, but in the winter of 1781 it sent a small group of Spanish soldiers and Indians from their post at St. Louis. They followed the Mississippi and other rivers north until they reached Fort St. Joseph at Niles, Michigan. Actually the British had left the fort. Only some traders and supplies stayed behind.

The Spanish raised their flag over the fort, took all of the

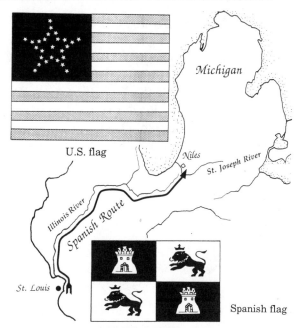

U.S. flag

Spanish flag

Spanish route to Niles

supplies they could carry, set the fort on fire and left. Because of that little expedition, the city of Niles can say it has had four flags during its history - French, British, Spanish, and American.

The Revolutionary War Ends

Most of the battles during the war were far to the east of Michigan. General George Washington, with the help of the French army and navy, finally forced the British to surrender at Yorktown, Virginia. The last battle was in 1781. But it took two more years to negotiate the final peace treaty. One reason the treaty process took so long was the problem of deciding the western boundaries of the United States.

What George Rogers Clark Did For Michigan

Even though George Rogers Clark did not capture Detroit, his actions had an impact here. First of all, the British were worried he would attack, so they built a new and stronger fort at Detroit, and they moved the fort at Mackinaw City to a better position on Mackinac Island. That fort is still on the island today. His actions also helped win the land north of the Ohio River for the United States. If Clark had not been successful, England would probably have kept this land after the Revolution; instead, it was included in the area given to the United States in the peace treaty of 1783. But the land we call Michigan was not a state at that time, it was only a part of the much larger area. It was part of the Northwest Territory.

What Are the Facts?

1.   Why didn't the people living in Michigan join those in the 13 colonies and declare independence from the British?
2.   What part did the British at Detroit play during the Revolutionary War? Mention at least two things.
3.   Were the British worried that George Rogers Clark might attack Michigan? Give a reason for your answer.
4.   How did the victories by George Rogers Clark affect Michigan after the Revolutionary War?

Use a map today!
Using a map showing the United States and Canada, make a new boundary which might have been used between the two countries after the Revolutionary War, if George Rogers Clark had not been successful.

Look!

KEY ❀ DATES

1754- Langlade & George Washington fight near Pittsburgh
       The French and Indian War begins
1759- Fall of Quebec, the French stronghold is lost
1760- Fighting ends in North America between French & British
       British take over Detroit from French.
1761- William Johnson meets with Indians at Detroit
1763 (May)- Chief Pontiac attacks Detroit
       (June)- Surprise attack at Fort Michilimackinac
       (October)- Pontiac stops attack on Detroit
1774- Quebec Act brings first civilian government to Michigan
1775- The American Revolutionary War begins
1777- British raiders from Detroit attack Americans in Kentucky
1778- Captain Dequindre from Detroit attacks Boonesboro, Kentucky
1779- Fort Michilimackinac is moved to Mackinac Island
1781- Spanish troops at Niles
1781- The British surrender and the American Revolution ends
1783- Peace treaty between U.S. and England
1783-1796   British stay in Michigan anyway

Michigan In Pictures

Upper Falls of the Tahquamenon River in Michigan's Upper Peninsula. The river has two picturesque falls located four miles apart. (*Courtesy Michigan Travel Bureau*)

French explorers and fur traders used Michigan's rivers as highways long ago. (*Theresa Deeter*)

A Port Huron steam engine on display by the Michigan Steam Engine and Threshers Club. The club has an annual meeting in late July near Mason. This type can weigh between 15,000 - 20,000 pounds. (*Courtesy David B. McConnell*)   **1**

Downtown Detroit, as it appeared in 1930. (*Courtesy Michigan State Archives*)   **2**

A *Ford Model T* car. The Ford Motor Company sold 15 million Model Ts in 19 years. (*Courtesy David B. McConnell*)

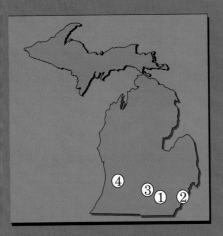

The Renaissance Center, a familiar sight on the Detroit skyline, was completed in 1977. The 73-story glass hotel is one of the world's tallest and is Michigan's tallest building. (*Courtesy Michigan Travel Bureau*)

The state of Michigan has had three capitol buildings. The first was located in Detroit. In 1847, the capital was moved to Lansing, but the building quickly became inadequate. The present capitol building was then built and dedicated on January 1, 1879. (*Courtesy Michigan Travel Bureau*)   3

The Gerald R. Ford Museum, located in Grand Rapids, was dedicated in September, 1981. The dedication was attended by numerous celebrities, including Bob Hope, Danny Thomas, and Sammy Davis, Jr. (*Courtesy Michigan Travel Bureau*)   4

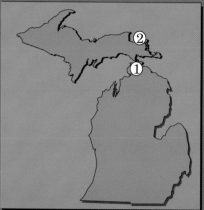

With its Great Lakes, 11,000 inland lakes and 36,000 miles of rivers, Michigan offers much to those looking for water recreation… whether swimming or fishing for salmon. (*Courtesy Michigan Travel Bureau*)

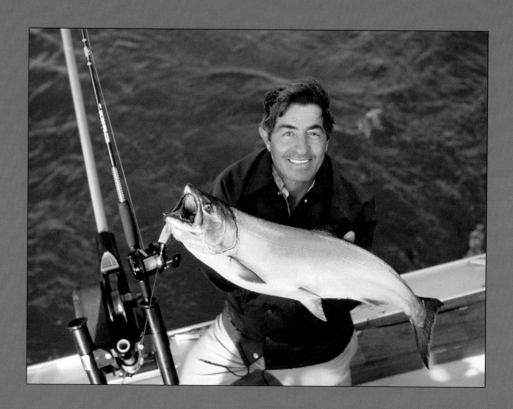

The 730-foot *John B. Aird* is passing in the background of this beach. The self-unloading freighter was launched in 1983. (*Courtesy Michigan Travel Bureau*)

This replica of the sloop *Welcome* was launched in 1980 and is harbored in Mackinaw City. The original was an armed ship stationed at Fort Michilimackinac during the Revolutionary War. The ship carried supplies to British outposts around the Great Lakes. (*Courtesy Mackinac Island State Park Commission*) **1**

In 1855 the first ship passed through the Soo Locks. These locks enable ships to pass between Lake Huron and Lake Superior, overcoming a difference in water levels of about 19 feet. Over 10,000 passages are made through the locks each year. (*Courtesy Michigan Travel Bureau*) **2**

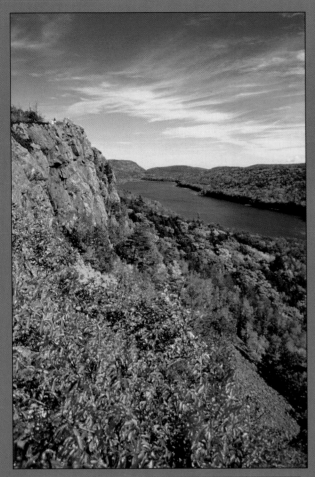

The No. 2 rock shaft house of the Quincy copper mine before it received new paint and siding. It is now one of the sites in the Keweenaw National Historic Park. The shaft is near Hancock and more than 9,000 feet deep! **2**

The Porcupine Mountain Range, located west of Ontonagon, is one of the highest elevations in the State. (*Courtesy Michigan Travel Bureau*) **1**

Eagle Harbor, on the Keweenaw Penninsula, was first settled in 1844 and was the site of early copper mining. (*Courtesy Michigan Travel Bureau*) **3**

The Mighty Mac, which connects Michigan's two peninsulas, is opened each Labor Day for those who wish to walk the five-mile suspension bridge. (*Courtesy Michigan Travel Bureau*)   **4**

The Eagle Harbor Lighthouse on the Keweenaw Penninsula. The first lighthouse here was built in 1851. The tower in the picture was built in 1871. (*Courtesy David B. McConnell*)

Fort Michilimackinac has been located in three places. It was established at St. Ignace in 1681, reestablished at Mackinaw City in 1715, and later moved to Mackinac Island by the British. It has now been restored at Mackinaw City. (*Courtesy Michigan Travel Bureau*)

Holland is famous for its Dutch heritage. A street vendor makes and sells wooden shoes, a part of the Dutch costume, during the annual Tulip Time Festival. The festival takes place each May. (*Courtesy David B. McConnell*)   **1**

Frankenmuth, home of the Bavarian Inn, is Michigan's top tourist attraction. About 3 million people visit each year. The Bavarian Inn seats as many as 1,200 people and cooks over 750,000 pounds of chicken a year! (Courtesy Michigan Travel Bureau)   **2**

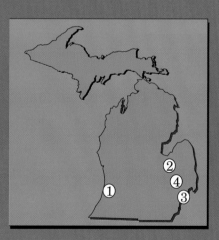

A Ukrainian-American woman at the downtown Detroit ethnic festival. Festivals are held every weekend from the first of May to the middle of September. Each festival emphasizes a different ethnic group. (*Courtesy Michigan Travel Bureau*)   **3**

The Renaissance Festival is held during the month of September in Holly. It includes the re-creation of a sixteenth-century village, and a crafts marketplace.   (*Courtesy Michigan Travel Bureau*)   **4**

Consider the Big Picture

The French lost control of the St. Lawrence River- their way into the Great Lakes- and thus they lost their empire of New France.

The British did not control Michigan for a long time- less than 40 years, but many things changed during this time.

The rules the British finally used when trading with the tribes upset them very much and caused a war led by Chief Pontiac.

Many Michigan area tribes switched from fighting against the British to fighting with them.

During the Revolutionary War, Detroit was a British base for raids to other parts of the country.

Building Your Michigan Word Power

Write each of these six words in a column. (lacrosse, massacre, rebellion, scalp, siege, tomahawk) Next to each one write the best definition from those below. There are extra definitions.

something from the top of a person's head; a large and heavy ax; an uprising against those in control; a short fight; a complete victory with the loss of most of the enemy; a very long attack against a fort or city; the French name for a Native American game; a small metal hatchet

Talking About It

Get together in a small group and talk about-

What does the discovery of a path up a steep hill in Quebec city have to do with the French leaving Michigan which is over 600 miles away?

In 1760 most tribes in the Michigan area were for the French, but by the time of the Revolutionary War they were fighting with the British. What happened? Why did they change sides? What was the goal of the tribes?

Pontiac's plans to force the British out of the Great Lakes was quite amazing. Can you think of any other time in history where native people have attacked so many forts with such success? What was the reason behind this success?

Put It To Use

Imagine you are a newspaper reporter based in Detroit for the *Michigan Frontier Gazette*. By writing four short articles, report the events of the Revolutionary War from the viewpoint of a person in Detroit.

Most of Michigan history to this point is about Native Americans, the French and the British– but the book also mentions three people from other places. Who are they and where were they from? Write a biography of each person.

Michigan Joins the United States

Chapter 5 Section 1

The British Hang On!

It is true. The British did not want to leave Michigan after the Revolution. They gave guns & supplies to the Indians so they could attack settlers moving west.

But Redcoats Still Rule!

The peace treaty with England stated Michigan would become part of the new United States. But there was one big hitch- the British did not leave their forts at Mackinac Island and Detroit! One reason they stayed was that many British fur traders were making money in the area. They also supplied the tribes with guns so they could attack American settlers in the Ohio River Valley. Perhaps the British thought the Indian attacks would weaken the United States and cause the young country to collapse.

In 1790 President Washington sent soldiers into Ohio to attack the tribes and humiliate the British. Indians under Chief Little Turtle massacred our troops and the United States was humiliated instead. A second army force was sent to Ohio the next year but it could do no better. President Washington was very concerned. A national crisis was developing.

Soldiers On the March

General Anthony Wayne was selected to lead a third army to wrestle control of the Ohio from the British and Indians. General Wayne had fought in the Revolution and was known for his bold actions in battle. He was determined not to be defeated.

He felt the soldiers in the first two battles had been poorly trained, so he spent months in training. The army

General Anthony Wayne carefully planned his march against the Indians in Ohio. (Courtesy Michigan State Archives)

slowly marched north through Ohio toward the Indian villages along the Maumee River. As it went north, several forts were built.

Little Turtle, Blue Jacket, and other Native American leaders decided to lure the Americans into a tremendous tangle of trees which had been blown down by a tornado. The place was known as Fallen Timbers. It was just south of Toledo, Ohio – only a few miles from Michigan. About 1,300 Indians and 53 British advisors had made their camp there.

BATTLE IN A TORNADO ZONE!

Battle at Fallen Timbers

Wayne had given the Americans orders to march into the trees and use their bayonets first and not fire their muskets until the enemy was on the run. Since their guns only held a single shot, that was wise advice. Many Indians and British were killed while trying to reload. General Wayne's army went on to destroy many of the Indian villages and their farms.

An Important Treaty

The next summer, Little Turtle, Blue Jacket, and other Indians came to Fort Greenville in Ohio and met with General Wayne. They made a peace *treaty* with the United States. Indians from the Michigan tribes also attended. They too pledged peace with the United States. *A treaty is a formal agreement to settle a conflict.*

In the treaty Indians gave up a large part of what became the state of Ohio and some land in Michigan. In exchange for their land, the Indians were provided $20,000 in trade goods and $9,500 in goods each year forever. It may not have been a fair trade, but much more could be purchased for a dollar at that time. The Treaty of Greenville was the first major Indian land treaty to affect Michigan. In this treaty, the Indians gave up land on the Detroit River and at the Straits of Mackinac, including Mackinac Island.

The Stars and Stripes Over Michigan!

And what about the British? The Battle at Fallen Timbers made them realize they risked war with the United States if they did not leave. The danger of General Wayne's large army so close to the British forts could not be shrugged off. Reluctantly, the British made a treaty and said they would leave their forts on the Great Lakes by 1796.

General Anthony Wayne and his soldiers were great heroes. Unfortunately on his way home, Wayne died from a leg infection. Eventually, a county in the territory was named for him. One of the officers with General Wayne was Lieutenant Colonel John Hamtramck (HAM tram ik). A Michigan city was named for Hamtramck .

The people in Detroit viewed the change of government with mixed feelings. William Macomb was a wealthy trader at Detroit who welcomed the Americans, though he died before they arrived, but many of the people did not want to have anything to do with the Americans. They moved across the Detroit River to live in Canada. The British soldiers left Detroit and built a new fort on the Canadian side of the river. There continued to be much British influence in Michigan.

Wayne, Hamtramck and Macomb were three people involved in events at the time when Michigan changed hands from being British to American. Places in Michigan are named after them today.

What Are the Facts?

1. Give two reasons why the British wanted to stay in Michigan after the Revolution.
2. How did General Wayne's victory at Fallen Timbers help open the way for settlers to come to Michigan?
3. Did the tribes receive anything for their land ? If so, what was it?
4. What did many of the British people living in Michigan do when the Americans took over?

This painting of Ojibwa leader Figured Stone was made during treaty talks in 1826 near Lake Superior. One day Figured Stone had a chance to show his feelings about treaties. He joined a U.S. government agent as he sat on a log. The agent moved over to make more space between them. But Figured Stone also scooted over. Again the agent moved, but the Ojibwa followed right next to him. When the agent got to the end of the log, Figured Stone gave a mighty push sending the government man sprawling. *Do you think the agent got the message?* (Courtesy Clarke Historical Library, Central Michigan University)

Express yourself:
Imagine you are a tribal chief from Michigan talking to a visiting chief. Tell your feelings how the Indians in this area were treated by the British and Americans in the 1790s. Use true examples where you can.

Chapter 5 Section 2

United States Takes Possession: 1796-1812

The pioneers couldn't just move in and build homes and start farms- several things had to be solved first.

Survey The Land

Could the settlers begin to move into Michigan now? Not quite. The land had to be surveyed so it could be purchased with a proper description. *A surveyor is a person who uses special instruments to find boundary lines for maps.*

Congress passed the Land Ordinance of 1785 (*ordinance means law*) which said the land must be surveyed before it was sold and not afterwards, as had happened in some places. The law also said the land would be divided into *townships*. *Townships are square blocks of land six miles on a side.* These townships are still used today.

The Land Ordinance also contained a new idea about how to help pay for schools. A section of each township would be sold to promote education.

To locate each township, two lines were drawn on the Michigan map. One line going east and west was marked across the Lower Peninsula. That is called the *base line*. Today 8 Mile or Base Line Road heads west along that exact line just north of Detroit. The base line continues across the north edge of the second row of Lower Peninsula counties.

Another line runs up the Lower Peninsula and into the Upper Peninsula reaching Sault Ste. Marie. This line is called the *prime meridian*. Each township in Michigan is east or west of the prime meridian and north or south of the base line.

This map shows the two key lines used by surveyors to locate townships in Michigan.

Even today property descriptions are based on the information gathered by surveyors tramping through underbrush over 150 years ago!

Buy the Land Through Treaties

There was just one more detail. The land had to be obtained from the Indians by the United States government. A treaty was made in 1807 for about a quarter of the Lower Peninsula. The Indians kept the right to hunt and fish on the land. The treaty process went on for many more years. Not until 1842 would the tribes give up the last major piece of Michigan.

Michigan as a Part of the Northwest Territory

Next came another ground-breaking law, the *Northwest Ordinance. This was a set of laws passed by Congress to give basic rules for this part of the country.* Many aspects of Michigan, which are taken for granted today, first came from that set of laws. Here are some things the Northwest Ordinance said:

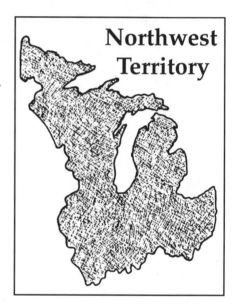

1. Slavery was prohibited. (People who already owned slaves were allowed to keep them.)
2. Indians were to be treated considerately. No land would be taken from the Indians without their consent.
3. Schools and education would always be encouraged because "religion, morality and knowledge are necessary to good government and the happiness of mankind."

Steps To Statehood

The Northwest Ordinance listed three stages to becoming a state. Each stage depended on the number of voters in the territory. In order to vote a person had to be a free white male who owned at least 50 acres of property. When a part of the territory had 60,000 free people, statehood was possible.

Birth Of The Michigan Territory

After Ohio became a state, Michigan was combined with the Indiana Territory. That did not please Michiganians because the capital of the Indiana Territory was in Vincennes which was just too far away. The people of Michigan asked Congress to set up a Michigan Territory so they could be closer to their own government. In 1805 the Michigan Territory was created. Its southern boundary was to be "an east-west line drawn through the southerly bend of Lake Michigan." At that time only a small part of the Upper Peninsula was included in Michigan.

The new Michigan Territory would have a governor, a secretary, and three judges, all appointed by the President of the United States. William Hull was the new governor. Hull had been a general in the Revolutionary War. Augustus Woodward was one of the three judges. All the laws for the territory would be made by the governor and the judges because there was no legislature at that time.

Disaster at Detroit!

In the summer of 1805 what kind of town did the officials find when they arrived at Detroit? No town at all- because it burned down on June 11! It started in John Harvey's stable. As flames burned through the roof, the wind picked up sparks and spread the fire to other buildings. Everyone pitched in to help. The fire wagon was brought out, but the suction hose on the fire wagon became clogged with pieces of felt from the hat maker's well and stopped working. In about three hours, all of Detroit was a pile of smoking embers except for the military buildings!

The 1805 Detroit fire which according to legend was started by ashes falling from a pipe. (Courtesy Michigan Bell an Ameritech Company)

Of course the people rebuilt Detroit. During these years, Detroit and Mackinac Island were really the only two major centers of activity here. Mackinac Island continued to be the headquarters of fur trade for the Great Lakes, but the British competed from a nearby island. Detroit was the capital of the territory and the center for the government. The town was growing slowly because it was quite difficult for settlers to reach Michigan. Soon the problems with the British and Indians would boil over and stop all progress for a while. The Michigan Territory would be at war!

What Are the Facts?

1. In 1800, was it clear that there would be a state called Michigan? Explain.
2. How much of the Upper Peninsula was included in the Michigan Territory?
3. What serious event happened in Detroit in 1805?

Digging Deeper:
Write a paragraph considering the following– What did the Northwest Ordinance say about taking land from the Native Americans? Analyze the contemporary factors contributing to the way the Indians were actually treated. That is to say, taking into account the events and thinking of those times, why weren't the ideas of the Ordinance better carried out?

Chapter 5 Section 3

The War of 1812: The Last Tussle for Michigan!

Find out about the two Indian leaders who united several tribes against American settlers between 1806 and 1813.

Hard to believe, but the British and Americans had a second war in 1812 and important battles took place in and near Michigan.

Irritations Lead to War

Even after treaties with the Indians and exit of the British, the Michigan pioneers faced problems. Tension was increasing between the Indians and American settlers. And why not! Settlers were hungry for Indian land

and were not shy about taking it. The Indians were beginning to realize what the land treaties with the Americans really meant for them.

Strong Indian Leaders to the South

Settlers had heard rumors about a Shawnee from Indiana who was becoming a powerful leader among the tribes. This man was known as The Prophet. The Prophet's Indian name was Tenskwatawa (tens QUA ta wa), which means "the one who opens the door."

The Prophet had a brother known as Tecumseh (ta KUM see). His name means shooting star. Tecumseh was also an able leader. He was very concerned about the settlers taking Indian land. When he heard the terms of one treaty he fumed, "Sell a country! Why not sell the air, the clouds and the great sea, as well as the earth? Did not the Great Spirit make them all for the use of his children?" Tenskwatawa and Tecumseh argued the land belonged to all Indians and not just those tribes who made the agreement.

Tecumseh is shown here wearing parts of a British military uniform.

Tecumseh traveled to many tribes telling them that they must unite and work together to fight the American settlers. He spoke to tribes in the north and as far south as Florida. Captain Sam Dale heard Tecumseh and commented, "His voice resounded....hurling out his words like a succession of thunderbolts.... I have heard many great orators, but I never saw one with the vocal powers of Tecumseh."

Get Rid Of The British!

Settlers in the Indiana Territory began to feel the pain of more Indian attacks. Indiana's Governor William Henry Harrison fought a large battle with The Prophet in 1811. It was a tough battle which the Indians lost. After the defeat, Governor Harrison reported that each Indian had a British gun, scalping knife, war club, and a tomahawk. Some of the guns were so new they were still wrapped. This led many Americans to feel the British should be driven from Canada.

America thought about war, but their defenses were not strong. In 1811 Michigan had only nine main settlements with about 4,700 non-Indian people. About four-fifths were of French background.

Michigan's territorial Governor Hull went to Washington to discuss the situation. Hull was made a general and given command of the northwestern army. His first goal would be to attack Fort Malden at Amherstburg, not far from Detroit.

The War of 1812

On June 1, 1812, President James Madison asked for a declaration of war against England. One detail was forgotten — no one told the frontier posts that war had actually been declared!

HEY, NO ONE TOLD ME!

The government sent Hull a letter by mail, but it did not arrive in time. The British commanders knew about the war before our own people! A ship bringing supplies to Detroit was captured and along with it the detailed plans to attack the British. The War of 1812 was not off to a good start and it only got worse.

Canada Is Invaded!

Nevertheless, General Hull invaded Canada in July. He made camp in Windsor. There was little fighting.

Hull was very cautious. He spent a month bringing cannons and supplies across the river. Then, news came that the British had captured Fort Mackinac! General Hull worried that the British and Indians would soon be coming south to attack. He left his plans uncompleted and returned to Detroit.

A Surprise Attack At Mackinac!

This is what happened at Mackinac Island. Landing in the darkness, the British and

General Hull served as Michigan's territorial governor and was made a general of the Northwestern Army in 1811. (Courtesy Michigan State Archives)

Canadians worked very hard to bring a cannon up the steep hill which was behind Fort Mackinac. By the next morning the cannon was aimed down inside the fort. Now the eight foot thick stone walls of the fort could not protect the American soldiers below.

Lieutenant Porter Hanks was in charge of Fort Mackinac. He didn't know war had been declared. He was beside himself when he realized the British cannon would slowly pulverize his fort and men. He surrendered without firing a single shot! Hanks and his soldiers were sent to Detroit.

Cannonballs Fall on Detroit!

About the same time a new commander, Isaac Brock, took over Fort Malden. The new British general was a man of action. Two days after arriving at Fort Malden he told General Hull to surrender. He warned that if the Americans did not give in, he could not be responsible if the Indians attacked people living outside Detroit. Hull did not give in, so the British began to fire their cannons across the Detroit River.

A cannon ball falls through the breakfast table of a Detroit family.
(Art by George Rasmussen)

Cannon balls came crashing down into the streets and homes of Detroit. As the Augustus Langdon family was beginning to eat breakfast, a cannon ball smashed through the roof of their home, through the ceiling, past their plates, through the table and into the basement! Judge Woodward had just jumped out of bed to see what was going on when a cannonball blasted through his bed! Lieutenant Hanks, who was under arrest and waiting to face a court-martial for surrendering, was killed in the bombardment.

Astonishing Surrender!

While all of that was going on, the British commander Brock crossed the Detroit River with his troops and joined a large number of Indians. General Hull became very concerned for the civilians. He was afraid of an Indian massacre. Without consulting anyone, he raised a white table cloth as a sign of surrender.

The British could not believe their good luck. The people in Detroit could not believe the surrender either! They could not believe that Hull would give in without a fight! Lewis Cass later wrote about the surrender:

"The general took counsel (advice) from his own feelings only. Not an officer was consulted. Not one anticipated a surrender, till he saw the white flag displayed. Even the women were indignant (upset) at so shameful a degradation (humiliation) of the American character."
Michigan Pioneer and Historical Collections, Volume 40

The British General Brock wrote his commander:

"I hasten to apprize (tell) Your Excellency of the capture of this very important post- 2,500 troops have this day surrendered... without the sacrifice of a drop of British blood. I had not more than 700 troops.... and about 400 Indians to accomplish this service. When I detail my good fortune Your Excellency will be astonished..." *Michigan Pioneer and Historical Collections*, Volume 40

Actually both Brock and Hull thought the other side had many more soldiers than they did. After the war, General Hull was court-martialed and sentenced to be shot. The army was not impressed with his concern about saving the lives of civilians. However, President Madison considered General Hull's Revolutionary War bravery and gave him a pardon.

What Are the Facts?

1. After the British left Michigan in 1796, did they still have influence over what happened in the area? Explain your answer.
2. What was Tecumseh's goal?
3. Name two places in Michigan which were captured by the British

early in the War of 1812. How did poor communications play a role in the loss of both places?

Express yourself:
Put yourself in the shoes of someone in Detroit when General Hull surrendered. Write about your reaction and what you might do or say.

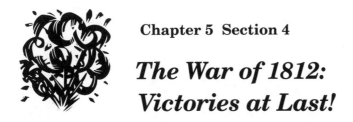

Chapter 5 Section 4

The War of 1812: Victories at Last!

A young officer in the American navy defeated the British in a battle on Lake Erie. With the Americans in control of the Great Lakes, the U.S. army chased the British into Canada.

Remember The River Raisin!

William Henry Harrison was given command of what was left of the American army in the area near Michigan. He planned to retake Detroit. Volunteers were gathered from Ohio and Kentucky. The American troops came north and camped just south of Toledo, Ohio, not far from Michigan's southern border.

On January 17, 1813, about 1,000 Americans marched to Frenchtown (Monroe, Michigan) on the River Raisin, and chased away a small group of British.

Before dawn on January 22, the British brought about 1,200 soldiers and Indians across Lake Erie over the ice. The Americans were not prepared for this surprise. A fierce battle began, the largest to ever take place in Michigan. Some of the Americans surrendered. The British commander, Colonel Procter, promised they would be protected from the Indians if they gave up.

However the British feared a counterattack and marched back across the ice taking the American prisoners who could walk. The wounded Americans were left with two British doctors in a couple of warehouses near the River Raisin.

After the British soldiers had gone, a terrible event took place. The Indians fighting with the British sought revenge. They set the warehouses on fire and killed the soldiers as they tried to escape. The Americans felt the British neglected the wounded men on purpose. The Americans were outraged and made "Remember the River Raisin!" a battle cry.

At Fort Meigs

In the meantime, the main group of American troops had built Fort Meigs on the Maumee River, near Toledo, Ohio. About 2,000 soldiers were inside. It was a rare occasion when anyone dared leave the fort because Tecumseh and his warriors were hiding outside ready to kill the unwary.

One day Tecumseh stood outside the fort and yelled to General Harrison:

"I have with me 800 braves.... Come out and give me battle. You talked like a brave man when we met at Vincennes, and I respected you, but now you hide behind logs in the earth, like a ground hog!" *American History Illustrated,* February 1972.

Fort Meigs was surrounded by Tecumseh's warriors and British soldiers in the War of 1812. (Courtesy Mackinac State Historic Parks)

In April 1813, British soldiers set up cannons and fired on the fort for five days. It was getting pretty bad inside. About the time the Americans wondered how much longer they could hold out, the British army left. No one really knows why they went.

Lake Erie Is the Key

On a small island on the western end of Lake Erie, stands a tall monument to Oliver Hazard Perry. It is in honor of a 28-year-old sailor who fought bravely for his country. General Hull had warned how much trouble British warships would be on Lake Erie. They brought important supplies to the British and kept the Americans from getting their own supplies by ship.

The Americans did not like this situation and decided to do something about it. They began to build several small war ships at Erie, Pennsylvania. Oliver Hazard Perry was given command of the makeshift navy. Some of the American sailors were Kentucky pioneers who had never seen a ship before!

The Battle Begins!

On the morning of September 10, 1813, the British sailed from Fort Malden into Lake Erie. Soon Perry spotted them. The ships slowly moved toward each other; there was not much wind. The sailors on both sides were impatient.

A puff of smoke came from one of the British ships; then the boom of its cannon carried over the water and the shell splashed harmlessly into the lake. A second British cannon fired—the *Lawrence* was hit! Perry could not even fire back; the British were out of range! But a fierce battle began once the American ships were close enough. The ships shook with the tremendous blasts from the cannons. The smell of gunpowder hung heavy over the water.

Perry's ship took a terrific pounding. Soon every officer on the *Lawrence*, except Perry and his younger brother, were dead or wounded. By 2:30 the *Lawrence* was out of action- only 20 of the 103 sailors were unhurt. The British thought the battle might be over. For some reason, one American ship, the *Niagara*, had stayed on the edge of the battle. Now the *Niagara* came closer and Perry made an unheard of decision.

He got into a rowboat and four brave sailors rowed him to the *Niagara* while the enemy ships tried to blast him to bits. He took command of the *Niagara* and sailed it right between the British ships! He fired the ship's guns all at once as he passed. By this time, the British commander had been wounded twice. The added firepower of the *Niagara* caused the British to surrender.

Lake Erie was the scene of a battle between British and American forces in which the British surrendered to Perry. (Courtesy Clarke Historic Library, Central Michigan University)

What Will The British Do?

Tecumseh could hear the booming cannon but the battle was too far away to see. He wondered what had happened but could pretty well guess when the British ships did not come back.

All of the United States was excited by Perry's victory! It opened the door for General Harrison to go after the British at Fort Malden. The British were in serious danger, so they decided to retreat and head northeast.

When Tecumseh heard about this plan he was shocked and angry. He made a passionate speech. He told the British he wanted to fight and keep Americans off Indian land. Throughout the war the Indians had hoped to get their land back from the Americans by helping the British. When he had finished talking, the Indians jumped to their feet with a shout, shaking their tomahawks!

A Quick Retreat

Tecumseh's speech did not stop the British from leaving on September 24. They made a hasty retreat with the Americans right behind them. The British couldn't move fast enough so they started leaving guns and supplies along the way.

About 35 miles west of Lake St. Clair, along the River Thames (TIMZ), the American army caught up with the British. The British troops were not very well organized. American bugles sounded and the Kentucky volunteers charged forward on their horses. They rode through the British line, then turned and charged back from the other side.

It was too much for the British and they were quickly overcome. Although the Indians fought bravely, Tecumseh was killed early in the battle. The fight became known as the Battle of the Thames.

This battle was the end of the Indian dream of keeping Americans off their land. It was also the end of a great leader, Tecumseh, who shaped that dream.

Peace At Last - The War Is Over!

The British eventually realized it was going to be too costly to win the war and peace was made on Christmas Eve, 1814. At last the War of 1812 was over.

If Perry had not beaten the British, then Harrison might not have been able to chase them into Canada and defeat them. Without these two victories, it is possible Michigan would have returned to British or Canadian control.

All worries about war with England and Canada did not disappear overnight. The United States kept Fort Mackinac active for many years and later Fort Wayne was built at Detroit.

Battles of the War of 1812 in and near Michigan

What Are the Facts?

1. Where, exactly, was the largest battle ever to take place in Michigan? Which war was taking place at the time? What took place after this battle that angered so many Americans?

2. Why was it important for Perry to defeat the British warships on Lake Erie?

3. How did Tecumseh feel about the British retreat after Perry's victory? What did Tecumseh hope to get by helping the British?

4. Since Michigan did not have many people at the time of the War of 1812, where did many of the men come from who fought on the American side?

Use a map today!

Water transportation was very important in the War of 1812. Soldiers and supplies had to travel great distances. Use a map to find out how many miles it is from England to Michigan by water.

KEY ⚘ DATES	
	1787- Northwest Ordinance passed by Congress
	1792- First election is held in Michigan- as a part of Canada!
	1794- General Wayne defeats Indians at Fallen Timbers
	1796- Troops raise American flag at Detroit. British leave Michigan
	1812- (June)- War of 1812 with England declared
	(July)- British capture Fort Mackinac
	(Aug.)- British capture Detroit
	1813- (Jan.)- Battle of Frenchtown (Monroe)
	(Sept.)- Perry's fleet defeats the British in Lake Erie
	(Oct.)- Battle of the Thames (Timz)
	1814- (Dec)- War of 1812 ends

Chapter ◀▶ Review

Consider the Big Picture

The British lost the Revolutionary War, but they did not leave Michigan.

They used their forts in Michigan to give guns to the tribes and to stir up trouble with settlers.

Finally an American army under General Wayne defeated the tribes and their British advisors.

Michigan was not yet a state. It was a part of the Northwest Territory.

In 1812 a second war started with the British. This is the only war where important battles took place in or near Michigan.

Building Your Michigan Word Power
Write a definition for each of the following words:

> base line, Northwest Ordinance, township, surveyor, treaty

Talking About It

Get together in a small group and talk about-

Compare and contrast the use of the tribes by the British to upset settlement and development of the young United States to the support of communist forces in South Vietnam by the North Vietnamese government.

If you had been George Washington or another leader in the early American government, what would you have done about the British staying in Michigan?

Compare and contrast what Pontiac tried to do to help his people to what Tecumseh did about 50 years later.

Read the third item listed on page 64 which says why there should be schools in the Northwest Territory. This law passed by Congress gives as the first reason "religion." If this is true, why do many people today say it is against the policy of "separation of church and state" to talk about religious things in public schools?

Put It To Use
Find out the name of the township where you live. If you live inside a city, you will need to choose a nearby township. Write down the location of this township using Michigan's base line and prime meridian.

6

Pioneers on the Way!

Chapter 6 Section 1

Yankees Move West

The Erie Canal helped bring the first big group of settlers to Michigan. Most of the early Michigan settlers were from New England and New York. They were nicknamed Yankees.

A New Route to Michigan— The Erie Canal

A full 200 years after the time of the French explorers, using rivers and lakes was still the easiest way to travel. But people were impatient with nature and wanted to travel new routes, to go places where no river flowed. In 1817 the governor of New York state decided to build a *canal* which would link New York City with the Great Lakes. *Canals are man-made rivers. A large ditch is dug and when it is filled with water, small boats can travel as if they are on a river.* It was named the Erie Canal and goes 363 miles west across New York State. It was a big project for those times. By building this canal across the land, people formed another great pathway to Michigan. The grand opening of the Erie Canal was in 1825. Then it was westward-ho!

Why Did the Settlers Come?

Why would anyone want to leave a business or farm in the East and move to Michigan? The main reason was the difference in land prices. Farming was how most people in the United States made their living

The Erie Canal opened the route to Michigan and thousands of families traveled the canal.

at that time. Farmland in the New England states was overworked and expensive. A young family seldom had enough money to buy farmland in the East. In contrast, land in Michigan and nearby states was quite cheap. Most land sold for only a little more than the minimum price of $1.25 per acre. Besides, the whole nation seemed to have an itch to move west.

Join a Family on the Way to Michigan!

John Nowlin and his family came to Michigan on the Erie Canal. He had bought some land that was near the present city of Dearborn. He wanted to move there with his wife and five children. Mrs. Nowlin was not so excited about his idea. Her son William wrote in his book, *The Bark Covered House*, "Many of her friends said she would not live to get to Michigan if she started...that if she did go, the family would be killed by Indians, perish in the wilderness, or starve to death!"

In spite of the concern of the Nowlin's friends, they headed for Michigan. They paid 1.5 cents per person, per mile, to ride on the canal boat.

After spending six to eight days aboard the canal boat, the Nowlins reached the shore of Lake Erie. They stayed at the rip-roaring city of Buffalo. The family found a room in a sleazy hotel where they worried about being robbed of their life savings. The next day the Nowlins took the steamship *Michigan* toward Detroit. Once the *Michigan* moved out onto Lake Erie the wind blew hard and cold, tossing the ship violently. Many passengers were really seasick. The ship made it to Detroit in 37-40 hours and the lucky Nowlin family was glad to step ashore.

Settlers crossed Lake Erie by ship. *The Michigan,* **one of several steamships which brought pioneers here, looked much like this.**

The Nowlins left Detroit on the Chicago Road which connected Detroit and Chicago. William Nowlin wrote, "I could just see a streak ahead four or five miles, with trees standing thick and dark on either side." After much effort, they reached their land near Dearborn.

The Chicago Road

Other families also used the Chicago Road to travel into the wilderness of Michigan. The road followed the Old Sauk Trail which was the ancient path used by the Indians. The Chicago Road, now known as U.S. 12, was started in 1825 and finished in 1833. It was not actually built to bring settlers west but to allow soldiers and military supplies to go from Detroit to Fort Dearborn at Chicago. The war of 1812 encouraged the federal government to build the Chicago Road and others like it.

The condition of the road was none too good. Some travelers complained they could hardly find it. Even so, much of the early settlement followed along the Chicago Road. Many of the oldest towns in the Lower Peninsula are on that route. Most of the early pioneers coming to Michigan went to live in the southern counties.

This map shows the major roads used by early settlers. Notice none of them reach the northern part of the state.

Michigan's Early Roads

Bay City
Saginaw
Grand River Road
Saginaw Road
Grand Rapids
Pontiac
Territorial Road
Detroit
St. Joseph
Ypsilanti
Chicago
Chicago Road

Title to the Land

Some early settlers were *squatters* on public land. *Squatters were people who did not buy the land where they lived.* It was hard to buy land at first because there was no federal land office in the western Lower Peninsula. In 1831 one was moved to White Pigeon. Later that office was moved to Kalamazoo and it was through the Kalamazoo office that much of the land in western Michigan was sold.

No land in Michigan could be sold to settlers unless the land had first been given over to the federal government by the Indians through a treaty. All of the treaties did not take place at the same time. Some were for big pieces of land and some were for small pieces. Generally, the Indians did not make the treaties with complete willingness. The federal government urged or forced them on the tribes. Sometimes the treaties were signed by Indians who had no claim to the land covered by the treaty.

Where Did They Come From?

Many of the early settlers in Michigan were from the New England states (Connecticut, Maine, Massachusetts, New Hampshire, Rhode Island, and Vermont) or New York. Because of the Erie Canal more settlers came to Michigan from New York state than from any other.

People from these states were often known as Yankees and kept many of their Yankee ways when they moved to Michigan. Often cities in Michigan were given the same names as the places which the settlers left behind. Utica, Rochester, and Litchfield are examples.

They brought many customs too. The idea of township government came from New England. A strong desire for education was common in New England. These settlers worked hard to begin schools in Michigan. Another idea from the New England area was a strong belief that slavery was wrong. Many of the ideas and customs these settlers brought with them helped forge and shape the way Michigan is today.

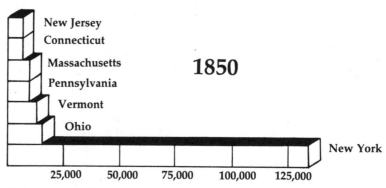

Michigan Settlers and the States They Came From

Why did they choose Michigan?

Why did settlers choose Michigan rather than Ohio or Indiana? Before the Erie Canal opened, it was hard to travel to Michigan. It was easier for settlers to reach Ohio and Indiana as they could sail down the Ohio River. The Erie canal offset that advantage. Probably the main reason was the best land in the two other states had already been claimed by the 1820s. Both Indiana and Ohio had much larger populations than Michigan at that time.

Still, choosing Michigan as a new home may not have been an easy choice. Several factors had kept settlers from deciding on a move to Michigan. There was bad publicity about the area which did not encourage people to move here.

Edward Tiffin sent surveyors to Michigan for the federal government in 1815. Their job was to see if Michigan land was fit to give to soldiers who had fought in the War of 1812. They picked a particularly poor spot to examine in the southeastern part of the Lower Peninsula. Tiffin's report said the land was quite swampy and sandy and that not one acre in a 1,000 would be good for farming. Today we know most of the land was not like that at all. But because of Tiffin's bad report, the former soldiers never had a chance to see what Michigan was really like.

Magdelaine la Framboise (1780-1846)

While settlers were coming to the southern part of Michigan, the rest of the territory went on much as it had for many, many years. Fur trading was still the main business activity.

Magdelaine la Framboise, a successful business woman, spoke French, English, Ottawa and Ojibwa. She owned a fine house on Mackinac Island, but she had also spent many years on the Grand River in the Lower Peninsula.

Magdelaine was born along the Grand in 1780. Her father was a French fur trader and

Magdelaine la Framboise

her mother was the daughter of an Ottawa chief. When she was 14 or 15 years old, Magdelaine married another French fur trader named Joseph la Framboise. She and her husband took their canoe from the Grand River to Mackinac Island each summer to sell what they had traded from the Ottawa.

A terrible event took place in 1806. Her husband was murdered because he refused to give liquor to a man. After that tragedy, Magdelaine had to keep the business going to feed herself and her children. She even managed to send her young daughter to Montreal so she could go to school.

Her daughter did well in school and returned to Mackinac Island where she met a young American soldier, Benjamin Pierce. Magdelaine's daughter and Benjamin Pierce were married in 1816. Later, Benjamin's brother became president of the United States.

Magdelaine la Framboise was always proud of both her French and Indian backgrounds and her home still stands on Mackinac Island.

Governor Cass

During the 18 years that Lewis Cass was governor of the Michigan Territory he did many things to help the early settlers. He urged the federal government to build better roads in Michigan. He helped explore Michigan and the Northwest Territory and he told about all of the benefits Michigan had to offer. He also served as the Indian Superintendent. In that job he made treaties with the different tribes so the land could be surveyed and then bought by settlers.

Angry Clash at the Soo

In 1820 Governor Cass and about 20 soldiers met with Indians at the Soo. He had heard they were friendly with the British. When they reached the Soo, Cass went to the home of John Johnston, a fur trader. John was away, but his Indian wife Susan and his son and daughter welcomed the visitors.

A council of chiefs was held with Cass on June 16. The chiefs were not friendly. Sassaba, an Ojibwa leader, was even dressed in a British soldier's jacket. Cass wanted to build a fort at the Soo but the Indians said the government could not have any land. Finally, Cass told them point-blank that a fort would be built whether they liked it or not! Sassaba became angry, threw his war spear into the ground, and kicked away the presents Cass had brought. It looked as if there would be some real trouble and Cass was greatly outnumbered.

Lewis Cass (1782-1866) lawyer; member of the Ohio legislature; soldier in War of 1812; Governor of the Michigan Territory 1813-31; U.S. Secretary of War 1831-36; ambassador to France 1836-42; member of the U.S. Senate 1845-48 and 1849-57; 1848 Democratic nominee for president of the United States; 1858-1860 U.S. secretary of state. (Courtesy Michigan State Archives)

Sassaba went to his lodge and raised a British flag on a pole. Next, Cass strode to the lodge and tore down Sassaba's flag and threw it on the ground. He told the Indians that if they put up another flag, they would be destroyed! What was Cass thinking of? He could have been killed! The Ojibwa were so amazed at the governor's behavior that they just stood there. But the Indians' anger increased.

Johnston's son, George, and his Indian mother, Susan, quickly went to the chiefs to try to cool things down. They talked to the chiefs and told them how dangerous it would be if they killed the Americans. They explained more soldiers would come to take revenge and the Ojibwa would lose in the end. Susan's speech to the Ojibwa was credited with saving Lewis Cass and his men. Later that night, the Indians signed a treaty with Cass giving up land for a fort. They kept the right to fish at the rapids and to camp on the shore.

Treaties with the Tribes

Cass made other treaties with the tribes. Always he was acting for the United States government and not the territory or state. These treaties opened up a large area for the pioneer settlers. Of course, this was not good for the Native Americans living in Michigan.

The treaty process was part of a clash between two completely different cultures: the European culture which believed in private ownership of the land and used the land for farming, and the tribal culture which believed in using the land as a group and only farming enough to provide sufficient food along with hunting and fishing. Many Indians had willingly given up small amounts of land in the past but were later shocked by the American demands for such large amounts. Many Indians resisted the treaties but there was great pressure to get the leaders to put their mark on the papers.

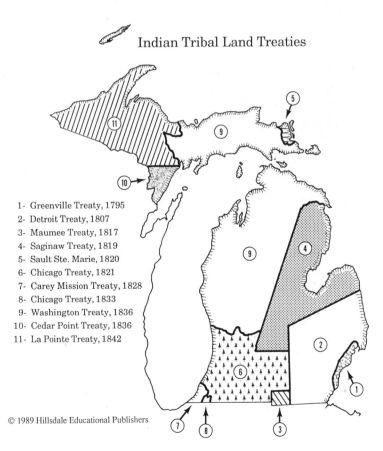

Indian Tribal Land Treaties

1- Greenville Treaty, 1795
2- Detroit Treaty, 1807
3- Maumee Treaty, 1817
4- Saginaw Treaty, 1819
5- Sault Ste. Marie, 1820
6- Chicago Treaty, 1821
7- Carey Mission Treaty, 1828
8- Chicago Treaty, 1833
9- Washington Treaty, 1836
10- Cedar Point Treaty, 1836
11- La Pointe Treaty, 1842

The tribes did receive money for their land but it was soon spent with the traders to get supplies. The supplies were often things which the Indians had once gotten from the land themselves. Very little of the money was left to use for things which would help them in the long run. Soon Michigan would be full of settlers clamoring for farmland. One Indian leader complained that plows were driven through their wigwams before they could even leave for a new home.

Michigan was changing from a land of native tribes to a land of farmers and settlers. In 1820, Michigan had about 9,000 settlers and probably about an equal number of Native Americans. One 1837 estimate stated there were 7,700 Indians in Michigan and that the rest of the population had grown to 174,543!

Lewis Cass was in charge of the affairs of Michigan for 18 years, longer than any other person. Not only was he in charge for a long time but it was an important time when Michigan was just beginning to develop. He wrote the state motto and designed the state seal.

In 1831 President Andrew Jackson asked Cass to become secretary of war. Then Cass left Michigan to become a member of the national government for the rest of his life. He traveled overseas and was himself nominated for president in 1848. Lewis Cass did much for Michigan and his nation.

What Are the Facts?

1. Early settlers to Michigan came from several states. Name all of the states mentioned in chapter six. Which state was home to the most Michigan pioneers? What was the nickname for people from these states?
2. What is significant about the Chicago Road?
3. Why did people from the East want to move to Michigan?
4. The tribes of Michigan were pressured to give up their land through treaties with the federal government. Could settlers buy land before it was covered in a treaty? According to the map on page 83, which Indian land treaty covered the part of Michigan where you live?
5. List three things Lewis Cass did for Michigan.

Use a map today!
Many pioneers came to Michigan from the New England states in the 1830s and 1840s. Work in groups to compare maps of Michigan and the New England area. Make a list of Michigan towns named after places the pioneers came from, such as Rochester (for Rochester, New York).

KEY ❀ DATES	
1816-	Indiana is a state
1817-	James Monroe is first president to visit Michigan
	First successful Michigan newspaper
1818-	Illinois is a state
	First steamboat stops at Detroit
1819-	Michigan sends delegation to Congress
1820-	Governor Cass explores Northwest Territory
1822-	Dr. Beaumont studies St. Martin's stomach
1825-	Construction begins on Detroit-Chicago Road
1825-	Erie Canal opens

Chapter 6 Section 2

Changing the Land- Farmers Arrive !

The landscape of Michigan was changed tremendously when
farmers began to cut down trees so they could plant crops.

Cabins were built with natural materials. The fireplace was made of logs and packed with
clay. Window glass was expensive and scarce, so settlers used animal skins instead. (Art
by David B. McConnell)

Farming was Tough

Today people often think about pioneer days with the fond desire to go
back in time and live in a log cabin, hunt in the woods, and fish beautiful,
clear lakes. But, early farming was a tough life for man, woman, and child.
The sons and daughters in farm families had to help do the work as soon as
they were old enough. One reason parents often had a dozen or more
children was that they could help keep the farm going.

War Against the Trees

Today much of Michigan has farms and open fields. That was not what
the early settlers saw when they arrived. They found a land which was
completely covered with trees. They could only see the trees as enemies
which kept the life-giving sun from reaching the crops they had to plant in
order to feed themselves. Trees had to be cut down, burned, and removed in
any way they could. From the instant pioneer farmers set foot in Michigan,
they were in a race to clear trees from their land and plant a crop which
would be ready to harvest as soon as possible.

Most settlers could only bring a limited amount of food with them—
perhaps a few barrels of dried beans, flour or corn meal, salted pork, and
maybe a cow or some pigs and chickens.

85

It was common for the early farmer to bring at least one or two pigs. Pigs would eat acorns which meant the farmer did not have to get food for them, especially during the first winter. The pigs also did a helpful service—they killed rattlesnakes. Much of Michigan was swampy in those days and provided a good home for rattlesnakes.

Oxen provided the muscle needed for many jobs done by early pioneers such as clearing land for farming. (Courtesy Michigan State Archives)

Gristmills and Waterpower

After the corn, wheat, oats, rye, and barley were harvested, they had to be made into flour at a *grist-mill* in order to be of much use to the pioneer. *At the mill two large heavy stones turned round and round and ground the gain into flour.* Water played an important part in the process. The gristmills were all powered by waterwheels then. Nearly every important town was settled next to a river which could give waterpower to run the mills. Sometimes the mill was the first building put up in a new town.

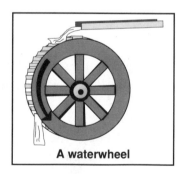

A waterwheel

Millponds were built to hold water which would go to the mill. Water from the pond flowed to a large waterwheel. It poured over the wheel and pushed it around. Inside the mill, big wooden gears transmitted the motion to a millstone which is what actually ground the grain and turned it into a powder, the flour.

Waterpower was important not only to run the gristmills but also the early factories. In addition, the rivers also gave the settlers a way to travel from town to town. Boats and rafts often carried people and equipment from place to place.

Got the Shakes Yet?

Imagine this scene. An early settler suddenly begins to shake and tremble. Then he or she has a raging fever, headache, and back pains followed with a severe chill. The crisis ends with a drenching sweat. One pioneer recalled this sort of incident: "You felt as though you had gone through some sort of collision with a threshing machine and came out not killed, but the next thing to it. "

That was what it was like to have the *ague* (AY g' you). Pioneers thought the disease was caused by gasses coming from the swamps. *Today we know it was malaria and was caused by a parasite transferred to people by the bites of mosquitoes.* Not many people died from that kind of malaria, but it could easily put a stop to getting any work done. Sometimes farmers were so sick they couldn't feed their farm animals or plant their crops. A popular rhyme was: "Don't go to Michigan, that land of ills; The word means ague, fever, and chills."

Early diseases caused a great deal of trouble for settlers. A person with ague would shake uncontrollably. (Art by Theresa Deeter)

A Quick Killer

The ague was a big nuisance, but *cholera* (KOL er a) was a deadly killer. It took its victims rapidly. One man was playing cards and seemed to be in perfect health when he gasped, "I've got it!" His friends tried to reassure him that it was probably just an upset stomach, but he was dead before the next morning! *People with cholera die from the loss of body fluids. Victims have uncontrollable vomiting and diarrhea.*

The disease reached Michigan in 1832 aboard the steamship *Henry Clay*. The ship was filled with soldiers on their way to fight an Indian uprising in Wisconsin. On the fourth of July, the ship docked at Detroit and the soldiers went ashore to join in the celebration. But by the next morning, 11 soldiers had died. The soldiers were terrified and jumped ship to get away from the sick and to try to save themselves. In the process of running away, they spread the disease.

The newspaper at Port Huron stated:

The dead bodies of the deserters are literally strewn along the road between here and Detroit. No one dares give them (the sick soldiers) relief, not even a cup of water. A person on his way here from Detroit passed six, lying groaning with the agonies of the cholera under one tree, and saw one corpse by the roadside....

People were so scared by cholera they set up roadblocks to stop travelers from coming into their towns. The upper floor of the territorial capitol building was made into a hospital to treat cholera victims. Father Gabriel Richard worked so hard to help the sick that he died from exhaustion.

In 1834 cholera struck Detroit once again. During the month of August about seven percent of the population died from the disease.

Bears and Wolves!

One winter night Mr. D. McClennand heard a great commotion from his hog pen. He raced outside in his nightshirt and saw a bear carrying off a 200-pound hog!

Wolves were another big problem. They would kill farm animals and keep pioneers awake with their howling during the night. Many pioneer communities paid a bounty for each dead wolf brought in to them.

Wolves are much like dogs but usually larger. Young William Nowlin said he shot a wolf which was six feet from the end of its tail to the tip of its nose. Few dogs grow to that size! Wolves were all the more fearsome because they always traveled in groups or packs. Today, the only wolves

(Art by Charles Schafer, Michigan Department of Natural Resources)

known to be in Michigan are on Isle Royale, but during the early 1800s wolves were often seen in southern Michigan.

Schools In the Wilderness

In pioneer days schools were usually a luxury. People were awed by the first elementary school in Ypsilanti in 1834. The township board taxed residents to pay for the school and its teacher. Since most families had very little money, people were allowed to supply materials to build the school instead. Parents also had to give the school half a cord of firewood for each child they sent. Ypsilanti paid their first teacher $90 to teach for eight months! Women found jobs as early teachers. Often, it was the only paying work they had.

In 1842 the elementary school in Detroit was made free for all students. In 1848 that city established its first high school.

Of course, some people had heard about the University of Michigan. Its first actual classes began in 1841. There were six students and two professors. The university was supported by state government, but most of the first colleges were started by church groups.

Scary Rumors in the Woods

The year 1832 brought startling news to Michigan settlers. An Indian chief named Black Hawk led an uprising of the Sauk and Fox tribes in Western Wisconsin. Those tribes were far from Michigan but people were concerned that the Potawatomi might join Black Hawk and attack settlers in southern Michigan. Others were worried Black Hawk and his followers would come along the Chicago Road and seek British protection at Fort Malden. Black Hawk had worked with the British in the War of 1812. He had taken scalps at the River Raisin massacre and had also been at the Battle of the Thames. Many wild rumors were heard in the towns and villages of Southern Michigan.

The great scare Black Hawk gave the people of Michigan caused many to think all Indians should be sent west. Then there would be no worries about possible attacks. Settlers were so agitated they forgot they had been living for many years without any problems with the Michigan Indians.

The southern part of the Lower Peninsula had the most settlers. Since the same area was home to the Potawatomi tribe, that tribe was the focus of plans to move the Indians. In 1838 U. S. soldiers forced about 300 Potawatomi to move to Kansas. It was a sad time for this tribe and its friends.

Dr. Beaumont and Happenings in the U.P.

The Upper Peninsula was a wild and rugged land too far away for most early pioneers to consider. It was a land visited by fur traders and the soldiers stationed at Mackinac Island and the Soo. Dr. William Beaumont was the army doctor at Fort Mackinac.

The American Fur Company store on the island was a busy place. There the French traders and Indians came to exchange their furs. On a spring morning in 1822, a trader named Alexis St. Martin was visiting the store when someone's shotgun accidently went off close to his body. Dr. Beaumont was called for help.

St. Martin was in serious condition. His shirt had been set on fire from the gun blast and part of his side was blown away. Dr. Beaumont believed "any attempt to save his life entirely useless." But the doctor did what he could. He was astonished that St. Martin was still alive two days later.

Alexis St. Martin improved very slowly. There was one unique thing about the wound; it never completely healed. A flap of skin formed but it left an opening into his stomach! Suddenly Dr. Beaumont realized he could see what actually happens to food by looking into St. Martin's stomach. By 1825 Dr. Beaumont was doing experiments with St. Martin's cooperation. These experiments were the first explaining what happens to food in the stomach. The doctor wrote medical papers which were read around the world.

What Are the Facts?

1. Why did farmers want to cut down so many trees? How did the farmers use the wood from the trees?
2. Explain how waterpower helped prepare grain so it could be used as food during early pioneer times.
3. How did pioneers know if they were having an attack of the ague? What is the modern name for this disease?
4. In what way did the settlers react to the Indians of southern Michigan after the Black Hawk uprising?
5. What was the name of the doctor who did experiments on how the human stomach works? What accident made his work possible?

Use a map today!
Waterpower was quite important to early towns. Check out your town. Did it have a millpond? Draw a simple map showing its location and the river which fed it. Where was the mill located? What did they use the waterpower to do?

Express yourself:
Read the short book *Night of the Full Moon* by Gloria Whelan which tells of a young pioneer girl who happens to be visiting a Potawatomi camp when soldiers come to take the Indians west. Then write your own short story about something relating to Indians being taken from Michigan.

Consider the Big Picture

Before 1825 Michigan was a large area with few white people, and many of them spoke French.

The Erie Canal and better ships on Lake Erie made it easier for new settlers to come here. There was a surge of settlers as land was cheap and plentiful.

Since the Erie Canal went through New York state, many of the new settlers came from there.

Getting here was just the beginning. Land treaties were made with the tribes; trees were cut down; cabins built, and much more. It was tough!

Building Your Michigan Word Power

Write each word below on a sheet of paper and next to it the phrase which is best related to it: ague, canal, cholera, gristmill, squatter.

quick death, didn't pay for it, unnatural river, flour made here, shaking and sweating

Talking About It

Get together in a small group and talk about-

Why were people living in the 1830s willing to go through such hardships and start new homes in Michigan? Compare this to people moving to another part of the United States today. Would it be similar to beginning a settlement on another planet?

Why was the southern part of the Lower Peninsula the part of the state where most settlers built their new homes?

Was it right to push the tribes to land far from their homes? If you had been in charge, how would you have dealt with getting land from the Indians? Was there a solution which would have been fairer?

Put It To Use

Suppose your home was first built by a relative moving from Albany, New York in the 1830s. Draw a map which shows the land between Albany and your home. Include the Erie Canal. Show the route your relative would have used. Figure the miles traveled and the number of days it would take for the trip.

Make a floor plan for a pioneer cabin where you will live. Give the number of square feet for each area. Where will your five children sleep? Where will you cook your meals and store your food safe from animals?

7

Almost a State.......
GROWING LIKE A WEED

Chapter 7 Section 1

Becoming a State:
Not a Simple Matter

Amazing- Michigan and Ohio almost went to war over the location of the border between them!

Michigan became the 26th state in the United States on January 26, 1837. It was not easy to get its own star on the United States flag and the path to statehood had some unusual twists.

Steps To Be a State

At first Michigan was just an unnamed part of the Northwest Territory. Congress formed Michigan into a separate territory in 1805. The governor of the territory was appointed by the President. The Northwest Ordinance of 1787 listed the steps in growing from a territory into a state. Once 60,000 people lived in a territory, it would be admitted to the United States and could form its own state government and write its own state constitution.

Ohio, Indiana, and Illinois all became states before Michigan. When those states had the minimum number of people, they asked Congress to pass a law saying they could write their constitutions. The Northwest Ordinance did not really require a vote by Congress, but it became the custom.

Ready To Be a State

Meanwhile, the population of Michigan was growing like a weed. We had become a popular place for settlers looking for a new home. Between 1830 and 1834 Michigan's population grew from 31,000 to 85,000. Stevens T. Mason, the territory's acting governor requested that Congress vote to see if Michigan could write a state constitution, but Congress voted no!

Why did that happen? The trouble was Michigan's argument with the

state of Ohio over the border between the two neighbors. They both
claimed a small wedge of land five
miles wide at the Indiana border
and eight miles wide at Lake Erie.

Neighbors Fight Over Land

The small wedge was not just
any piece of land. It contained the
mouth of the Maumee River which
flowed into Lake Erie. During the
era of great canal projects there
were plans to connect the Maumee
River to the Ohio River and from
there to the Mississippi River.
People in Ohio had invested in land
around the river and in the canal
projects. Meanwhile, people from
Michigan began to build two railroads which would end at the
Maumee. Many believed the area of
land would become a great center
for the shipping business. They
thought a great port city would grow
up there. At that time both Ohio and
Michigan felt their whole future depended on owning that little strip of
land!

Stevens T. Mason, became acting governor
when he was only 18 years old! Sometimes he
is called the "boy governor." (Courtesy Michigan State Archives)

Territory of Michigan

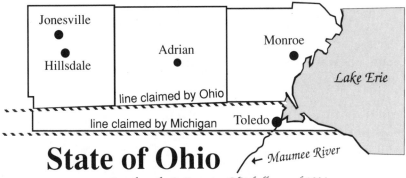

Jonesville
●
●
Hillsdale

Adrian
●

Monroe
●

Lake Erie

line claimed by Ohio

line claimed by Michigan   Toledo ●

State of Ohio   ← *Maumee River*

Based on the S. Augustus Mitchell map of 1834

Information from an 1834 map shows the famous strip of land claimed by both Ohio and
Michigan.

Why wasn't it clear who controlled the land? The Northwest Ordinance said the northern border for Ohio was to be a line touching the south end of Lake Michigan and going east from there to Lake Erie. A border made along that line would put the mouth of the Maumee River in Michigan.

That was fine, but when Ohio wrote its state constitution in 1803, it put the river in Ohio and when Michigan became a territory in 1805 it put the river in Michigan. The two descriptions overlapped and Congress accepted both of them!

Neither side was going to give in. They were becoming serious. Each state called for its *militia* to march into the land, now often called the Toledo Strip. *The militia is a group of people who volunteer as soldiers and are usually under local control.* Ohio and Michigan planned to go to war with each other! Today that sounds quite funny, but both sides meant business. William Nowlin, the Michigan pioneer, said: "When we heard that Governor Mason had arrived at Toledo, we wondered if we should hear the roar of his cannon. Sometimes I listened. We thought if it was still and the wind favorable, we might hear them, and we expected every day there would be a battle."

Constitution Written

On June 24, 1835, delegates representing the people of Michigan got together and wrote a state constitution. Acting Governor Stevens T. Mason felt Michigan was entitled to become a state even if Congress had said no! From that time on, Michigan acted as if it were a state and passed its own laws.

The 'Toledo War' Heats Up !

Events at the Ohio border became a comedy. Both Michigan and Ohio sent officials into the Toledo Strip to control it. Several Ohio surveyors were spotted south of Adrian. A posse gave chase during the night. The next morning they found nine surveyors hiding in a log cabin. Eventually the men from Ohio gave up and came out. But suddenly they made a mad dash to escape. The Michigan posse fired their guns over the surveyors' heads. Soon all were recaptured without injury. Luckily, no one died during those "Toledo War" days of 1835.

Mason Must Go!

During the "Toledo War" President Jackson decided to remove Stevens T. Mason from office. Since Michigan had not officially become a state, he could do that. The President hoped it would help calm the situation, but it didn't.

The people in Michigan ignored the new governor sent by President Jackson. They continued to act as though they were a state. An election for the governor of Michigan was held in October and Mason won. In Michigan he was considered the governor of the *state* of Michigan, but in Washington he was considered to be some kind of nut!

Michigan patriots chased surveyors from Ohio along the disputed border during the Toledo War. (Art by Tim Pickell)

The Rule Of Politics

The law was on the side of Michigan, but Ohio was stronger politically. President Jackson knew he would need their votes during the next election. Since Michigan was not really a state, its people could not vote anyway.

Michigan tried to influence politicians in Washington by naming nine counties in southern Michigan after President Jackson and members of his cabinet, but it did not help.

A Compromise From Congress

Congress finally decided on a plan for solving the border problem. They felt the best idea would be to have Michigan trade the Toledo Strip for the western three-quarters of the Upper Peninsula. The people of Michigan were outraged. Everyone thought any land north of Saginaw Bay was a cold wasteland.

Slowly, Michigan's people realized they would have to go along. Delegates trudged into Ann Arbor on a very cold day in December 1836. After two days of haggling, they voted yes. Their last-minute winter meeting was known as the "Frost-bitten Convention." About four weeks later, Congress voted to let Michigan join the rest of the states. As a result of the border dispute, Michigan lost 450 square miles to Ohio and the eventual port city of Toledo, but gained 9,000 square miles of the Upper Peninsula. The people of Michigan later found it was a peninsula which has some of the nation's most beautiful scenery and which is also rich in copper, iron, and timber.

The Capital Takes a Trip

In 1848 the people of Michigan felt the original capital in Detroit was too far from the center of the state. Many cities went all out to lobby for the honor of being Michigan's new capital. Someone suggested Lansing as a joke because almost no town existed there. Amazingly, the vote went to Lansing because of its central location. There were few towns that far north then.

What Are the Facts?

1. When did Michigan officially become a state? What year did Michigan write its constitution and begin to act as if it were a state? Why aren't the two dates the same?
2. What problem kept Michigan from becoming a state when it first applied to do so? How was this problem resolved?
3. What city was the first capital of the state of Michigan? Where was it relocated and why?

Use a map today!
On a map of the Upper Peninsula draw the Toledo Strip. Be sure to use the same scale. Compare the size of the Toledo Strip with the size of the part of the UP received in the trade.

Chapter 7 Section 2

Boom and Bust

Learn how people moved to Michigan in record numbers from 1830 to 1840 and land prices rose rapidly. It became a fad to buy land in Michigan in hopes of getting rich.

Michigan Fever!

The number of people coming to Michigan kept growing. Pioneers had "Michigan Fever" and wanted to move to the state. In just one day, October 7, 1834, ships brought 900 new settlers to Detroit.

> Population recorded by U.S. census:
>
> 1810— 4,762
> 1820— 8,896
> 1830— 31,639
> 1840— 212,267
> 1850— 397,654

Just as the number of people increased, the demand for land went wild. The Kalamazoo land office sold over 1,600,000 acres in 1836. Business was so brisk the office had to close for 18 days just so the clerks could bring the books up-to-date.

Kalamazoo was then just a small village and only had four hotels. It quickly overflowed with people who came to do business at the land office. Everyone wanted rooms and often three strangers slept in the same bed and late arrivals paid to use the floor!

Land could be sold as soon as it had been surveyed. Each area of land was put up for auction for two weeks. During that time, people would bid against each other for the best parcels. All of the land which was not bought at the auction was sold at the minimum price of $1.25 an acre.

Get Rich Quick!

With so many settlers moving to Michigan, it was only natural that the price of land would go up. It became a fad in Michigan during the late 1830s to buy land with the hope of selling it at a higher price. That was known as land *speculation. Speculation is going into a risky venture where something is bought with the idea of selling it when the price goes up.* An example was the Porter farm in Detroit. It was purchased for $6,000 in 1833 and sold for $20,000 in 1835. At that time, a dollar might be a good day's wage!

As the fad continued, people became rather careless; often they did not even go to see the land they were buying. Antoine Campau (ahn TWAN kam POE) is a good example of such carelessness. Mr. Campau had bought a parcel well out into Lake Michigan!

Settlers From Overseas

Most of the settlers coming to Michigan during the 1830s were from New England and New York. In the 1840s the mix of settlers began to change. More started to come from Europe.

A series of problems of that time in different parts of Europe caused many people to *immigrate* or move to the United States. Significant numbers of people moved to Michigan from Germany, Ireland, Holland (also called the Netherlands), and a part of England called Cornwall. Later, more people arrived from other countries. Here is more about each group.

Germans

Many of the early immigrant groups looked toward religious leaders for guidance. The Germans were no exception. Reverend Fredrich Schmid led 34 German families to mid-Michigan in 1833. The Germans began to settle the Ann Arbor area and the Saginaw River valley, forming towns like Frankenmuth. Catholic Germans started Westphalia in the central Lower Peninsula. These immigrants left Germany because of crop failures and a revolution in 1848.

Irish

The Irish were driven out of their homeland by a potato disease in 1845. These people rented the land they farmed and could not continue to pay the rent when their crops failed. Because of that, most of the Irish were often very poor when they arrived in the United States. Since they did not have much money to start farms, a large number of Irish worked in the cities, mines, and factories. Detroit had a big Irish population for many years.

Dutch

The Dutch came to find religious freedom. The Dutch government had started a government-run church and many people there disagreed with its policies. Since they could not change the government church, these people left the country. Reverend Albertus C. Van Raalte led the first Dutch settlers to America. They first arrived in western Michigan in 1847 and started Holland, Michigan. Grand Rapids also has many people with a Dutch background as does Zeeland.

Cornish

The Cornish came from Cornwall in southwest England. Cornwall had been a major center of copper mining but the ore was nearly gone. In the 1850s they were sought out to come to Michigan and work in the new Upper Peninsula copper mines. They moved to towns like Houghton and Eagle River.

This map shows some of the places in Michigan where groups from other countries have settled. The modern flags of these countries are pictured. The flag of Saudi Arabia represents the many countries of people from the Middle East. Many cities also have people of African heritage. The flag of Ghana represents one of the areas in Africa where those people first lived. (Art by David B. McConnell)

A Panic in 1837- the Bubble Burst

In 1837 the land speculation bubble burst. President Jackson put the breaks on when he said that only gold or silver could be used to buy land at the federal land offices. The new order made it hard for people to buy land and the prices went down. It was a big blow to people who had used all of their money to buy land hoping to get rich quickly.

There was also a second problem. In those days banks could print their own paper money, but trouble developed because many did not have enough gold and silver in their vaults to back up all the paper money they printed. Soon farmers and merchants would not accept paper money at full value.

The loss of value in land and paper money really slowed down the economy. The time was called the Panic of 1837.

Since Michigan was growing so fast, many new banks had started here. No one had been watching the situation carefully and many of the banks were unsound and others downright dishonest. Even so, new settlers continued to come. Several new counties had also been organized. In 1828 Michigan had 10 counties, but by 1836 the number had increased to 27.

At the time of early banks in Michigan, each could have its own paper money printed. Here are several samples. (Courtesy Clarke Historical Library, Central Michigan University.)

What Are the Facts?

1. How much greater was the population of Michigan in 1840 than it was in 1830?
2. Where did settlers need to go to buy land?
3. Give some reasons why people moved from Europe to Michigan.
4. Name the four main ethnic groups who came to Michigan during the 1840s and 1850s. Name one city or town which had many settlers from each of these groups.

Express yourself:
Make a crossword puzzle or word search using names of immigrant groups and some of the towns they settled in Michigan.

Canals & Copper

Did you know a copper "rush" took place in the Upper Peninsula during the 1840s? In 1844 iron ore was discovered by surveyors in the Upper Peninsula! Then we had to solve the problem of getting it to market.

Government Goals

Once state government was started, there were two major goals- build a strong economy and set up a statewide transportation system. These goals went hand in hand. Michigan could not have profitable industries without good transportation.

Railroads Begin

By the late 1830s, people could see that railroads would be an important part of the future. The state government decided to add railroads to the list of projects it planned to develop.

In 1837, Michigan had the first steam locomotive west of New York state. That railroad went from Toledo, which was considered to be a part of Michigan, to Adrian. Then the Michigan Central line started between Detroit and Ypsilanti. Its grand opening was flawed when the engine broke down and horses had to pull the trainload of officials back home!

Even the first railroads were great time-savers. The few roads that existed were really bad. The Michigan Central could take passengers or freight to Ypsilanti from Detroit in about two and a half hours. A wagon on the road would need *two days* for the same trip! The cost of food and products began to fall as soon as railroads reached more Michigan cities.

The first trains were slow by today's standards as they traveled an average of 25 miles an hour. But they were still an important improvement in transportation. (Courtesy Michigan State Archives)

Who Was Dr. Houghton?

Douglass Houghton was the person who helped do much to develop Michigan, especially the northern part of the state. Houghton came to Michigan in 1830 to give lectures in Detroit on the latest scientific wonders from the East. The talks that Houghton gave were very popular. He opened a medical office in Detroit in 1831. By 1836 Dr. Houghton gave up his medical work so he could concentrate on making money in the great Michigan land boom. But while he was doing all of these other things, he told many officials that there should be a complete study of Michigan's animals, plants, and minerals.

Douglass Houghton served as Michigan's first state geologist. He lost his life when a sudden Lake Superior storm caught his boat in October 1845. (Courtesy Michigan State Archives)

What Is Out There?

Everyone was interested in learning more about what Michigan was like. People wanted to know what useful things could be found in the region.

After Michigan became a state, Governor Mason chose Dr. Houghton to find out exactly what resources were here. Houghton was given the job of state geologist. In 1837 he began to explore every part of the state. At first Houghton and his assistants traveled all over the Lower Peninsula. They looked for things like salt springs and clay deposits which could be used to make bricks. They found material which could be used to make glass and they found deposits of coal.

In 1840 Dr. Douglass Houghton took several assistants and headed to the Upper Peninsula. They planned to really study the copper situation. People had known there was some copper, but not the amount and location. Dr. Houghton's report told about huge amounts of copper. One piece weighed over 3,700 pounds!

The Copper Rush!

Copper! Copper! Pure copper just lying on the ground? When the news reached the public, guess what happened next? The first great mineral rush in the United States started in Michigan's Upper Peninsula! Adventurous miners arrived by the boatload.

People expected to become wealthy by just picking up pieces of copper off the ground. While they searched, they had to swat great swarms of mosquitoes and black flies. During the winter they found themselves dangerously cut off from any source of supplies by huge snowdrifts and frozen lakes. But still thousands came.

Angus Murdock told what it was like in his book, *Boom Copper*:

Listen!

"Soft palmed clerks, whose heaviest work had been lifting ledgers and pushing quill pens, came ashore with picks slung over rounded shoulders. Tidewater Easterners arrived in fishermen's outfits.... Others were ex-lawyers, ex-preachers, ex-husbands, ex-everything you can think of except expert miners."

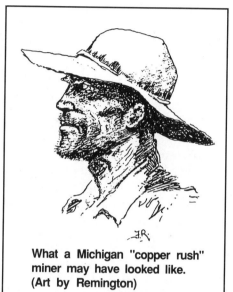

What a Michigan "copper rush" miner may have looked like. (Art by Remington)

There was also concern that the Indians would resent the arrival of so many miners. In order to be certain no trouble would take place between the miners and Indians, Fort Wilkins was built at Copper Harbor. The fort only operated until 1846. There seemed to be little need for it. The fort probably did more to protect the Indians from the miners than the other way around.

The Cliff Mine Story

John Hays helped get the first actual copper mine going. He was known as Old Blind Hays because of serious eye problems. Hayes had been a druggist in Pittsburgh. Hays paid $1,000 for a one-sixth interest in another man's claims.

They started to dig a mine shaft near Eagle River. There they found a piece of copper so large it had to be broken up before they could continue. Afterwards, many more large boulders and hunks of nearly pure copper were found. One old prospector said, "Most of them were bigger than my outhouse back there!"

What finally happened to the person who started it all? Dr. Houghton was doing more exploring in a small boat in October 1845. He was near the Eagle River on the Keweenaw Peninsula when a sudden storm came up. The boat tipped over and he drowned along with one other man. His body was not even found until the next year!

Compass Confusion

A man named William Burt was assigned to be the deputy surveyor with Douglass Houghton. Burt and his assistants were working on the township lines for Marquette county near Teal Lake. Then something most unusual happened. Jacob Houghton, Douglass's brother, gave this account:

"On the morning of the 19th of September, 1844, we started to run the line south. As soon as we reached the hill to the south of the lake, the compassman began to notice a fluctuation... of the magnetic needle.... The compassman called for us all to 'come see.' Mr. Burt called out, 'Boys, look around and see what you can find!' We all left the line, some going east, some going to the west, and all of us returned with specimens of iron ore."

A new billion dollar industry was born in Michigan! The discovery of iron was even more surprising than the discovery of copper because people had known the copper was there all along. No one had any idea Michigan had iron ore. Douglass Houghton had made careful studies just a few miles from the location of a 150-foot high mountain of solid iron ore and never saw a trace of it!

They Came from Jackson

Some men from Jackson, Michigan, made the first try to mine the iron ore. The group formed the Jackson Mining Company, even though not one of them knew much about mining nor about the land where the minerals were found. In July 1845, the men headed north. The trip took 21 days.

At the Sault they met Tipo-Keso, an Ojibwa woman. She told the greenhorns about a mountain of mineral ore near her uncle's camp on Teal

Members of the Jackson Mining Company found bright iron ore under the roots of this old tree. (Courtesy Michigan State Archives)

104

Father Baraga, also known as the snowshoe priest, came to the Great Lakes from Yugoslavia in 1830. He began preaching to the Ojibwa in the Lower Peninsula. He moved to L'Anse in October of 1843 and spent the winter of 1844-1845 at Fort Wilkins in Copper Harbor. (Courtesy Michigan State Archives)

Lake. They went to the camp and were met by her uncle, Marji-Gesick, who entertained them. The next day Marji-Gesick led them to the area of the mountain of ore. Under the roots of a big pine tree which had fallen down they found some bright iron ore. Today the city of Negaunee is near that spot.

The Jackson mine proved that the Upper Peninsula had high quality iron ore and attracted the attention of people far and wide. The Michigan Iron Industry Museum is now located nearby.

Bottleneck at the Rapids

Some miners had great success, but many wasted their time and money. It was the cost of shipping which ruined most miners' hopes of a profit. It cost $18-$20 to ship a ton of ore to Boston and the markets on the East Coast. About that same time it only cost $15 to ship it from South America! The big problem was the mile-long St. Mary's rapids. At that spot the water falls about 20 feet pouring from Lake Superior into Lake Huron.

The rapids made it impossible for any ship to sail in or out of Lake Superior. Everything had to be unloaded at Sault Ste. Marie and hauled by man or beast to the other end of the rapids and reloaded.

The answer to the problem was to build a canal and *lock* which could take ships around the rapids at the Soo. *A lock is a waterway used to raise or lower ships*. This idea had been discussed along with other early canal projects in Michigan, but no one had been able to get the project started.

Michigan had tried to get help from the federal government. The great leaders in Washington did not feel kindly to building a canal and locks in far away Michigan. In 1840, Senator Henry Clay said such a project was, "a work beyond the remotest settlement of the United States, if not the moon!"

Eventually, the resistance was overcome. President Fillmore signed a bill in 1852 which authorized the building of the Soo locks and allowed 750,000 acres of federal land in Michigan to be given as a reward to those who built the locks.

Locks at the Soo

An unlikely group came together to build the locks and claim the 750,000 acres of land. It started with the imagination of a 24-year-old weighing scales salesman, Charles Harvey.

Lots of politics took place in Lansing over the canal project. It was decided that everything had to be finished in two years. Perhaps two years seemed reasonable because the canal was only one mile long.

Charles Harvey hardly knew what he had gotten himself into. Supervising most of the work on the canal and locks fell on his shoulders. The U.S. Army loaned an engineer to help with the technical details. Work started on June 4, 1853. Eventually 1,600 men came to work on the project.

In the winter the workers ate breakfast before daylight and went to work as soon as they could see. Many times the first thing they had to do was to find their tools which were often covered by a foot of snow during the night. Sometimes they had to chop through ice to even get to the rock they were trying to take out. What the workers did was a miracle under the worst conditions.

The job of building the canal was much more difficult than people had predicted. In spite of all the problems, the canal and locks were finished five days before the deadline!

**These workers are building a new set of locks at the Soo in 1894.
This larger lock is 800 feet long. (Courtesy Steelways Company)**

On June 18, 1855, more than a thousand people came to see if the locks would really work. Indeed, the first ship passed through without any problems. More and more ships passed through each year. By 1865, over 280,000 tons of freight shipped through in one season. The freight was mostly copper, iron ore, and grain.

The locks were made larger in 1876 and many times since. The Soo Locks became a key link between the Peninsulas. The locks made it possible to develop the great copper and iron resources in the Upper Peninsula. All from land that was once traded for the Toledo Strip!

What Are the Facts?

1. Did the Indians know there was copper and iron in the Upper Peninsula? Did they realize the full value of these minerals?
2. What is the most important thing Douglass Houghton did?
3. What are the Soo Locks and what do they do? Why are they important?
4. How long did it take to build the Soo Locks and when did they open? What did the company that built the locks get in return?
5. What property of iron ore allowed surveyors to find it?

Math challenge!
It is said the Ontonagon Boulder was 20 cubic feet of pure copper. Measure some everyday items and try to find one that has about 20 cubic feet. Report your findings to the class.

KEY ❀ DATES		
	1831	Stevens T. Mason becomes acting governor of Michigan Territory
	1832	Detroit hit by cholera and Chief Blackhawk war scare
	1834	Michigan claims statehood but Congress disagrees
	1835	The Toledo War
		Stevens T. Mason elected governor by the people of Michigan
	1836	Erie and Kalamazoo Railroad begins operating
	1837	(Jan. 26) Michigan officially becomes the 26th state
	1840	Population of Michigan over 6.5 times that of 1830
	1841	University of Michigan opens in Ann Arbor
		Douglass Houghton's report on copper in the Upper Peninsula
	1842	Detroit has the first free, tax-supported school in Michigan
		All land in Michigan has been "acquired" by treaty from Indians
	1844	Fort Wilkins built at Copper Harbor
		William A. Burt discovers iron ore near Teal Lake in U.P.
	1847	German settlement is started at Frankenmuth, MI
		Albertus VanRaalte starts Dutch settlement at Holland, MI
		Michigan leads U.S. in copper production
	1848	Lewis Cass is the Democratic candidate for U.S. President
		Legislators meet for first time in Lansing
	1851	First college degree granted to a woman in Michigan

Consider the Big Picture

Michigan population grew very quickly in the 1830s. By 1835 the people felt it was time to switch from being a territory to being a state. Becoming a state provided more privileges and a voice in national government.

Plans for statehood became tangled with a border argument with Ohio. A small, but important, strip of land around Toledo was claimed by each.

In the late 1830s and 1840s Michigan had lots of excitement. It got its first railroad; had a "copper rush" in the Upper Peninsula; iron was discovered, and the capital was moved from Detroit to Lansing.

In 1855 the Soo Locks were finished. Now ships could sail between all of the Great Lakes for the first time.

Building Your Michigan Word Power

Write a short story which includes each of these words used correctly: immigrate, lock (used for ships), militia, speculation.

Talking About It

Get together in a small group and talk about-

Why did people in Michigan think it was important to be a state? Why did it matter to them? Didn't they have enough things to worry about starting farms, building homes and developing their towns?

Would people today become so upset over a land conflict with another state? Was it really important to anyone? What if your neighbor said he or she really owned part of your yard and was going to put up a fence? How would you react?

Why was it important to build the Soo Locks? Which do you think is more important today- the Soo Locks or the Mackinac Bridge?

Put It To Use

Find a simple state outline map of the United States. On it write the date when each state east of the Mississippi River achieved statehood. Use an almanac or encyclopedia to find the dates for the other states.

Work in a small group to survey the ethnic groups represented in your own class. Have each student find which country or part of the world his or her family originated. List each place and the number of students related to each. Make a graph to show the information.

8

A Stand Against Slavery

Chapter 8 Section 1

A Way to Freedom: The Underground Railroad

Many people in Michigan were against slavery. Once slavery was made illegal in Canada, escaped slaves passed through Michigan on their way there. What was the Underground Railroad?

A Question of Freedom

The idea of allowing slavery in a nation founded on freedom was a sort of poison which began to slowly create more and more problems for the United States. But the use of slaves had become the economic way of life in the South. This conflict finally ripped the United States apart when many states left the union. This led to the Civil War. What follows is the story of Michigan from the 1830s through the 1860s.

By the time Michigan was admitted as a state, Congress was forced to balance each new state which did not allow slavery with one new state that did allow it. Arkansas was the slave state admitted about the same time as Michigan. The Northwest Ordinance stated slavery was illegal in the Northwest Territory- including Michigan. Apparently those who already had slaves could keep them because the 1830 census listed 32 slaves living here.

By 1832 Michigan had a group whose goal was to abolish slavery. This was one of the first groups of its kind in the U.S. Members were called *abolitionists* (AB oh LISH un ists). *Abolitionists wanted to abolish or end slavery.*

Laura Haviland—One Woman With a Cause

Laura Haviland was a quiet and gentle woman who devoted her life to helping others. In 1837 Laura and her husband started a school for orphans on the Raisin River near Adrian. It was the first Michigan school which accepted African American children.

In 1845, disease took the life of Laura's husband and one of their children. With great effort Laura raised money to keep the school going, care for her six remaining children, and pay taxes on their farm.

Not content to assist those who had already managed their escape, Laura actually helped slaves to make their getaway! Outraged slave owners put up a $3,000 reward for her capture. This was a huge amount of money then. Laura never was caught and today there is a statue of her in front of the Adrian City Hall.

Pamela Thomas

Pamela Thomas was only twenty-three when she learned about escaped slaves through her husband who was a *Quaker. The*

Laura Haviland holding a slave neck collar. (Courtesy Michigan State Archives)

Quakers were a religious group against violence and slavery. Many Quakers were members of the *Underground Railroad.* Beginning in the late 1830s, a number of Michigan people started working with the Underground Railroad.

The Underground Railroad did not have steam engines and passenger cars. It was a loosely organized group of people who were willing to help the runaway slaves. It was called underground because it was supposed to be secret.

It wasn't easy for the Thomas family. Pamela said, "They began to arrive in loads of from six to twelve. This brought much hard work to me and great expense to my husband. Often after my little ones were asleep and I thought the labor of the day over, a friend would drive up with a load of hungry people (escaped slaves) to be fed and housed for the night."

Not all escaped slaves knew about the Underground Railroad or used its services. Their journey was a hard and dangerous one in any case. The worst part of the trip, through the southern states, was made on their own.

Through Michigan to Canada!

In 1834 Canada outlawed slavery. This meant slaves from the United States who reached Canada would be safe. They could not be brought back across the border by slave catchers.

The Routes They Used

Several routes were used by the escaping slaves. The routes went through New York, Indiana, Ohio, and Michigan. One route was known as the "Michigan Central Line." It had the same name as a real railroad.

It is very difficult to know how many escaped slaves used the Michigan route of the Underground Railroad. Since the work of the railroad was secret, few people kept any records and probably no one knew all of those who were "conductors." Some historians guess as many as 40,000 to 50,000 slaves passed through Michigan, while others think those numbers are too high.

Not Everyone Felt the Same

Not everyone in Michigan approved of helping escaped slaves. The Battle Creek office of an antislavery newspaper was burned. Many felt hiding runaway slaves was illegal and would tell the sheriff.

A sailor with connections to Michigan, Captain Jonathan Walker, was helping seven slaves escape in Florida. He was caught and convicted in 1844 as a slave stealer. With a red-hot iron they branded the letters S.S. in the palm of his right hand so all who met him would know what he had done. There is an historic monument in Muskegon, Michigan, in honor of the "Man with the Branded Hand."

Look!

Slave Catchers In Marshall!

A well-known event took place at Marshall, Michigan. In 1843, Adam Crosswhite and his family ran away from Frank Giltner's Kentucky plantation because Crosswhite learned that his four children were to be sold. The Crosswhites made the tough journey north and finally settled in Marshall.

On the morning of January 2, 1847, the slave catchers and a local deputy sheriff were pounding on Adam's door. His neighbors heard the noise and came running. The cry of "slave catchers!" was yelled through the streets of Marshall. Soon over 100 people surrounded the Crosswhite home.

Threats were shouted back and forth. One of the slave catchers began to demand that people in the crowd give him their names. They were proud to tell him and even told him the correct spelling. Each name was written down into a little book. Finally, the deputy sheriff, swayed by the crowd's opinion, decided he should arrest the men from Kentucky instead. By the time the slave catchers could post bond and get out of jail, the Crosswhites were on their way to Canada. But the story does not end here.

Next the Giltners went to the federal court in Detroit. They sued the crowd from Marshall for damages! Since they had many of their names it was easy to decide whom to sue. They wanted to be paid the value of the Crosswhite family. In Kentucky, the Giltners were neighbors of United States Senator Henry Clay. Clay said Michigan was a "hotbed of radicals and renegades." Because of the Crosswhite case and others, Senator Clay helped pass the Fugitive Slave Law in 1850. This national law had stiff penalties for anyone helping an escaped slave!

111

She Spoke the Truth—Isabella Baumfree

Elizabeth Chandler wrote about an African American woman losing her child as it was sold. She wrote about the pain and agony but Isabella Baumfree *felt it*! Her son Peter was sold as a slave and taken to Alabama.

Isabella was born in 1797 in New York state where she lived as a slave. She knew the humiliation of being sold along with some sheep when she was a young girl. Isabella was a strong, proud, six-foot tall woman who took matters into her own hands. In 1826 she gathered up her belongings and left with her youngest daughter. A Quaker family took her in and paid her master money so he would quit bothering her. About this time New York state stopped allowing slavery.

However, during that time, she discovered her son Peter was no longer at the old master's house. She was told the shocking news that he had been sold and taken into the deep South. It meant he would probably never be free. But Isabella was a fighter and went to court, finally winning his release.

Sojourner Truth. (Courtesy Michigan State Archives)

Isabella became very religious over the years. In 1843 she started traveling throughout the North and speaking against slavery and for the equality of women. When she began speaking, Isabella changed her name to Sojourner Truth. She said that God had sent her on a sojourn or trip for the truth.

In the 1850s, Sojourner Truth came to Battle Creek where she began to work with the Underground Railroad. She is buried in the Battle Creek cemetery, but her spirit lives on.

As the years passed, life in the North and the South differed more and more. The invention of the cotton gin in 1793 allowed plantations in the South to process cotton easily and thus more slaves were needed as cheap labor to harvest the cotton. The Northern states relied on new methods of industry and manufactured an increasing number of products. Over the years in the North, the number of people farming kept decreasing. Slavery had no economic value in the North as it did in the Southern states.

What Are the Facts?

1. What human rights struggle created conflict in Michigan and the whole nation from 1830-1865?

2. Briefly tell what each of the following women did: Laura Haviland, Pamela Thomas, and Sojourner Truth.

3. Write an overview of the Adam Crosswhite case.

4. Take the main events from this section and put them into a timeline with dates for each event.

Use a map today!
Draw a map of a real or imaginary Underground Railroad line through your home town. Show how it will reach Canada and label eight towns along the way.

Digging Deeper:
Which core democratic values were denied to slaves?

Chapter 8 Section 2

New Politics From the Wolverine State

The Republican party was started in 1854 in Jackson, Michigan. The party was against slavery and fought to change proslavery laws. Abraham Lincoln was the first Republican president.

Punish the Abolitionists

Because of the Fugitive Slave Law it was very risky for anyone to help an escaped slave. But the work of the "conductors" went on as usual and business even picked up. Some "conductors" were even free African Americans, including William Lambert and George de Baptiste (bap TEEST) of Detroit.

Equal Treatment Still Hard to Find

In spite of the fact that many in Michigan were against slavery, they were not always ready to admit that blacks and whites were really equal. In 1850, Michigan made a new state constitution and the issue of allowing African-Americans to vote was considered, but not included.

The Birth of a New Political Party

By the mid-1850s, the nation was losing any idea of compromise about slavery. The two major political parties, the Whigs and the Democrats, were coming unglued. People who were strongly antislavery were not satisfied with either party.

In 1854 a small group gathered in a meeting house in Ripon, Wisconsin. They were thinking about starting an anti-slavery party. The editor of the *Detroit Tribune* also called for a meeting with people from all parties to support a new political group. On July 6, 1854, supporters poured into Jackson to organize and make a list of candidates for office. The meeting in Jackson, Michigan was so large there wasn't enough room in any building to hold all of the people. They met under the oak trees on Morgan's Forty, a farm on the edge of town. The 1,500 people at the meeting decided to form the Republican party.

They chose the name because they felt republican meant having

This plaque marks the spot where the Republican Party was organized in Jackson. (Courtesy Michigan State Archives)

personal freedom where each person was on an equal level. The Republicans decided on a ticket of men who would run for state offices in Michigan. Kinsley Bingham was nominated to run for governor and he won!

Not Everyone Is Excited

Even though many people in Michigan were strongly against slavery, the new party was ridiculed. The *Detroit Free Press* (July 8, 1854) said the men on the Republican ticket were not qualified to hold office and that Bingham was dishonest. The newspaper felt the Fugitive Slave Law was following the ideas in the United States Constitution, the supreme law of the land.

The editors of the *Free Press* must have been among the many who were surprised when Bingham was elected governor and the Republicans also won control of the Michigan legislature.

A Visitor Who Becomes Famous

Other Republican meetings took place around Michigan. On August 27, 1856, a tall, slender lawyer from Illinois was invited to speak at a Kalamazoo meeting. Zachariah Chandler, the prominent abolitionist and a Republican leader, was quite disgusted with the fellow because he just did not speak out strongly enough against slavery. Who was the lawyer from Illinois? He was Abraham Lincoln!

The Republicans Have a Great Impact

The Republican party had a great impact on Michigan and the United States. Up to that time, Michigan Democrats had won every election for governor except one. Then the tables turned. Except for three terms, Michigan had all Republican governors during the next 78 years!

The Republicans nominated Abraham Lincoln for president in 1860. Austin Blair was the new Republican governor of Michigan. After the election, most people in the South were quite alarmed. They felt they had lost control of the national political process.

Many states in the South began to leave the union and form their own government- the Confederate State of America. Earlier, Lewis Cass resigned his post as Secretary of State because President Buchanan refused to force all the states to stay together. The slavery issue had finally torn the country in two.

Zachariah Chandler, a powerful U.S. senator, controlled the Michigan Republican Party much of the time from 1835 to 1860. (Courtesy Michigan State Archives)

What Are the Facts?

1. Exactly where and when did the Republican party first meet to organize? Who was the first Republican governor elected in Michigan?
2. Why did Zachariah Chandler not like Abraham Lincoln's speech in Kalamazoo?
3. Explain what impact the Republican party had on the state of Michigan over the years.

Express yourself:
Put yourself back in time to the year 1854. Write a Michigan newspaper headline and editorial about the new Republican Party.

Chapter 8 Section 3

Michigan and the Civil War: 1861-65

No fighting took place in Michigan; but once the war started, Michigan quickly sent soldiers and nurses to help. Several people from Michigan became famous and one was George Custer.

It Looks Like War!

Michigan's new governor, Austin Blair, said: "The Union must be preserved and the laws must be enforced in all parts of it at whatever cost.... *Secession* is a revolution, and revolution...is treason...." Most people in Michigan were ready to fight to keep the southern states from leaving. *Secession means for one part of a nation to leave the rest.*

The tension between the North and the South was broken when Confederate forces attacked Fort Sumpter near Charleston, South Carolina. That blaze of cannon fire in the darkness of the early hours of April 12, 1861, began a great and terrible civil war– a war between two parts of the United States. The North, or the Union side, fought the South or Confederate side.

Volunteers Came

Neither side was prepared for war. The North had a regular army but it was not nearly large enough. Right away President Lincoln asked each state in the North to send volunteers to fight. Men throughout Michigan were ready. Each city or town formed local units.

Of course, very few of the new soldiers had any kind of military training. Commanding officers were usually chosen from each town's leading citizens. Governor Blair appointed the top commanders himself. Most of the units traveled to Fort Wayne in Detroit for some training. Many of the men found that practicing marches and drills was rather boring. Some complained when they did not get pie with supper!

The first group from our state was called the "1st Michigan" and sent to Cleveland, Ohio by ship. From Cleveland they traveled by train to Washington D.C. At 10 o'clock on the night of May 16, 1861, the 1st Michigan marched down the streets of Washington, D.C. Abraham Lincoln said "Thank God for Michigan!" He was glad to see troops willing to serve from the western states.

Michigan Soldiers There in the Beginning

People thought that the war would be over as soon as the Union troops marched south and thumped the Southerners. On a hot summer day, in July 1861, the soldiers from Michigan saw action with the enemy for the first time at the Battle of Bull Run. They had to load their single shot muskets and take aim at another human being. They smelled the burnt gunpowder and heard the cries of the wounded. They faced the whistling cannon balls and the gleaming, sharp Confederate bayonets. War was not as easy as they had been led to believe and things went badly.

When the dust had settled after the day's fight, the 1st Michigan found six of their men were dead, 37 were wounded, and 70 had been captured, including their commanding officer. The dazed survivors straggled back to Washington, walking more than 60 miles in 24 hours without food or sleep. Detroit and the North were shocked. The *Detroit Free Press* said: "We are beaten; it is a defeat and a rout."

This photo shows three Civil War soldiers from Michigan's 4th Infantry. The Afro-American man is not in the army, but probably helping with chores around camp. At first, black men were not allowed to fight for their own freedom. (Courtesy National Archives, Washington D.C.)

The Civil War was violent and bloody. This photo of a Civil War reenactment shows nurses helping a wounded soldier. Doing this work could be as dangerous as fighting!

Cavalry from Grand Rapids

Later that fall, 1,163 men joined the 2nd Michigan Volunteer *Cavalry* at Grand Rapids. *The cavalry is made up of those soldiers riding horses into battle.* They were one of the few units outfitted with Colt repeating rifles. Captain Russell Alger rode with the 2nd. He would become governor of Michigan after the war.

The Grand Rapids soldiers went south down the Mississippi River and were soon deep in Rebel country reaching Booneville, Mississippi. Then, on July 1, 1862, the Confederates sent 6,000 troops to wipe them out.

The Confederates were confident as they marched forward. They came in hard. Suddenly the 2nd Michigan let loose with their repeating rifles. The Southerners had never faced such a concentration of bullets. It was hair-raising!

Captain Alger took a group of cavalry charging around behind the enemy, yelling all the way. Alger might have been the hero of the battle except, in the excitement of the charge, he rode into a tree and was knocked out! The cavalry went on without him and succeeded in driving off the Confederate soldiers. The 2nd Michigan was saved from destruction.

Turned Down At First

Even though one of the reasons for the Civil War was to stop slavery, black men were not allowed to join the Union army at first. Some tried to, but they were turned down.

It wasn't until 1863 that black units were formed in Michigan. Blacks who were living in Canada came back so they could go into the army too.

The black soldiers from Michigan fought bravely. Many times they faced greater risks—some Confederates would not take black prisoners alive! By the end of the war, over 1,600 men had fought in the black units from Michigan. Some Native Americans also served from Michigan. Many of those were in Company K, 1st Michigan Sharpshooters.

Helping the Sick & Wounded

There was no Red Cross at the time of the Civil War. In its place, brave and dedicated women helped in the Sanitary Commission. This group gathered food,

Kinchen Artis came to Michigan from Ohio. He served as a corporal in Company K, First Michigan Colored Regiment. (Courtesy Michigan State Archives)

blankets, books, and newspapers for the soldiers on the battlefields.

The more adventurous women actually went as nurses. They helped with the gruesome task of aiding wounded soldiers. Julia Wheelock, Anna Etherage, Elmira Brainard, and "Michigan Bridget" Devins all worked in terrible conditions to do what they could for the wounded.

Anna Etherage was about 21 years old when the war began. She volunteered immediately in Detroit. It is hard for people today to realize what it must have been like to try to treat battlefield wounds with the crude equipment and lack of drugs during the Civil War. Women nurses were often ready and willing to run into battle to help the wounded. They had to be cool to do their work among the bullets and exploding cannon shells. Once Anna was bandaging the wounds of a soldier when he was torn to pieces by a cannonball! Many times bullets and pieces of cannon shells tore holes through her dress but somehow she was never injured. She was held in the highest regard by Union soldiers.

Besides wounds from battle, the Civil War nurses and doctors had to face a great deal of disease. One of Michigan's past governors, Moses

Wisner, joined the army and then died of typhoid fever in 1863. One astonished soldier said, "We have lost about 30 by disease since the regiment was organized and have not lost one by the bullet."

A Most Unusual Soldier!

Not every woman involved in the war effort was a nurse. Michigan had at least one who enlisted in the army. Sara Emma Edmonds had been traveling around the country as a Bible *salesman*. Yes, salesman! She ran away from home in Canada and felt the only way she could earn a living was by pretending to be a man.

She was living in Michigan when the war started and she enlisted as a man. How she kept her secret is a mystery. But Sara served for two years as Franklin Thompson in the 2nd Michigan. At that time she was wounded and wanted to leave the army. She was probably afraid she would be discovered when the wound was treated.

Sara Edmonds, the woman who disguised herself as a man and fought in the Union army. (Courtesy Michigan State Archives)

A Very Young General

George Armstrong Custer was one of the most controversial people to come out of the Civil War. He was born in Ohio and moved to Monroe, Michigan, a few years before the war began.

Only three days after graduating from West Point, Lieutenant Custer found himself at the Battle of Bull Run. Almost immediately, Custer became known for his bold manner on the battlefield. Later in the war, Custer was promoted to the rank of general because of his daring leadership in a cavalry charge. This was two days before the battle of Gettysburg in Pennsylvania.

The battle on the rolling hills around the little village of Gettysburg was considered to be the turning point in the war. The Confederates considered it a daring advance into Union territory. At an important moment, the Confederate cavalry planned a surprise charge into the back of the Union troops. That is when General Custer and Colonel Alger led their

Michigan cavalry units out of hiding and into a counter charge against the Confederates.

The Awesome Charge

Custer led his soldiers while waving his sword and shouting "Come on you Wolverines!" The cavalry charge by the two sides was awesome. Six thousand Confederates commanded by J.E.B. Stuart faced 5,000 Union soldiers. The earth shook from the thousands of running horses and their thunderous noise rolled across the fields.

Both sides claimed victory. But the result was that the Confederate's surprise attack was stopped. If it had succeeded, Gettysburg might have been a Confederate victory instead of one for the Union side.

The War & Michigan's Resources

The Civil War increased the need for many natural resources. The demand for copper and iron went up and so did the need for food. Michigan provided the Union with wheat, wool, and nearly 70 percent of the copper used during the war. Manufacturing businesses increased during the war. There were nearly four times as many

General George Custer, the well-known commander of a Michigan cavalry unit. (Courtesy Michigan State Archives)

companies making things in 1870 as there were in 1860. It was the beginning of Michigan's change from a farm state into a manufacturing state.

It Is Over!!!

In 1865 General Robert E. Lee surrendered. The Civil War was over and the country was united again. One soldier exclaimed,

"Everyone is wild with joy. As for myself, I cannot write! I cannot talk; only my glad heart cries...."

Grown Men Seen Crying

Shock and sorrow came over Michigan just three days after Lee's surrender. President Lincoln was shot and killed. The President was often affectionately known as Father Abraham in Michigan. Grown men were seen crying along the streets when they heard the news.

The Human Cost

Michigan soldiers came back home— the homes some had not seen for three or four years. And there were many who never came back. Over 4,100 were killed in battle or died from wounds and about 10,000 more died from disease. Michigan sent more than 90,000 men and at least one woman to fight and end the southern rebellion. All except about 5,000 had volunteered to go. Three times as many Michigan soldiers were in the infantry (soldiers who walked) as were in the cavalry (soldiers who rode horses). Some were also in the navy.

The soldiers and sailors came back to a state which had changed in many ways. Michigan was becoming an industrial state. Great demand would build up for the state's natural resources: its lumber, copper, and iron. Nature's storehouse was full and ready to be used in Michigan!

What Are the Facts?

1. What happened at the Battle of Bull Run? What did the *Detroit Free Press* say about the battle?
2. List three people from Michigan who were in the Civil War. Explain what each person did.
3. How many Michigan soldiers fought in the Civil War? Compare how many of these died from wounds and how many died from disease?

Express yourself:
Put yourself in the place of a Michigan soldier or nurse who fought in the Civil War. Write a short story about something you did in the war.

Digging Deeper
How did the development of the Erie Canal have anything to do with Michigan's strong antislavery attitude and its strong response to sending soldiers to fight in the Civil War?

1832	First Michigan anti-slavery society formed	
1840	William Woodbridge becomes Michigan's second governor	
1843	Isabella Baumfree speaks against slavery using the name Sojourner Truth	
1847	Adam Crosswhite escapes slave catchers in Marshall	
1854	Republican Party holds first statewide convention at Jackson	
1856	Abraham Lincoln speaks in Kalamazoo	
1860	Lincoln elected U.S. President	
1861	Austin Blair becomes governor	**KEY ✿ DATES**
	Civil War begins	
1862	(July) Anti-war riot in Detroit	
1863	Many Michigan soldiers fought and died in Battle of Gettysburg, PA	
1864	Michigan passes law to draft men into army	
1865	General Lee surrenders– the Civil War is over	
	Colonel Pritchard helps capture the Confederate president, Jefferson Davis	

Consider the Big Picture

Before the Civil War, most Michigan people were against slavery. Some people even worked to help slaves who escaped from the south.

Many escaped slaves passed through Michigan on their way to the safety of Canada. Those who helped them were part of the Underground Railroad.

In 1854 Michigan was the place where a new political party started which was against slavery. Members of this party called themselves Republicans.

In 1861 several pro-slavery states tried to leave the United States or Union and start their own country. This soon led to a civil war with two parts of the nation fighting each other.

No Civil War battles were fought in or near Michigan, but about 90,000 people, mostly men, joined the army to fight. Of these, over 14,000 died during the war.

Building Your Michigan Word Power

Choose two Michigan related words from this chapter. Write what each word means on separate slips of paper. All slips from the class will be placed in a box. Each person will take out two slips. Read aloud the definitions and the correct words which go with them.

Talking About It

Get together in a small group and talk about-

Compare and contrast the people who helped escaped slaves in Michigan to those who helped Jewish people hiding from the Nazis in World War II.

What do you think would happen today if one or more of the states decided to leave the United States? Is this same kind of thing happening elsewhere in the world? What about the former Soviet Union?

Put It To Use

Go to the internet and find sites about slavery or the Civil War. Try to find sites which include Michigan information. List four of the sites you like best and tell what can be found there.

Work with a small group of other students and your teacher to visit a local cemetery which has Civil War veterans. Carefully check the tombstones to find some and write down as much information about each one as you can. Include the year of birth and death. Did some actually die during a battle? Make a report or video for the rest of the class.

9

We Take from
Nature's Storehouse

Chapter 9 Section 1

Lumbering: Rugged People and the Smell of Sawdust

The development of Michigan was driven by our location, natural resources, climate and the cultures of the people who settled our state.

Find out how Michigan became the number one lumber-producing state. It seems no one planted new trees and today only a very few original ones are left in Michigan.

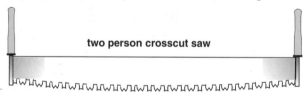

two person crosscut saw

Everyone Wanted Lumber and We Had it!

One of Michigan's most exciting times was the lumber era. It was a time of lumberjacks and sawmills. Here, the lumber business really got going after the Civil War. Wood was needed to rebuild war-damaged buildings and for new houses in fast-growing cities like Chicago. Michigan was growing fast too. The state's population increased almost 60 percent during the 1860s.

Everyone wanted lumber and Michigan had it. For years, Maine and New York had been the leading lumbering states, but their supply of trees was shrinking. Michigan had plenty of trees! The one the loggers wanted most was the white pine. It is now Michigan's state tree. The northern two-thirds of Michigan was covered by straight, majestic pines reaching well over 100 feet toward the sky. Some of the best trees reached 200 feet and were five to seven feet across. These giants were about 300 years old.

There were so many trees that many people thought it would be impossible to ever cut them all, but they were wrong. There is only one place where original trees were left standing in the Lower Peninsula. This is at Hartwick Pines State Park near Grayling. Many people will never have the chance to see the glory of one of these 200-foot giant white pines.

124

Rivers were an important way to move logs to the sawmills. (Courtesy Michigan Department of Natural Resources)

The Rivers Were Important

There were very few roads in the northern woods but Michigan's streams and rivers were just right for floating logs to the sawmills. Some of the great logging rivers were the Muskegon, Manistee, Au Sable, Tittabawassee, Menominee, Escanaba, and Manistique.

The Saginaw River Valley was the first main lumbering region and logging operations continued there until the 1900s. When lumbering was at its peak, there were 112 sawmills between Saginaw and Bay City! The other major lumber area was along the Muskegon River. "Two out of every three pine trees that came crashing to the ground in Michigan's Lower Peninsula in the 19th century ended up in Saginaw or Bay City or Muskegon." (Jeremy Kilar, *Michigan's Lumbertowns*)

Logging moved farther north and into the Upper Peninsula as the years passed. Nearly all cities and villages in the northern part of the Lower Peninsula and in the eastern end of the Upper Peninsula had their start during the lumber era.

A Winter's Work

In the earlier years, cutting and moving the trees was a winter job because it was easier to haul logs through the woods with snow or ice on the ground. The cut logs were hauled on horse-drawn or ox-drawn sleds.

Men left their families and friends and spent the winter months in the forests cutting the trees. They were called *"shanty boys." The loggers got this name because of the crude bunkhouses where they lived.* Many of the loggers were immigrants. Some were from Sweden and others were born in Finland, Norway, or Canada. The lumbering business was full of colorful people. Dynamite Jack, Chris Crosshaul, Cedar Root Charley, and Slabwood Johnson were just a few of the characters cutting down the pine.

125

These two Native Americans were cutting down huge trees near Manistee about 1888. (Courtesy Michigan State Archives)

The shanty boys were up and out of their bunks before daylight. They gathered in the cookhouse and ate an enormous breakfast in silence. Talking was always forbidden while eating.

Once in the woods, the *swampers* would get the brush away from the bigger trees. The *fellers* used axes or long crosscut saws to cut down the trees. As soon as the mighty pines hit the ground, the *limbers* chopped off the small branches and *buckers* worked hard at sawing the trees into logs about 16 to 20 feet long.

At noon, a meal was brought out to the men. It was eaten right in the woods. The men worked until the sun started to go down. Then they heard the sound of the cook's *"gabriel." The gabriel was a very long tin horn blown to bring the shanty boys back to camp.* The tired, weary, and hungry men walked back ready to eat. After supper it was time to dry out their clothes and socks around the bunkhouse stove and then turn in for a night's rest.

The River Drive

By spring, each camp had carefully stacked thousands of logs at the rollway. All the logs were stamped on one end with a specific mark. The mark was like the brand used to identify cattle. Then, each lumber company could spot its own logs. Each river might have dozens of camps scattered along it all sending logs down at the same time.

The river drive was the next step in taking the logs to market. The drive was complex and dangerous. When all was ready and the water flowing fast from the spring snow melting, the logs were released. They rolled into the river with a thunderous splash! The men who worked on the river drive were called river hogs. They stood on the logs as the timber bobbed and weaved with the current. The rivers became a mass of moving logs. At the end of the river drive millions of logs came floating into the ponds by the sawmills.

Sometimes there were so many logs the river became clogged and there was a logjam. A logjam stopped everything from moving on the river. The tremendous weight of all the logs pushing down on a jam could make it seem as solid as concrete. There were several famous logjams. A granddaddy of all jams took place in Grand Rapids in July 1883. The whole river was blocked back for seven miles! When the jam broke free, a sea of logs moved down the river, sweeping bridges and everything else out of its path.

Mountains of Sawdust

What was a sawmill really like? The first ones were powered by water, much like a gristmill. By the 1870s, most mills were using steam engines to run their equipment. They were also using large circular saw blades, 50 inches or more across. The logs were pushed into the blade and one board was cut off with each pass. Much of the finished lumber was put aboard ships and transported on the Great Lakes.

The circular saw cut one board at a time which made slow work of sawing so many logs. Later it was replaced by gang saws which could cut a whole log into boards in one pass. (Courtesy Michigan State Archives)

New Ways to Work Faster and Better

At the sawmill, circular blades were replaced by band blades, which were like a ribbon of steel. Gang saws were also introduced. Each gang saw had many blades, sometimes up to 40. In a gang saw, two or three whole logs could be sliced up in a single pass.

Improved technology helped loggers to do the impossible task of cutting down almost all of Michigan's pine. In the 1870s the ax was replaced by the two-man crosscut saw. Early saws did not work well to cut thick trees because their blades became clogged with sawdust. The simple addition of shorter teeth, called raker teeth, pushed the sawdust out.

Silas Overpack's invention of big wheels made it possible to haul logs in the summer when sleds could not be used. The logs were chained to the axle between the wheels and lifted off the ground. (Courtesy Michigan State Archives)

Big Wheels Overpack

Silas Overpack was not even in the lumber business but he was the fellow who made it possible to log the whole year round. Overpack made wagons in Manistee. One day a farmer came to him and said he was trying to clear the trees from his farm. It was a hard job to move them over the rough ground. He asked Overpack to build him the largest set of wooden wagon wheels he could. The farmer used the wheels successfully to haul his logs. Overpack soon began to market the idea of using his nine to ten-feet-tall "big wheels" to the loggers. Big wheels made in Manistee were shipped to every lumbering area in America for 50 years. Using Overpack's wheels pulled by horses or oxen, logs could be hauled over the bumpy ground in the woods without a sled. The logs were chained to the single axle and lifted up under the axle when it was hitched to the animals.

Lumber Barons — the Lucky Ones

The shanty boys did the hard work of cutting the trees but it was the owners of the lumber companies who frequently became rich. *The wealthy owners were often known as "lumber barons."* Many times they used their money to influence lawmakers in Lansing. Five lumber barons actually became governors. Russell Alger, Josiah Begole, Aaron Bliss, Henry Crapo [This unusual last name is pronounced with a long "a" like CRAY], and David Jerome all served in the state's highest office.

Charles Hackley was just one of the 40 lumber millionaires living in Muskegon during the 1880s. He eventually owned railroads, ships, and much timberland outside of Michigan. Hackley worked hard to improve Muskegon and gave the city several million dollars for various projects. His house still stands in Muskegon and can be visited.

Louis Sands was born in Sweden; just as were many others in the lumbering business. He came to America trying to find a better way of life. Eventually he found work as a shanty boy in Michigan. He saved his money and finally had enough to buy his own timberland. Most of Sand's operations were near Manistee. Over the years, Sands earned a great deal of money.

The great Mr. Sands was very thrifty and didn't spend a penny he did not need to. He was well known for serving his loggers beans- which were cheap. A song was even written about life in a Louis Sands lumber camp. Jim McGee was his foreman or "big push." Here are a few verses:

Who feeds us beans? Who feeds us tea?
Louis Sands and Jim McGee.
Who thinks that meat's a luxury ?
Louis Sands and Jim McGee.
We make the big trees fall ker-splash.
And hit the ground an awful smash!
And for the logs, who gets the cash?
Louis Sands and Jim McGee.
        from *Lore of the Lumbercamps* by Earl C. Beck

Traverse City was another booming lumber town and it became the home of Perry Hannah. Hannah moved to Michigan when he was just 13 years old. He worked in the woods and became an office clerk with one of the lumber companies. He too started his own outfit, Hannah, Lay & Company. Hannah owned much land in Traverse City and also ran several other businesses.

Often lumber barons owned many different businesses which were related to timber in some way. There were factories which made wooden shingles, matches, toothpicks, and more. For many years there was a big demand for bark from hemlock trees to use in the tanning of leather. And large amounts of scrap wood were used to evaporate salt brine.

What Trees Meant to Michigan

Logging operations had a big impact on Michigan. From the end of the Civil War to 1900, the lumbering industry dominated Michigan's economy. During that time, about 160 billion board feet of pine were cut here. That was an awesome quantity of wood; it was enough to build 10 million six-room houses! Michigan produced more lumber than any other state from 1869 to 1899. The years of greatest production were the late 1880s.

The Michigan trees were called "green gold" by the loggers. The average wholesale price of 1,000 board feet of lumber was $13.00. Multiply that by the amount of wood cut, and you can see that wood worth over $2 billion was taken from Michigan forests during the peak lumbering days. It has been said that Michigan's green gold was worth more than all the gold taken from California during the same period.

Loggers and their improved technology stripped the pines from Michigan faster than any shanty boy ever thought possible. By 1905 the amount of trees cut in the Lower Peninsula had dropped drastically. Lumbering continued in the Upper Peninsula for several more years but the end was near. After the loggers were through, they left tens of thousands of acres of *cutover country. This was land with stumps as far as you could see. It was land with very few trees growing, but with piles of brush and wood waste left behind.*

After They Trashed the Land

The cutover country became a problem. At first some lumber companies tried to sell it to potential farmers. Those people who tried to raise crops on the land soon discovered that it lost its minerals quickly and could not support farming.

The removal of all the trees by loggers destroyed the ground cover. Without plants to hold the topsoil in place, wind and rain washed it away and the area was badly damaged by erosion. This photo shows cutover country in Clare County. (Courtesy Michigan State Archives)

Incredible Fires!

The second problem for the cutover country was that of forest fires. When fires started, the results could be terrible. Michigan had many fires in the timberlands but two stand out. On Saturday October 7, 1871 fires started at several places in the northern part of Michigan. Some say campfires had been left by railroad workers near Escanaba. Perhaps some farmers had set fires trying to clear the slashings off their land. The fires became so large the heat of the flames developed a wind which whipped the flames and pushed them along faster and faster.

One fire moved toward Menominee. People tried to protect themselves by going into the Menominee River. This is what someone said:

Listen!

"The heat was so intense that the instant they rose out of the water, their clothes caught fire and when they inverted wooden buckets over their heads, the bottoms of the buckets would catch fire.... A bottle at the edge of the river melted and ran with a hiss into the water."

Several towns were wiped out. Fire scorched 14,000 square miles in Michigan. Needless to say, many people died horrible deaths in the blaze. Ironically this was just one day before the great Chicago fire. Also there were bad fires in Wisconsin at the same time. The Midwest had been a dry tinderbox!

Just 10 years later, on September 4, 1881, the thumb area of the Lower Peninsula was hit hard by another forest fire. Several villages were consumed by the fire. Four hundred people ran to the Bad Axe courthouse. It was the only brick building in town. In order to remain safe inside, the crowd had to pass buckets of water up to the roof and keep it damp.

After the fire, there was much concern for the well-being of those who had lost their homes and loved ones. That was the first disaster where the American Red Cross came to provide assistance.

Forest fires were a reminder of careless lumbering. Fires burned thousands of acres and killed both people and animals. (Courtesy Michigan State Archives)

Thinking It Over

Looking back at Michigan's famous lumber days, it was a time of colorful adventure. Many people became rich through logging, though most of the shanty boys spent their money without much thought for the future. Little attention was paid to the land after the trees were gone. Even though it has been nearly 100 years since logging stopped in some places, the giant trees have not returned. It may take another 100 years or more before that begins to happen.

What Are the Facts?

1. What were the years of greatest lumber production in Michigan?
2. How large were the tallest white pine trees cut by the early loggers? How long did it take for the trees to grow so big?
3. What invention first made it possible to log the whole year round?
4. Explain how logging practices contributed to forest fires. Where and when were some of the worst forest fires in Michigan?
5. Design your own unique log mark and tell why you made it that way.

Express yourself:
Write a short essay about why you think lumber companies were careless in cutting down so many trees all at once. Why didn't they practice conservation and plant new trees?

Chapter 9 Section 2

Copper and Iron by the Ton

It is true! Michigan produced a large percentage of the nation's copper for many years and much iron ore too- all from the Upper Peninsula.

Fast Growth In Mining

Just as the lumber industry was being affected by new equipment and better ways of doing things, so were the iron and copper mines of the western Upper Peninsula. Early miners used picks and their own muscles to chip rock from beneath the ground.

By the 1870s and 1880s, steam engines were compressing air to run big drills and hammers. The compressed air was sent into the mines in pipes and hoses to where the miners were working. Miners were lowered deeper and deeper into the dark pits. Eventually, some of the mines went below 5,000 feet!

Large new deposits of copper were found in the Keweenaw Peninsula. "The most famous copper mine in the world!" is what they called the Calumet and Hecla. Just two years after it opened, it was producing 46 percent of Michigan's copper!

Many New Workers

With the great increase in mining came the need for more and more workers. The population of the mining towns grew rapidly. Houghton County had 88,000 people in 1910 and was the county with the 4th largest population in Michigan!

People came from many places to work in the mines. In 1900, half of the people living in Houghton County were born in another country. Immigrants came from Canada, Cornwall (in England), Czechoslovakia, Finland, Germany, Italy, Norway, Poland, and Sweden. Large numbers arrived from Finland. They even started the only Finnish college in the United States, Suomi College (SUE mee). Suomi, located in Houghton, still operates today.

Man engines or man cars were like elevators which quickly raised and lowered workers into deep copper and iron mines. The cars were open and safety was not the greatest concern. (Courtesy MTU Archives and Copper Country Historical Collections, Michigan Technological University)

133

The Cornish from Cornwall were very respected for their mining knowledge. Many of the mine captains, superintendents and shift bosses were Cornish. The Cornish also gave us the *pasty* (PASS tee)—*a sort of meat pie made with potatoes, turnips, and onions. A pasty was the miner's "box lunch." The men carried them into the mines wrapped in newspaper.*

Benefits & Danger

Michigan's big copper mine owners respected their workers. They wanted to have a stable group of happy employees. Over 1,000 rental homes were built for the people who worked for the mines. Their homes were repaired free and the garbage hauled away by the company. The companies built schools, libraries, hospitals, and bathhouses. In 1898 a local newspaper said "No mining company in the world treats its employees better than the Calumet and Hecla." In spite of these many benefits, being a miner was hard and dangerous.

Many miners were killed or permanently injured. Between 1855 and 1975, about 2,000 miners died in Michigan copper mines. They were not all strong men; many young boys were given jobs in the mines. For their work they were paid half of a man's salary. Today, it is against the law to hire children in any industry.

The 1890 Report of the Mine Inspector for Houghton County listed this accident:

> Accident 9.—Charles F. Carlson, John H. Sullivan, and a boy named Andrew Adamsky were at work in the...No. 4 shaft in the Osceola Mine....They had with them...about eight pounds of dynamite and a full box of blasting caps. An explosion occurred. What caused this explosion is not known, but it is supposed that fire dropped from a burning candle on the box of blasting caps, which caused them to explode. An inquest was held before Justice Vivian ...

Troubled Times at the Copper Mines

Changes were coming to Michigan's copper mines. By 1913 some miners talked about starting a union so they would only have to work eight hours a day instead of twelve. They also wanted to have a minimum wage. Miners in some western states had already started unions.

The copper mining companies in Michigan were facing their own problems. Now they had lots of cheap competition. New mines were producing copper in Montana and Arizona. These mines were cheaper because they were open-pit mines working on the surface. How could the mines in Michigan compete? The Michigan mine owners began to cut costs. At that time, drill crews had two men. The mine owners felt the answer was to only have one miner work each drill.

One-Man Drill Means A Strike...

The miners were really upset over the new policy. They were afraid many men would lose their jobs. They were worried that miners might be injured and no one would know about it because each man was working alone.

July 23, 1913, a strike was called by the union against the Calumet and Hecla mine. Miners stood in picket lines around the entrances to the mine. Mine captains and supervisors crossed the picket lines because they felt they should keep working. The towns around the mines were divided by the strike. Were the miners right or wrong?

The sheriff did not think he could keep the peace. People in the area sent telegrams and told Governor Woodbridge Ferris that the situation was desperate and that troops were needed. He sent the entire Michigan National Guard, about 2,500 men, to the Copper Country.

A miner with a one-man drill. The miners only have candles to see in the dark mine. Can you imagine how hard it must have been to see with so little light!

Bloodshed at Keweenaw

The situation got worse. Two miners were shot and killed. Also, 139 miners were arrested for picketing. The company started to throw striking miners out of their company-owned homes! Later, three strike breakers were cut down in a hail of gunfire. Then the worst event of the strike took place. The union gave a Christmas party for some 600 miners' children and their mothers. The party was held on the second floor of the Italian Hall in Calumet. About halfway through the party someone shouted "Fire!" A mass of children tried to run down the stairs but the doors opened toward the inside. No one could get out. Seventy-two women and children were crushed to death at the bottom of the stairs— and there never was a fire. Years later some people thought they knew who yelled the false alarm, but they never told because the person still lived in town.

The Strike is Over

Finally, in April 1914, the long and tragic strike ended. The miners did not win much. An eight-hour day was the only demand met. The 1913 copper strike took the spirit away from the copper industry in Michigan. Many people felt it was never quite the same afterwards.

The National Guard was called in after the copper strike began. These soldiers had the unpleasant job of keeping order among the strikers. (Courtesy MTU Archives and Copper Country Historical Collections, Michigan Technological University)

Not Much Mining Now

Michigan copper mines have closed one by one. The White Pine Mine in Ontonagon County was Michigan's last. It closed in the fall of 1995 because of the cost of eliminating pollution problems. The Keweenaw Peninsula still has plenty of copper, but most of it is too far below ground to mine at a profit.

Iron Mining Grows Too

Michigan iron mining began near Marquette. Later, new deposits were discovered further south near the Menominee River. These deposits were not developed because it was impossible to take the iron ore anyplace where it could be used. Lack of a good way to move the ore to the Great Lakes stopped development of the iron range until the railroad arrived in 1878. The first railroad connected the mines to the port city of Escanaba.

In 1879 the largest known deposit of iron ore was found in the Menominee range at a place which came to be called Iron Mountain.

Visit a Mine

What was it like to work in one of Michigan's mines? This is what one man saw deep inside an iron mine in 1877.

Listen!

"Standing on the edge...we look downward and see...the small lamps of the busy miners, whose forms are only dimly outlined by the feeble rays, making them appear more like evil spirits; an impression which is enhanced by the clanging of the drills and hammers, the heavy reports of the blasts (explosions to loosen rock), the rumbling of the skips (ore cars) moving up and down the shafts, and all these sounds echoed and re-echoed from invisible walls...create an impression of awe and fear."

The inside of a mine was dark and dirty. For many years miners depended only on candles for light, even while operating heavy equipment. (Courtesy Michigan State Archives)

Charlotte Kawbawgam (Laughing Whitefish) fought the Jackson Iron Mine to get her father's stock in the company. He was the man who led the miners to the iron!

137

The Copper and Iron Ranges in Michigan's Upper Peninsula

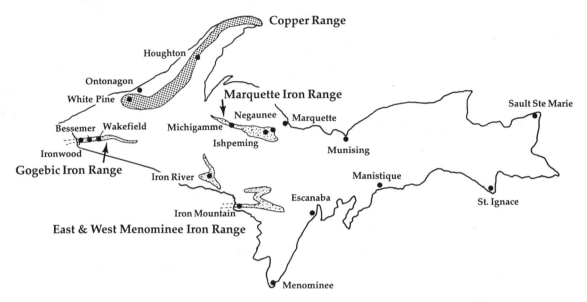

More Iron Ore

Look at a map of the Upper Peninsula and you can see where the iron mines were. Each area has at least one town with "iron" in its name! In 1880 there were only 150 people in Iron Mountain, but by 1890 the population had jumped to 8,000. Other mines and towns started nearby.

As the railroad reached to the most western end of the Upper Peninsula, more iron ore deposits were explored. Boomtowns sprouted up around a new iron range, the Gogebic (go GEE bik). It was the third major iron range in Michigan. Ironwood soon had 5,000 people, three newspapers, and five schools. Other Gogebic Range mines were at Bessemer and Wakefield. All three of Michigan's iron ranges helped to make the state one of the leading iron ore producers from the 1880s until the early 1900s. It was then the open-pit mines were developed in Minnesota where the iron ore was near the surface. These mines cost much less to run than the ones in Michigan.

These open-pit mines, being on the surface, were much cheaper to run than the Michigan mines which were deep underground. Once the Minnesota iron mines opened, it was hard for Michigan miners to compete. Now there are only two working iron mines, the Empire and the Tilden. These mines are both near Marquette. Even though there are only two left, they still produce about 25 percent of the nation's iron ore! Both are open-pit mines, just like the ones in Minnesota. Because they are expensive to operate, they may be forced to close at any time.

New Processes Help

The two open-pit mines near Marquette have been successful and cost effective because they use new processes. The iron ore mined now is low grade ore and it must be concentrated before it can be used to make steel. As a part of the process, Michigan's ore is made into small pellets and baked at 2,400 degrees. These iron-ore pellets look like gray marbles. The pellets are taken by train to the ore dock at Marquette where they are poured into the holds of waiting Great Lakes freighters.

Gold in Michigan!

Copper and iron are not the only metals which have been mined in Michigan. In 1881, Julius Ropes opened a small gold mine north of Ishpeming. Some silver has been mined in Michigan, too.

What Are the Facts?

1. Why do you think people came to Michigan from other countries to be miners?
2. What caused the 1913 copper strike? In your opinion was the strike a victory for the miners or mine owners? Please give examples to support your thoughts.
3. What fact of geology makes it more expensive to operate mines in Michigan compared to those in some other places?
4. What is a pasty?

Use a map today!
On a map of the Great Lakes, trace the routes that iron ore freighters take from the iron mines of Michigan to the ports of Gary, Ashtabula, Erie, and Buffalo where steel is made.

KEY ❀ DATES

1860	3,700 workers mine 75% of U.S. copper at 33 Michigan companies
1870	Michigan cuts an average of 3 billion board feet of lumber each year
1871	Forest fires burn from Holland and Manistee to Saginaw Bay
1874	Silas Overpack introduces "Big Wheels"
1876	Band saw replaces circular saw in many mills
	Narrow-gauge railroads used in Michigan logging
1883	Grand River log jam—one of the biggest
	Between 1847 and 1883, half of copper mined in U.S. came from Michigan
1886	Cliff Copper Mine closes
1888	Peak of lumber output in Michigan
1892	Lumber markets look at pine grown in southern states
	Smelting operations close at Fayette
1894	Iron miners strike in Ironwood
1913	(April) Copper strike begins. Workers want $3.50 for 8 hour day!
1914	(April) Copper strike ends
1916	Peak Michigan copper production year- 133,500 tons

Consider the Big Picture

After the end of the Civil War, Michigan began to sell its natural resources in a big way. It was a leader in providing lumber, copper and iron.

The lumbering moved north as the trees were cut. Rivers were a key to moving the logs. Muskegon and Saginaw became two major logging centers.

Logging was done in a rather thoughtless and greedy way. Little care was given to saving trees for the future or what would happen to the land without any trees.

Michigan mines were rich with ore, but they went deep underground to find it. When surface mines opened in western states, Michigan mines could not compete. Mining companies tried to cut costs and miners went on strike. The last copper mine in Michigan closed in 1995.

Building Your Michigan Word Power

Write these words in a column. Next to each one write as many words or phrases as you can which are synonyms (means the same thing): cutover country, lumber barons, pasty, shanty boys

Talking About It   Get together in a small group and talk about-

During the boom times of lumbering few people cared or noticed what was happening to the forest land. Today Michigan may have another crisis with its land which few people notice. Good farm land is quickly being used for new housing, highways, and shopping malls. Should we do anything about it? What can be done to save farmland for farming? What will happen if we do nothing?

How important is wood as a building material today? Would we be better off to stop using wood or should we use more wood and less steel and concrete?

Today the Upper Peninsula faces many problems because there is little business left to support its people. What do you think can be done to bring jobs to the U.P.? Is it important, or should everyone just move elsewhere?

Put It To Use

Become a lumber baron. Choose a Michigan river along which to build your lumber camps. Measure the river's length. A longer river should let you reach more trees. Decide where to build your camps and sawmill. Put all your information on a map which you design.

You are a lumber camp cook! Plan to feed the 50 loggers in your camp for a day. Make a menu and figure how many pounds of each food item you will need. Remember loggers work hard and are hungry people!

10

Let's Eat-
Michigan Food

Chapter 10 Section 1
Farming the Land

Did you know? Farming at one time touched most people's lives in Michigan. Eighty-five out of 100 people lived or worked on a farm.

Once, Most Lived On Farms

It is difficult for most Michiganians to understand what it was like to live on a farm. The reason is simple: only 1.5 percent of the population now earns a living by farming. In the 1850s nearly 85 percent of Michigan's people depended on agriculture for their way of living.

It was the pioneer farmer who settled Michigan's countryside. The main purpose of the pioneer farm was to grow food for the family. At first it was difficult to get extra food to market, so it was either used by the farm family or traded to neighbors.

Farming Becomes A Business

The ability to ship food by railroad helped to change farming. So did the increased demand for food caused by the Civil War. Many farmers went off to war and the ones left behind had to produce extra food for the soldiers and their families. Also, farmers made good profits because of the high prices. As a result, farmers had their profits to spend for better equipment and many new farm inventions became available.

Better Power Sources

First, the farmer used his own muscles; then he harnessed the ox. After the 1850s the oxen began to be replaced by horses as it was easier for the farmers to care for them. In the 1870s, steam started to provide power for the farm. A primitive steam tractor was developed by using a small railroad locomotive. Its wheels were replaced with bigger ones which would move the machine over the soil.

Other ideas were used to get more work with less effort. Small wooden and steel windmills were popular for pumping water.

About 1900, farmers began to buy smaller portable gasoline engines. These engines powered farm equipment like corn shellers. After the invention of the electric light bulb, these engines were used to run electric generators. With their use the lucky farmer could have electric lights in the house and barn. No more kerosene lamps!

Windmills were used to pump water from wells. Wind power made it easier to water livestock, do laundry, and cook. (Courtesy Grand Rapids Public Library-Michigan Room)

Slowly the Horse Is Replaced

Could the gasoline engine be used to power a machine which might replace the horse? Today we know that machine as the tractor. But many years of experiments were needed to take the bugs out of the concept. As late as 1920, Michigan farmers still used over 600,000 horses to pull their equipment. By 1940, a time when most families had a car, they continued to use about 300,000 horses for farm work!

A Great Woman Farmer!

Not all Michigan farmers were men. Sarah Van Hoosen Jones used her knowledge and education to run the family farm in Rochester. In 1921 Sarah received a Ph.D. in animal genetics. At college she learned how to breed better types of cattle. Many of her animals were award winners at state and county fairs. Officials came to her farm from other countries to purchase cattle for their own herds. She made many contributions to agriculture in Michigan.

A wood or coal fire gave steam tractors their power. In the 1880s they began to replace horses for some farm work. This engine is connected to a threshing machine. (Courtesy Michigan State Archives)

Specialized Farming

The pioneer farmers grew and raised many things on their farms because they needed a bit of everything to get along. As farming became more of a business, Michigan farmers began to specialize. Farmers realized that some land was better suited to certain activities.

Celery

In the late 1800s, Kalamazoo became widely famous as the celery capital of America. Celery was not really eaten very much as a vegetable until it was developed in Michigan. Two Scotch immigrants brought celery seeds to the area in the 1850s. Later, Dutch farmers started growing celery in quantity. In the early days Kalamazoo went a little nuts over celery. It was made into sodas at the drugstore; there was also celery soup and celery soap, celery chewing gum and even Celerytone— a medicine which was supposed to improve your love life! Michigan no longer leads in the production of celery. Most of the celery land was used for homes and buildings as Kalamazoo grew. Today, Michigan is second among the states in the amount of celery grown.

Michigan Mint

Did you know Michigan is a source for the flavor used in chewing gum and toothpaste? Yes, spearmint and peppermint are Michigan crops. Many years ago Albert M. Todd started a company to extract the mint oil and helped Michigan become the leading producer. In 1900, ninety percent of the world's supply of peppermint was grown within 75 miles of Kalamazoo! Much mint was also grown near St. Johns, Michigan.

Michigan no longer leads in the production of peppermint after a disease killed much of the crop. We still produce an average of 68,000 pounds of spearmint per year along with some peppermint. Most of the mint grown today comes from Clinton and Sanilac counties.

A Sweet Harvest—Sugar

**A sugar beet
(Art by Diane
Hayward)**

If you believe the bag of sugar you bought in the store came from some far away place, think again! Many Michigan grocery stores sell sugar which is grown right here. This sugar is not made from sugar-cane but from sugar beets. Each year Michigan farmers grow about 3,500,000 tons of sugar beets. The Saginaw River Valley has the right kind of soil for these beets and is the "Sugar Bowl" of Michigan. Huron County is the leading sugar-producing county.

The Nation's Bean Pot

Besides producing sugar beets, the Saginaw Valley is known as the nation's "bean pot." The counties around Saginaw Bay grow almost 24 percent of the United States' supply of edible dry beans! That is over 735 million pounds of beans a year- a lot of chili and bean soup! Michigan grows white navy beans, red kidney beans, and six other types.

navy beans

The Fruit Belt

Many Michigan farmers specialize in growing fruit. Michigan's fruit belt is in the Lower Peninsula along the coast of Lake Michigan. This part of the

cherries

state is perfect for fruit because Lake Michigan softens the impact of the weather. Cool fall breezes blowing from the west are warmed when they pass over the water. The water then cools warm air during the early spring. Otherwise, the warm air might cause the fruit trees to blossom too soon and be damaged by a late frost. The Traverse City area is well known for producing red tart cherries. Michigan is the largest producer of red tart cherries in the United States.

We Are Tops...

Today, Michigan's farmers produce almost $3.5 billion worth of food each year. The state leads the nation in growing blueberries, pickling cucumbers, navy beans, and red tart cherries. Michigan grows nearly 45% of all

144

blueberries consumed in the U.S. The most valuable Michigan farm products, however, are those in the dairy group like milk, cheese and butter. Our dairy products are worth from $750 to $800 million dollars a year!

   Michigan agriculture is also about things other than food. Michigan produces more Christmas trees than any other state. Also, Michigan ranks second in the bedding plant market. Bedding plants are small plants sold to farmers and gardeners so they don't have to start them from seeds. In addition, Michigan has an expanding wine industry.

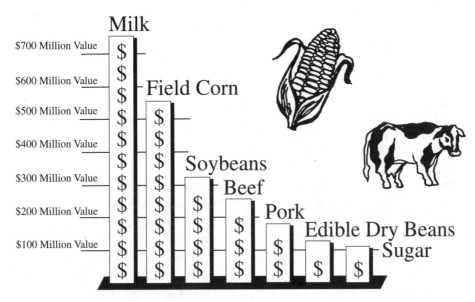

The value of some of Michigan's major farm products

What Are the Facts?

1. What was the first type of transportation which helped farmers get their produce to markets far away?

2. In the late 1800s Michigan was the #1 producer of two rather unusual agricultural products. What are the two products? List two agricultural products in which Michigan currently leads the nation.

3. Which part of Michigan concentrates on growing fruit? Why does fruit do well in this area?

Use a map today!
Make a food products map on a large Michigan county map. Paste pictures from magazines showing crops like apples, sugar beets, and grains. Include processed food products like breakfast cereal, milk, and cheese. Be sure all the pictures are in the correct areas.

Chapter 10 Section 2

Fishing On the Great Lakes

The Great Lakes were full of delicious fish when the pioneers arrived, so a big fishing industry started. By the early 1900s, fishing was declining. Too many had been caught in too short a time. Also, a nasty creature called the sea lamprey killed millions more.

A Wonderful Source of Food- the Great Lakes

For many centuries the waters of the Great Lakes provided fish for Michigan's Native Americans. Fish was important in their diet. For as long as anyone could remember, Indians had been fishing the rapids at the Soo.

When the first European explorers and missionaries arrived in Michigan, they marveled at the quality and size of the fish they saw. After the settlers came, it was natural they would fish in the Lakes too.

Fishing Becomes a Business

It was not long before pioneer settlers began fishing to make a profit. That was the beginning of commercial fishing in Michigan. They sold their fish to those who lived in the nearby villages. Detroit became a fishing center. As Michigan's population became larger, the demand for fresh fish increased. More men and some women caught fish to sell.

Whitefish was the favorite kind of fish. On the average, about half of the catch was whitefish.

One problem was how to keep the fish fresh long enough to get them to market. No method of refrigeration had been invented yet and fish didn't stay fresh long after they were caught. Fresh fish could only be sold in places very close to the fishing ports. Indians had been smoking and drying fish to preserve them and that method also worked for the commercial fishermen. Fish could also be mixed with salt and packed in barrels. The trouble with salted or smoked fish was they didn't taste as good as they did when they were fresh.

Railroads Help the Fishing Industry Expand

The new railroad lines helped fishermen just as they helped farmers. As railroads connected all parts of the state, it was possible to ship fish to market in a day or two. Large amounts of fish were taken by train to Detroit, Chicago, Milwaukee, and Cleveland.

By the time of the 1870s and 1880s, commercial fishing boats were going out of many port cities. Especially busy were those ports on Lake Michigan. The fishing industry was growing quite rapidly and in some northern counties it was the largest industry.

One Fisherman's Story

In June 1886, Anthony Hamel and his crew of four were fishing in a sailboat near the Les Cheneaux Islands (northeast of Mackinac Island). He was using a kind of trap net. It was a difficult job to set that kind of net and the crew had spent the entire day putting just one net into the water and fastening it down.

The next morning they wanted to check the net. They were disappointed when they arrived because they didn't think there were any fish in the net. Concerned that something had gone wrong, the men decided to bring the net up to take a look. Then they had a real surprise. When they started to move the net, it seemed to be alive with fish. There were thousands of them! They brought in so many fish they were afraid the boat might sink. Hamel and his helpers had to go to shore and return for the rest. Altogether they caught 6,300 pounds of whitefish from one net!

More and More are Caught— Perhaps Too Many!

Lake Michigan catch for selected years

1872	7,500,000 pounds	
1875	12,000,000 pounds	
1880	23,000,000 pounds	
1908	47,000,000 pounds	(largest catch)
1911	23,000,000 pounds	

New technology was changing the fishing industry about the same time it was changing the lumbering industry. Steam-powered boats were replacing sail boats and steam-powered equipment was pulling in larger and larger fish nets. In 1885 there were over 1,400 fishing boats, of all kinds, on Lake Michigan alone.

Many of the fishing boats used *gill nets. Gill nets look like tennis nets and catch fish by the gills when they try to backup and get out. This kind of net hangs in the water like a curtain.*

The use of gill nets tends to kill many fish. They can suffocate even while in the water because they can't use their gills to take in oxygen. In spite of this, many fishermen used gill nets on the Great Lakes because they were less expensive and easier to use.

Hamel used a Mackinac boat similar to these. (Courtesy the Library of Congress)

They Forgot About Conservation

The Great Lakes had always been so full of fish that no one ever thought fishing in these big lakes would have to slow down. That was the same way most people felt about Michigan's forests. By the 1880s some fishermen noticed they were not catching as many whitefish as before. They were not sure why. Some even started to use gill nets with smaller openings so they could capture smaller fish.

To help the fish population increase, state and federal governments put millions of baby whitefish into the Great Lakes starting in 1875. But it did not help. Each year the number of whitefish caught was a little less than the year before. Each fisherman reacted to the problem by trying to catch more fish so he could earn a living. One kind of fish, the grayling, completely disappeared from the Great Lakes.

Great Lakes fishing was definitely on the decline. In Lake Michigan, 1908 was the peak year. Only three years later less than half as many fish were caught.

Some kinds of Great Lakes fish must always be restocked by adding more from hatcheries. Here a DNR employee holds a hose which is releasing thousands of small Grayling from a tank truck. (Courtesy David Kenyon, Michigan Department of Natural Resources)

A New Killer—
The Sea Lamprey!

To make matters worse, a new villain came into the picture during the 1920s. It was the *sea lamprey*. The lamprey is a creature that once lived only in the oceans. *A lamprey has a long snake-like body with a gray-green color.* Anyone who has seen a lamprey will not easily forget its mouth. It is a round opening with many sharp teeth in a circle. The tongue is rough and sharp and can cut through the side of a fish. *Lampreys use their mouths as suction cups and attach onto fish; then slowly kill them by feeding on their blood.* Fishing crews found the disgusting sea lampreys on every kind of fish. Scientists believe lampreys must have attached themselves to the bottoms of ships

149

coming through the Welland Canal. Once again, human activity helped damage the Great Lakes.

Men and women scientists in the United States and Canada were busy studying the sea lamprey, hoping to find a weakness they could use to eliminate it. They knew that lampreys went up rivers each spring to spawn and lay their eggs. After spawning, the adults die. The lamprey eggs hatch and the little lamprey larvae burrow into the riverbed and stay there for four to seventeen years. In 1958, workers at the U.S. Fish and Wildlife Service finally found a chemical which killed lampreys without hurting fish. Soon a vast program was started to treat all the rivers going into the Great Lakes. The program has helped, but lampreys are still found on many fish.

The sea lamprey punctures the skin of the fish with its sharp, rasp-like tongue and sucks the blood from its victim. This is the only part of the fish it eats. After a while the fish dies and the lamprey moves on.

A New Invader

In recent years a new creature has entered the Great Lakes. It is the *zebra mussel which is a small water animal with a hard tough shell having unique stripes.* Scientists are almost certain it entered the Great Lakes from extra water carried by oceangoing ships from Europe. A few tiny mussels were probably sucked up with the water when the ships were in Europe and dumped out when the ships were in the Great Lakes.

A zebra mussel doesn't look danger-ous, but it creates many problems be-cause it multiplies so fast. Many parts of

The little zebra mussels cause many problems by attaching themselves to everything. (Photo Courtesy David Kenyon, Michigan Department of Natural Resources)

of the bottom of Lake Erie are covered with the muscles like a carpet. The zebra muscles fill water pipes of power plants and sewage treatment stations. Their shells are very hard and expensive to remove. Since the little muscles can cover the lake bottom so completely, they can also destroy the places fish need to lay their eggs. Over time this may cause some kinds of fish to die out and upset the balance of life in the Great Lakes.

The problem of the zebra muscle could have been stopped if people using the Great Lakes had given a bit more thought to what they were doing.

The Sport Fishing Boom

Starting in 1966 Michigan decided to try a new idea to build up the fishing industry in the Great Lakes. The state added two new kinds of salmon to the Great Lakes. Almost a million four-inch to six-inch coho and Chinook salmon were brought in from the West Coast and "planted" in Lake Michigan and Lake Superior. The coho and Chinook grew rapidly, sometimes reaching 20 inches in a single summer.

The salmon brought a change to the fishing industry. They are game fish and fun to catch. Many people along Michigan's shores bought big fishing cruisers and earned good money by taking people into the Great Lakes to fish. It is not unusual for a group of people to pay $100-$125 per hour to charter a fishing boat!

Adding salmon to the Great Lakes has led to a boom in sport fishing. These big fish also eat smaller kinds of fish which people don't want. (Courtesy Michigan Travel Bureau)

151

The sport fishing industry boomed, although it was not long until conflicts took place between the sport fishing people and the commercial fishing operators. Which group should have the right to catch the fish? The owners of the sport fishing boats believed the commercial fishing boats were catching too many of the good game fish.

Fishing Rights By Treaty

A third group interested in fishing was Michigan's Native Americans. The Indians were given the right to fish by the federal government in many land treaties. Their rights were not just in Michigan but in other states too. Sport fishing people were concerned that Indians were still using gill nets. They said the Native Americans were taking too many fish and killing young fish in their gill nets.

The state government felt the state had the right to say how everyone should fish since the government pays to have new fish added to the Lakes each year. So many fish are taken from the Lakes that new ones must be added constantly.

The question about Indian fishing rights finally ended up in federal court. In 1979, Judge Noel P. Fox decided the Ojibwa tribe living in the Upper Peninsula had unlimited fishing rights because of their treaty with the federal government. It was a matter between the federal government and the Indians. The judge said state government didn't really have control over the rights listed in the treaty.

Since that time, Michigan's Department of Natural Resources has been working on an agreement with Michigan's tribes to set some limits on what can be caught and where. Many parts of the Lakes have been divided into fishing zones and complex rules control fishing in each zone.

The Pollution Problem

Sometimes there are signs at beaches warning people not to eat any fish caught nearby. Many kinds of poisonous and cancer-causing chemicals have been found in some Great Lakes fish at certain places.

Researchers say these chemicals come from many different sources. Sometimes an industry may give off poisonous by-products. The by-products contaminate a stream which flows into the Great Lakes and the pollution is spread over a long distance. Other types of pollution come from burning coal in the many power plants around the Lakes. Coal contains very small amounts of poisonous chemicals. But so much coal is burned that the small amounts begin to add up and can cause trouble when they are washed out of the air by rain.

Acid rain is also formed from the small amount of sulfur in coal and oil. *The burned sulfur makes weak sulfuric acid when it mixes with water in the air. In some lakes the acid rain injures young fish and can also damage the trees and plants.* Large amounts of coal with traces of sulfur are burned to generate power. Acid rain does not effect the Great Lakes too much, but it does cause trouble in smaller lakes in the Upper Peninsula and nearby Ontario.

Canada and all of the states touching the Great Lakes now have strict controls over wastes going into the Lakes. In 1986 the governors of eight states signed a toxic waste agreement. But, many of the problems are hard to fix. Some kinds of polluting chemicals remain in the mud at the bottom of the Lakes for years.

Human activities have caused numerous problems for the Great Lakes in the last 150 years. People working closely together have been able to solve or reduce some of the problems, but it will take thoughtful use of the Great Lakes and the rivers and streams which empty into them to finally help the Lakes to recover from the damage.

What Are the Facts?

1. Explain how human activity helped the sea lamprey and zebra muscle to harm the Great Lakes.
2. Use the headings in this section to help you divide the history of commercial fishing on the Great Lakes into several stages. List these stages.
3. Explain, at least in theory, how fishing on the Great Lakes can be an important source of food. Use some facts presented in this section in your explanation.

Express yourself:
In our country many people say everyone should be able to do any kind of business activity they want, and do it in any way they wish. Others will say that some activities need to be controlled by the government. What do you think? Use examples from this chapter.

Chapter 10 Section 3

Breakfast Cereal Invented Here

Learn how breakfast cereal was invented by Dr. John Kellogg in Battle Creek and how Charles Post beat him to market.

A New Food Idea— Breakfast Cereal

Travel to another country and ask for corn flakes and they usually know what you want. Think about it— Michigan was the place where a food known around the world was first developed! Today, many people wouldn't know how to start the day without breakfast cereal.

Just imagine, before the 1890s cold breakfast cereals were unknown. It was Dr. John Harvey Kellogg who first thought of the idea. Dr. Kellogg was in charge of a large sanitarium in Battle Creek. The sanitarium was much like a hospital; patients came to rest and improve their health by using a better diet and exercise. Many well-known men and women came to the sanitarium.

What Dr. Kellogg wanted was an appealing food which was made from grain. He wanted something which he could give to patients and they could also take home.

Breakfast cerals are used all over the world. A Japanese boy holds his box of frosted flakes. (Art by George Rasmussen)

A Patient Profits

Charles Post was a patient at the sanitarium in 1891. He became very interested in the unusual foods served there. Within four years Post developed a coffee substitute called Postum. It was similar to one of Dr. Kellogg's. Post marketed Postum aggressively and his business grew and became very profitable. Before long he added his first cereal, Grape-Nuts. So the Post Company became the first cereal company in Michigan.

What happened to Dr. Kellogg, the man with the original cereal ideas? He was too busy running the sanitarium and working with religious missionary activities. It was Will Kellogg, the doctor's brother, who wanted to make the cereals widely known through national advertising.

Better Late Than Never

Will Kellogg couldn't stand to see all of the opportunities in cereal go to others. In 1906 he started a company on his own— the Battle Creek Toasted Corn Flake Company. It started in a big old barn-like building. At the same time Charles Post sat in a magnificent office and earned a million dollars a year. Before long though, Kellogg caught up with the competition.

There were others who thought they could make breakfast food too. At one time Battle Creek had 42 different cereal companies making cereals like Malta-Vita and Try-A-Bita. Most of the companies and their cereals didn't last long. Today, Kellogg's, General Foods (which bought Post), and General Mills (which bought the Chex cereals from Ralston Purina) are the only ones left. These giant companies make Michigan the "breakfast food state."

What Are the Facts?

1. Who first invented breakfast cereal and who started the first company to make breakfast cereal in Michigan?
2. Which Michigan city has three cereal companies today?

Express yourself:
Invent a new food or dessert using Michigan farm products. Make a list of things you will need to do if you want to make and sell this new food idea.

KEY ❀ DATES

1850s	About 85% of Michigan's people depend on farming for their way of living
1898	First factory to process Michigan beet sugar
	Charles Post begins to make breakfast cereal– Grape Nuts
1906	Will Kellogg starts a breakfast cereal company using his brother's ideas
1908	Year of the largest fish catch on Lake Michigan
1940	300,000 horses still used for farm work
1947	The sea lamprey has spread throughout the entire Great Lakes
1966	Coho and Chinook salmon added to Lake Michigan
1970	First health advisory about Great Lakes fish from the DNR
1979	Famous court case about Indian fishing rights
1986	Zebra mussel gets into Lake St. Clair from European ship

Consider the Big Picture

150 years ago nearly 85 percent of the people in Michigan lived or worked on a farm. Today, less than 2 percent are farmers; however, almost $3.5 billion worth of food is produced each year.

Fishing in the Great Lakes was big business, but by the 1900s it was declining. Too many fish had been caught and the sea lamprey had killed millions more.

Breakfast cereal, a food known around the world, was first developed and produced in Battle Creek, Michigan.

Building Your Michigan Word Power

A newspaper reporter is interested in your opinion about dangers to the well-being of the Great Lakes. Write a paragraph and rank each of these from the most dangerous to the least dangerous: acid rain, gill nets, sea lampreys, zebra mussels.

Talking About It

Get together in a small group and talk about-

Think how little we know about feeding ourselves today. If there were a national disaster which closed all grocery stores and cut off all transportation, how would you feed yourself for the next six months?

In our modern age do you feel the rights of sport fishing or the fishing rights of the Native Americans are more important? What steps are being taken so both groups can use the Great Lakes?

What problems must be solved before a new food product will be successful on today's market? Compare this with the problems the Kellogg brothers had in putting breakfast cereal on the market.

Put It To Use

Prepare the menu for a meal using just Michigan food products.

List five food items which were not available a few years ago.

Solve this riddle and then make another one based on this chapter.

> I dine on fish, but not from a restaurant dish;
> Though my mouth is big, talking I don't "dig".
> My tongue is rough and sharp enough
> To attack my victims until they give up.
> In the Great Lakes I am a pest. Can you guess the rest?

The Focus Changes-
FROM FARM TO FACTORY

Chapter 11 Section 1

We Made It Here!

Learn how Michigan began to make items used across the country and even the world!

The Vehicle City

Northwest of Detroit is Flint. People in Flint said "We put the world on Wheels," but it was wagon wheels they were talking about. Several wealthy lumber families used their money to start wagon and buggy factories in Flint. Josiah Begole started the first in 1882, just before he became governor.

The wagon business really got going when William "Billy" Durant started his company in 1886. His company made both two-wheeled and four-wheeled buggies. Business was great and by 1900 Durant was selling 100,000 buggies a year. And that is how Flint started to put the world on wheels!

The Furniture Capital

Even in the 1830s a few people were making furniture in Grand Rapids carpenter shops. They used wood from the maple and hardwood trees in the area. As the furniture industry grew, it changed from a few men working in a small shop into hundreds of people working in large factories. Grand Rapids had a good supply of wood and water power from its river, but natural resources alone did not provide the reason why the city became the furniture capital of the United States.

In 1863, C. C. Comstock decided to work hard at selling his furniture outside of Michigan. He used the new invention of photography to make pictures of his furniture and hired sales people to go around the country and contact customers. Perhaps more than anything else, it was the clever use of advertising, promotion, and a supply of skilled workers that made Grand Rapids the furniture capital.

Railroads were very important to the furniture business, just as they had been to other industries. They allowed shipments to be sent far away. Furniture made in Grand Rapids became known across the nation and was sold in Europe and South America. Even a Japanese emperor used office furniture from Grand Rapids!

The markets for furniture have changed. Today the area around Grand Rapids is best known for office furniture. The Steelcase Company and the American Seating Company have replaced those that made furniture for the home.

Inside a Grand Rapids furniture factory about 1900. (Courtesy Michigan State Archives)

The Bissell Carpet Sweeper

Whack, whack, whack! Each spring and fall, millions of women around the country dragged their carpets outside and beat them with brooms to get out the dust and dirt. In the days before vacuum cleaners, Melville Bissell invented a carpet sweeper which could clean carpets without so much trouble. It was a little push sweeper with rotating brushes.

It was not long before Mr. Bissell realized he had a product which was in great demand and Grand Rapids had another growing business. The Bissell Carpet Sweeper Company was making 1,000 sweepers a day in 1893. Not only were they sold in the United States but England as well. Mrs. Bissell was involved in the business too. By 1900 she was president of the company.

Medicine From Kalamazoo

A new Kalamazoo industry began with a young doctor who drove in his horse-drawn buggy to visit patients. The doctor's name was William Upjohn. Dr. Upjohn was concerned about the pills he was giving patients. Some of them seemed "as hard as bullets" and he didn't think they could possibly dissolve in the patient's system.

Upjohn began to experiment with ways to make better pills. He was successful and patented his ideas in 1885. Soon, three other Upjohn brothers joined him in the pill business. Things went fairly well and by 1900 Upjohn

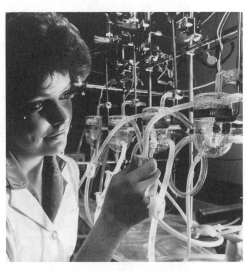

The Upjohn Company in Kalamazoo is a major center of medical research. (Courtesy Upjohn Company)

159

pills were sold as far away as Egypt. Over the years, the Upjohn Company has grown larger and larger. Today it is a major employer in the Kalamazoo area.

Herbert Dow— What Can I Make From Brine?

Herbert Dow was interested in salt *brine* which had been found at Midland and other parts of Michigan. Most of the Lower Peninsula has a thick layer of salt under it. Brine is formed when water found underground dissolves the salt.

When Herbert Dow was in college, someone gave him a bottle of brine. He used the school's chemistry lab to study what it contained. Like most brine, there were small amounts of chemicals besides salt. Dow began to wonder if there could be a use for the other chemicals.

In 1890 Dow arrived in town and viewed the scattered crude wooden towers of the brine wells. Success came after much hard work. Making useful products from brine became Dow's whole life. By the time he died in 1930, his company had grown into one of the greatest industries in the world. One of Dow Chemical's best-known consumer products, until it was sold to the S.C. Johnson Company, was Saran Wrap. One of the chemicals which is used to make it can come from salt brine.

This photo shows a large bubble of Saran Wrap in one step of its manufacture. (Courtesy Dow Chemical Company)

Many Kinds of Industry

The examples given in this section are only a few of the many industries which developed in Michigan. There was a great increase in the number of factory workers between 1860 and 1890. Michigan was becoming

160

a major industrial state. More and more people were leaving the farm and making their homes in the city. The skills needed were changing, and the problems the state faced were also changing.

What Are the Facts?

1. What type of vehicles first made the city of Flint famous?
2. What things helped make Grand Rapids the furniture capital of the United States during the late 1800s?
3. What underground resource contained the chemicals Herbert Dow used?
4. Design and draw a time line showing when and where at least three Michigan products were first made.

Digging into the past!
Talk to someone from a local historical society or check in your public library and find out some of the early industries in your town. Make a list of them and tell what each made. Did any of them use raw materials which were found nearby? Can you discover why each started in your town?

Chapter 11 Section 2

Great Lakes Ships and Cargoes

Since the time of LaSalle's *Griffon,,* large ships were an important way to move people and cargo on the Great Lakes. Ships are still an important way to move certain kinds of cargo, but there are few passengers today.

Travel on the Great Lakes

The vast, blue waters of the Great Lakes have been a transportation route for Michigan people beginning with Indians in their canoes. As Michigan grew, the Lakes became more important. La Salle tried to carry furs on his sailing ship the *Griffon*. Today huge freighters over 1,000 feet long slice through the cold waters carrying up to 60,000 tons of cargo. Few ships carry passengers now, but that wasn't always so. At one time many passenger ships also crossed the Lakes.

Early sailing ships carried all kinds of cargos on the Lakes. This ship is shown in dry dock so that the bottom or hull can be repaired. (Courtesy MTU Archives and Copper Country Historical Collections, Michigan Technological University)

Steamships Replace Sailboats

In 1818, the *Walk-in-the-Water* was the first steamship to reach Michigan. It carried 29 passengers and had a paddle wheel on each side. By 1850 most passengers traveled in steam powered vessels. The steamships could stay on schedule without worrying how the wind was blowing.

Fewer People On Ships Today

As more roads and highways were built, cars took people where they wanted to go. By the 1920s and 1930s there were fewer passenger carrying ships and today there are almost none left. People still use ships to reach a few places, mostly islands in the Lakes. Ships take passengers to Beaver Island, Isle Royale, and Mackinac Island each summer. Or you can take your car across Lake Michigan on a car ferry from Ludington.

Once, many passengers traveled on Great Lakes ships. Here people are boarding two steamers docked at Port Huron. Competition between ships sometimes led to races. (Courtesy the Library of Congress)

Ships & Freight

Michigan's natural resources became important bulk cargoes for the freighters. Bulk cargoes are such things as wheat, iron ore, limestone or coal. Bulk cargo is normally poured into the hold of the ship. After the Civil War, Michigan produced more bulk cargo materials and lumber. The increase made business very good for cargo ships.

Don't Forget the Locks!

Each new freighter was a little longer and bigger than the one before. There were limits, however. The ships could not be any bigger than the locks at Sault Ste. Marie or those in the Welland Canal between Lake Erie and Lake Ontario. If they were, the ships could not travel between these places and they could not go into some of the Great Lakes. A larger lock was built at the Soo in 1881 and an even larger one was finished in 1896. From time to time, larger locks are built for the longer ships using the Great Lakes.

Modern Cargoes

Freighters still haul millions of tons of bulk cargo on the Great Lakes. Almost 30 percent of the cargo is iron ore— the biggest percentage of all cargo shipped. Most of the iron ore no longer comes from Michigan, but from

Minnesota, and is taken to steel mills in Indiana, Illinois or Ohio.

Ships carry a large amount of limestone too. A total of 23 million tons of limestone is shipped each season. Another important item is cement, which totals over 3.4 million tons. A large cement plant is located at Alpena. Coal mined in southern Illinois and West Virginia is brought to Great Lakes ports by train. From there it is taken by ship to power plants and factories located along the Lakes. Nearly 20 million tons of coal is shipped each shipping season.

Ships from overseas can also reach Michigan and the Great Lakes. These oceangoing ships are called "salties" because they sail on the oceans which have salt water. To reach Michigan they use the St. Lawrence River, which connects the Great Lakes with the Atlantic Ocean.

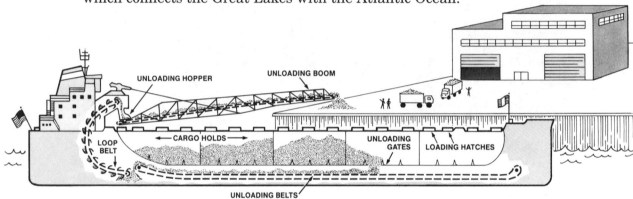

A modern self-unloading freighter. The bulk cargo is brought from the hold using conveyor belts and scoops. Then it travels over the side on the unloading boom. A 1,000 foot ship can carry 70,000 tons of cargo on each trip. (Art by Theresa Deeter)

A Link to the Ocean

For a long time it was impossible for ships to reach the Great Lakes from the Atlantic Ocean because Niagara Falls blocked the way. Now ships use the *St. Lawrence Seaway* to reach the Lakes. Part of the Seaway called the Welland Canal was built to go around the falls. This canal has several locks. These are needed to raise and lower ships a height equal to Niagara Falls! *The St. Lawrence Seaway is made up of the St. Lawrence River plus the Welland canal and its locks.*

The Seaway was finished in 1959. It was a big project and Canada worked on it with the United States. Over 22,000 workers were needed to build it and they dug up 210 million yards of earth and used 6 million yards of concrete. As many as 4,500 ships have used the Seaway in a single year.

Shipwrecks and Accidents

Danger has always lurked on the Great Lakes. Over the years, an incredible 6,000 ships have sunk or been destroyed! Terrible storms have flooded sailboats and steamers alike.

November is an unlucky month for sailing the Great Lakes. As the winds turn cold, many bad storms have suddenly caught captains by surprise. Year after year at least one ship sank in the Lakes during October or November storms. But few sailors were prepared for what nature handed them in November 1913. It turned into one of the greatest storms in Great Lakes history!

Captain Lyons on the freighter *Sheadle* was in Lake Huron near Harbor Beach and remembered what it was like.

"In about four hours the wind had come up from 25 to 75 miles an hour.... The bell rang for supper at 5:45 P.M.... when a gigantic sea mounted our stern (a large wave washed over the back of the ship)... sending torrents of water through the passage ways... breaking the windows... The supper was swept off the tables and all the dishes smashed.... Volumes of water came down on the engine through the upper skylights, and at times there were from four to six feet of water in the cabin." From a letter given to K.T. Lyons, by his father the captain of the *Sheadle*.

Amazingly, the *Sheadle* made it through the storm and reached its destination on November 12th. Her crew was lucky. In the November 1913 storm, 12 ships sank with the loss of all the crew members. Experts believe 251 sailors died. Fifty-seven ships were damaged as a result of the weather.

The Edmund Fitzgerald

In another November, years later, sailors again faced a great storm. The 729-foot *Edmund Fitzgerald* left Duluth with a load of 25,116 tons of iron ore pellets in 1975. At first it was sunny, but the following evening

The raging storm which sank the *Edmund Fitzgerald* pounded one of its life boats and badly damaged it. (Courtesy Nancy Hanatyk)

Lake Superior was in a nasty mood. The captain of the *Fitzgerald* radioed the captain of the *Arthur M. Anderson* to keep an eye on the *Fitzgerald* because its radar was not working.

It was snowing and dark as the waves grew larger. The *Anderson's* captain frequently looked for the *Fitzgerald* in his radar. At 7:25 P.M. as the ships neared Whitefish Point, he glanced at the radar screen and was shocked to find the *Fitzgerald* gone. He tried the radio but there was no answer. That was because the *Edmund Fitzgerald* was at the bottom of Lake Superior under 529 feet of water, broken in two pieces! Her whole crew of 29 drowned and no one would ever know exactly what had happened. The *Edmund Fitzgerald* was the most recent, but probably will not be the last ship to have a tragic end on the Great Lakes.

It's gone!

The *Stewart J. Cort* as it passes Detroit on its first voyage. The ship is 1,000 feet long and 105 feet wide. It carries 51,500 tons and can travel at 16.5 miles per hour. Amazingly, the *Cort* can unload in less than three hours. (Courtesy Bethlehem Steel Corporation)

Imports and Exports on the Lakes

The Great Lakes and the ships which travel on them continue to be important to Michigan. The state has 40 ports where "lakers" and oceangoing ships can load and unload cargo. Detroit, Escanaba, Rogers City, and Stoneport handle most of the cargo by weight, usually 10 million tons or more per year. Rogers City and Stoneport are next to large limestone quarries. Detroit, Marysville, and Muskegon receive much more than they send.

Certain ports specialize in *imports*, and others in *exports*. *Imports are products from another country which are shipped to the United States and sold. Exports are items from the United States which are taken to other countries and sold.* Saginaw is an important port for the overseas export of edible dry beans. Many products are imported and exported through Detroit. A foreign ship at Detroit may unload olive oil and wine and return with a cargo of military tanks.

As we look to the future, there remain some questions about Great Lakes shipping. Should new, larger Soo Locks be built for the bigger freighters? Should Coast Guard icebreakers be used to clear paths through the ice so ships can operate in the winter? No matter what happens, Michigan and the Great Lakes will always be linked together as one— both part of a vital transportation system.

What Are the Facts?

1. What is the St. Lawrence Seaway and what does it allow ships to do?
2. Explain why experienced Great Lakes sailors were not completely surprised that the Edmund Fitzgerald sank during a November storm.
3. What are the main kinds of cargo shipped on the Great Lakes today?
4. Design your own time line for this section. Include what you think are the most significant events about shipping on the Great Lakes.

Use a map today!
Using a map of the Great Lakes, locate and name as many ports and locations mentioned in this section as you can. Tell what is significant about each one.

KEY ❀ DATES

1869	Eli Peck builds first design of a unique Great Lakes freighter
1875	Bissell patented carpet sweeper
1876	Grand Rapids furniture sales take off
1880	Detroit's most valuable industry is tobacco products— mostly cigars
1885	Upjohn Company formed in Kalamazoo
	Michigan child labor law passed
1886	Billy Durant starts Flint Road Cart Co. Sells 4,000 buggies 1st year
1891	Featherbone Corset Co. opens and soon moves to Kalamazoo
1897	Dow Chemical Co. starts in Midland, MI
1900	25% of Michigan workers have jobs in factories
1905	Burroughs Co. begins to make adding machines near Detroit
1907	Huron Portland Cement Co. begins in Alpena
1912	Steelcase Co. starts business as Metal Office Furniture Co.
1934	Tecumseh Products begins to make refrigeration equipment
1947	Sales of Grand Rapids furniture exceeds $100 million a year
1972	Stewart J. Cort is the first 1000 foot Great Lakes freighter
1975	Edmund Fitzgerald sinks in Lake Superior

Consider the Big Picture

In the late 1880s Michigan was changing from a farm state to a state where many things were made- a manufacturing state.

Michigan factories were making home furniture, carpet sweepers, wagons, chemicals, and medicine.

At that time the use of ships was very important to move cargo and people. There were not many good roads yet.

Today, most large ships on the Great lakes only carry bulk cargoes, such as iron ore, limestone, and coal.

Building Your Michigan Word Power

Write each word on a sheet of paper and next to it the word or phrase which is best related to it: brine, bulk cargoes, exports, imports. There are extra phrases.

plastic used to wrap sandwiches, cars, made in Michigan, iron ore, made in Ontario, salty well water, those with lots of fiber, 100% salt, cities with docks for ships

Talking About It   Get together in a small group and talk about-

When many people left Michigan farms to have jobs in factories, how did this affect their families and society?

Billy Durant was looking ahead when he realized that his carriage business would die out because of the car. Can you think of some businesses today which will die out because of new technology?

Should Great Lakes shipping be stopped each fall at a certain date to make certain the ships are safe from storms and bad weather?

Put It To Use

You are living in Michigan in 1880 and you are traveling from Flint to visit relatives in Traverse City. Plan this trip and remember you can only use a train, a ship, or both. To make your plans more realistic, find a map of railroads and ship routes from that time. To find some railroad maps, look in the book *All Aboard* by Willis Dunbar on page 104, etc.

Imagine you are a television reporter and there was one sailor who survived from the Edmund Fitzgerald. Form a team with another member of your class. Let that person be the survivor and your job is to do the interview. Plan your questions and answers ahead of time so they make good sense.

We Put the World on Wheels

Chapter 12 Section 1

Horseless Carriages to Giant Corporations

Inventors built some early cars with little engines and bicycle tires. And guess what! It was the start of the two biggest industrial companies in the United States. All right here in Michigan.

Few Good Roads Then

We did not have good roads until quite recently. Michigan only had 200 miles of paved roads as late as 1890! The reason for few roads was no one took much time building them— including the state government. Early versions of the state constitution did not provide money for roads and highways. Road work was done by each township. Usually a farmer took care of the roads along his or her property. As a result, most roads were in poor condition.

Take the example of a certain wooden bridge over the Muskegon River. It had been built by John Fleming. Fleming felt he had done his duty to build the bridge in the first place, so he did nothing to keep it repaired. Neither did anyone else. In 1903, along came William Conn and his wife in their buggy.

When they were halfway across the bridge, it collapsed! Down went the Conns. Down went their buggy. And down went their horses into eight feet of water!

Everyone just shrugged their shoulders and shook their heads. What could they do?

Eventually, more attention was given to better roads and new laws were passed. In 1893 counties were allowed to vote on whether to tax their citizens to take care of road work.

Bicycles, Bicycles

Bicycles became quite popular in the 1890s. Bikers wanted better roads. One bicycle rider was Horatio "Good Roads" Earle. In 1905 he helped change the state constitution so a highway department could be formed. At first good roads meant a place to ride bicycles, but that changed. Soon, young people were attracted to the automobile. That new invention was just as exciting to them as computers, CDs, and the Internet are today.

Detroit's First Cars

On an early spring night in 1896, Charles King finished building his very own car in Detroit. But he waited to try it out until after 11 P.M. so he would not scare horses or people! King was a good machinist and inventor; he even made parts for another person who was trying to build a little car of his own— Henry Ford.

Ford finished his car in June the same year. It was called the *quadricycle*. Ford used that name for his first car because *it used four bicycle wheels and quad means four*. Ford had been so excited he did not realize the car was wider than the door of the shed where he worked. He had to knock out some bricks so it could fit through the doorway!

Henry Ford started down the road to automotive history in this small Detroit workshop where he built his first car. Today the workshop has been rebuilt on the grounds of Greenfield Village. (Courtesy Henry Ford Museum and Greenfield Village #833.67782)

All those who saw the little cars King and Ford had built thought they were interesting— nice toys to use for a spin around the park, but most people had no idea horseless carriages would actually become a major kind of transportation. While these men were continuing their experimenting, someone else was already to go into production. That person was Ransom Olds.

Michigan's First Car Company!

After 10 years of experimenting, Olds was able to start the first Michigan automobile company. The year was 1897. His Olds Motor Works began to make cars in Detroit. Because of a fire in his factory, Olds moved his business to Lansing.

He built 425 cars the first year. That model was called the "curved-dash Olds." It was so popular, the song "In My Merry Oldsmobile" was written about it. The reason many people bought the Olds car was that it only cost $650. That was still a large amount in those times, but much less than the cost of other cars. The next year Oldsmobile sold 2,000 cars.

OLDSMOBILE CURVED DASH RUNABOUT
BUILT FROM 1900 THROUGH 1904

Many New Companies Begin

When he made his first car, Henry Ford was working in one of Thomas Edison's power plants. Meanwhile, he used every spare minute to develop new automobile ideas. Then he quit his job at the power plant and started a company to make cars, but it went broke. He tried again but failed once more. He looked for others who would join him in a third try.

Ransom Olds, the first really successful car maker in Michigan, at home with his family in Lansing. This picture was probably soon after he started his company. (Courtesy Michigan State Archives)

His efforts became easier after Olds sold 2,000 cars, for suddenly people could see there was a profit in making them. In 1903 Henry Ford got his wish. He found people willing to put up money to start another company. The backers were a coal dealer Alex Malcomson and some of his employees, including James Couzens. Couzens had to borrow every dollar he could find to have enough money to join the company. Others who invested in the new business included John and Horace Dodge. Their own company would be making the engines and parts for the Fords. That is how the Ford Motor Company began.

The year 1903 not only saw the start of Ford, but also Buick, Cadillac, and Packard. Those were only a few of the new car companies in Michigan. Of course there were car companies in other states and other countries too. But Ransom Olds' early success helped Michigan become a leader in making cars.

Michigan Became the Leader

What things helped Michigan become the leader in the automobile industry? There were several people experimenting with cars here and they often helped each other. There were people with money willing to invest in the new idea. Also, Michigan had many skilled workers who could use tools and make parts for cars. In addition, Michigan had many of the raw materials needed for early cars. Iron, copper, and wood were all close by. All of these things helped make Michigan the leader in an exciting new business.

The Model T was once the most popular car in America. (Courtesy Henry Ford Museum and Greenfield Village #833.4502)

A Ford For Everyone

Henry Ford believed cars should be sold for a low price. He felt everyone would want a car, if they could afford one. In 1908 he made a car for the average family. That car was the Model T.

The Model T was designed for the conditions at that time. It could go over bad roads and even drive across fields. It was not fast, but most people found it impossible to drive over 40 miles an hour on the bumpy dirt roads which existed. The Model T could be fixed by the average person if it broke down, and it did break down often. It had other advantages. Farmers found the Model T was handy for jobs. They would jack up the back, take off a tire and attach a pulley to the wheel and power a saw or electric generator.

The last year for the Model T was 1927, and by the time production ended, 15 million had been sold. That was more cars than any other model except the Volkswagen "Beetle."

Cars Sold Each Year

	FORD	*BUICK*	*OLDS*
1908	6,398	8,820	1,055
1912	78,440	26,796	1,155
1916	500,000	90,925	10,263
1925	2,024,254	201,572	34,811

From Carriages to General Motors

In Flint, William Durant had one of the country's largest companies making carriages. Durant looked into the future; he realized it belonged to the car- not the horse and buggy. He knew he must go into that new field or his business would fade away. He heard that David Buick's car company had problems in 1904; so Durant bought it.

Henry Ford and many of the other automobile pioneers were mostly interested in the mechanical aspects of cars. Durant was different. He spent most of his time thinking about finances and company organization.

By 1908 the Buick had become the largest selling car in the United States. Durant began to use his profits to buy other car companies. He planned on a grand scale. He began the General Motors company. GM then began to buy dozens of other companies making cars and car parts. Some of the most important ones were Oldsmobile, Cadillac, Oakland (which became Pontiac), Champion Spark Plug, and the Fisher Body Corporation. One time even Henry Ford agreed to sell, but Durant found he could not borrow enough money for the deal.

William (Billy) Durant began the General Motors Company in 1908 which was the same year Henry Ford started making the Model T. (Courtesy Michigan State Archives)

Eventually the low-priced Chevrolet built in Flint became a serious threat to the Model T. Ford and General Motors began a competition which still continues. These two large companies had many advantages over the smaller car companies. Today they are the largest American car companies.

In 20 years the auto industry had grown up. It was not a fad. It was a major part of Michigan's economy. By 1914 almost 78 percent of the nation's cars were made here and they had a value of nearly $400 million. Thousands of men and women worked in the state's auto plants. The attraction of these good jobs brought more people to the state each year.

What Are the Facts?

1.   In what year did Henry Ford build his first car? Did Henry Ford invent the automobile?
2.   What was the first company formed in Michigan to make cars?
3.   List three things that helped Michigan become a leader in the car industry
4.   Who started General Motors? Why does GM have so many divisions like Buick, Chevrolet, and Fisher Body?
5.   Imagine that you lived in 1900 and you want to start a company to make cars. Choose a name for your new car. List the main things you will need to start your company. Pick a Michigan city to build your factory in and tell why you made this choice.

Digging Deeper:
Use the internet to find sites about cars. List the four you like the best and explain what can be found at each site.

This picture shows automobile workers before the moving assembly line. These early car bodies actually had wooden frames with metal only on the outside! (Courtesy Michigan State Archives)

Chapter 12 Section 2

Ideas Help the Auto Industry Grow

Henry Ford was a leader in the auto industry. He had some dramatic new ideas, like the assembly line and doubling workers' wages. Meanwhile Billy Durant started General Motors and bought up every car company he could find! GM brought better styling and new models each year.

In the Factory— Making the Cars

What did new workers see when they started to work at a car factory? It must have been a bewildering experience. Take the Ford Highland Park plant as an example. It had thousands of people producing cars. Workers were scurrying back and forth gathering parts going this way and that. Some workers put engines together in one place and others put the body together in another. Much of the car body and parts of the wheels were made of wood in those early days. When the engine was finished, it was put on a cart and pushed over to the body. Then the crew worked to install it. Making cars was not very efficient.

Henry Ford was about to change that. The Ford company had so many orders for the Model T they could not make them fast enough. In 1913, Ford and his engineers realized they had to develop a new process. A unique idea came to them. Could parts be brought to the workers instead of the workers gathering up the parts?

Better ways of making cars came quickly. This photo shows an assembly line of the 1920s. (Courtesy Michigan State Archives)

The Assembly Line is Born!

That simple idea was a new idea in manufacturing. It was called the moving *assembly line. Each worker stood in one place and the parts came by on a moving belt. A worker might just place a nut on a bolt. The next worker would tighten the nut, and so on.* The new process really worked. Before the moving assembly line, it took 12.5 hours to put each car together. After the assembly line, the time was cut to 1.5 hours. It also meant that workers with fewer skills could do almost any job.

People from other companies were allowed to visit the Ford factory and see how the assembly line worked. One person said,"It was so simple and logical, so easy to comprehend.... It spread like wildfire." The year after the assembly line went into operation, the Ford company was making 42 percent of all the cars in the United States.

Workers Don't Stay Long

There were many workers who did not like the assembly line. To meet their quotas they often had to work without any breaks..."no allowance was made for lunch, toilet time, or tool sharpening." It had always been hard to keep workers, but the problem became worse. In 1913 the Ford company had 15,000 employees, but only 640 of them had been there for 3 years or more. Ford was spending a fortune to train thousands of workers who only stayed a short time.

MOTOR AGE   January 8, 1914

Ford Company to Divide $10,000,000 Among Employes

Profit-Sharing Plan Announced Whereby Minimum Wage for Males Is Advanced from $2.34 to $5 a Day—Hours Decreased from 9 to 8 Daily

SECRETARY OF COMMERCE REDFIELD PRAISES FORD'S GENEROSITY

Washington, D. C., Jan. 6—Special telegram—A "social advance" and a "recognition of the value of a man in industry," were Secretary of Commerce Redfield's characterizations today of the Ford Motor Co.'s plan to distribute $10,000,000 to its employes.

Note that Ford's great salary increase only mentions male workers!

The Five Dollar Day

In January 1914, Henry Ford decided to double workers' pay. Ford workers would earn $5.00 a day. In today's money that is probably like $250 to $300 a day!

The response was amazing. Headlines across the country had FIVE DOLLAR DAY! in big letters. Other business leaders were not pleased with the idea of trying to match those wages. One said, "the most foolish thing ever attempted…" and another cried "it would mean the ruin of all business in this country." Ford later said the five dollar day was "one of the finest cost-cutting moves we ever made."

News of Ford's high wages started a rush of people moving to Michigan. There were many people without good jobs in 1913, and they immediately came to Detroit.

In spite of the better wages, not everyone was excited about working for Ford. This is what the wife of one Ford employee wrote to Henry Ford. "The system you have is a slave driver! …My husband has come home and thrown himself down and won't eat his supper— so done out! Can't it be remedied? …That $5 a day is a blessing — a bigger one than you know, but oh they earn it."

General Motors Passes Ford

While Ford was spending all of his energy on ways to make the Model T for less money, other companies were paying more attention to what people wanted in a car. Times had changed. As more and more roads were paved, people wanted cars which could travel 50 or 60 miles an hour. Women wanted cars with style and nice colors— not just black.

In 1927 Henry Ford finally listened to his son Edsel and replaced the Model T with the Model A. The Model A was a much better car and had good sales. But Ford had waited too long. After 1930, GM became the largest car company and Ford has been in second place ever since. Although in some years Ford has made more money than GM.

In the late 1920s the entire nation was eager to see what Ford would do to replace the out-of-date Model T.

The GM Approach

General Motors used a different approach. Much of GM's success was due to its president Alfred Sloan. Sloan thought about research and styling. General Motors began the idea of bringing out new models each year. That was quite different than Ford's having the same model for 19 years!

End of an Era

During an economic slowdown in 1920, William Durant lost control of General Motors. Then in the great stock market crash of 1929, he lost millions of dollars. By the 1940s the founder of General Motors, was working in a bowling alley and selling hamburgers to GM workers.

The two great pioneers of the auto industry, William Durant and Henry Ford, both died in 1947, just a few weeks apart.

Olds Fades From the Scene

And what happened to Ransom Olds, the founder of the first car company in Michigan? He left Oldsmobile and started another company in 1904 called REO. The REO name came from his initials. REO made cars and trucks in Lansing. After 1907 Olds was not very active in the company and spent his time traveling and boating. Ransom Olds faded away from the auto industry. He died in 1950. Even his mansion in Lansing was torn down to make room for a freeway.

Years later, Henry Ford poses in an early Ford race car (Courtesy Henry Ford Museum and Greenfield Village # 188.21670)

What Are the Facts?

1. Explain what the assembly line is. Why did the Ford Motor Company install the moving assembly line in its factories?
2. Why did Henry Ford want to double the wages of his workers in 1914? What problem was he trying to solve?
3. Briefly explain how the approach used by General Motors was different than that used by Ford for making and selling cars in the 1920s.

Express Yourself:
Are there factories which make car parts in your town? In your opinion, how has the auto industry affected the town or city where you live?

KEY ❊ DATES

1886	Durant starts business making buggies
1896	(March) Charles B. King drives first car in Detroit
	(June) Henry Ford builds "quadricycle" car
1897	Olds starts first car factory in state
1903	Buick begins making cars
	Cadillac Motor Company builds first car in 1903
	Ford motor Company begins & Barney Oldfield races "999"
1908	Durant forms General Motors Company
	(Oct.) First Model T Ford
1911	Chevrolet Motor Company starts
	Kettering invents self-starter
1913	Ford introduces moving assembly line
1914	Five-dollar day for Ford workers amazes world
1919	State driver's licenses required
1920	Ford's River Rouge Plant, world's largest industrial complex, opens
1925	Chrysler Corporation organizes
1931	Ford makes 20 millionth car

Albert Kahn, a world famous architect who was well known for his designs of factories, including many automobile plants in Michigan. (Courtesy Michigan State Archives)

Chapter Review

Consider the Big Picture

Beginning in the early 1900s, cars and modern roads created a transportation revolution. Within a few years Michigan was making three out of every four cars built in this country!

People from Michigan developed giant companies to make cars, trucks, and tractors. Some of these became the world's largest businesses.

The moving assembly line was developed in Michigan. This idea changed forever the way work is done in factories.

The business of making cars has been the most important business in Michigan ever since.

Building Your Michigan Word Power
Write a short story about working on an assembly line.

Talking About It

Get together in a small group and talk about-

Henry Ford felt a car should be made so that almost everyone could afford it, so he designed the Model T. Are any car companies doing this today? Why or why not?

Some companies are undoing their assembly lines and letting workers make a product from start to finish. Why would they do this? Does it make the product cost more? What are the bad points of working on an assembly line?

Today the percentage of cars made in Michigan is much less than it once was. What happened? What problems do Michigan car companies face today?

Find out how many cars there are in the United States. What are the good points and bad points of using so many cars? Should we try to increase the use of other kinds of transportation like trains?

Put It To Use

Make a crossword puzzle using car related names and words from this chapter.

Go to your library and find as many names of old Michigan cars or car companies as you can. Here are some examples: Jackson, Deal, REO. Make a map and show where each one had its factory. As a hint, George S. May has written some books about Michigan car companies. You might also get help from an antique car club in your city.

WORLD WAR I
and Afterwards

Chapter 13 Section 1

From Peace to War

An awesome idea- two Michiganians, Rebecca Shelley and Henry Ford, tried to stop World War I. It did not work though. Eventually, Michigan factories made huge amounts of war supplies, including ships and planes.

Michigan saw the year 1914 begin in a quiet way. At first, few people really noticed the disturbing news reports from Europe. There had been an assassination in some tiny country and a war had started. Almost everyone thought it was not our problem.

Look!

July 1914 newspaper headlines tell of trouble ahead in Europe as World War I begins. (Courtesy Michigan State Archives)

The war in Europe quickly grew in size. Soon it was of awesome proportions. A number of Americans felt Germany was in the wrong. But there were some who did not support England either. To confuse the issue even more, Michigan also had many people whose families had come from Germany. It was hard for people to choose one side or the other.

Should We Help?

The countries at war soon ran short of ammunition and supplies. England and France started to order war supplies from American companies. Many business people welcomed the orders and hired new workers. But one of Michigan's most important business owners, Henry Ford, was completely against the idea. He said, "I hate war because war is murder, desolation, and destruction." He remarked he would rather burn his factories than make materials for war.

Ford's top executive, James Couzens, had English parents and he thought Ford should make supplies for England. Ford and Couzens argued over the war.

Couzens said, "All right. Then I quit."

"Better think it over, Jim," advised Ford.

"I have. I'm through."

James Couzens kept his word and left his important job with the Ford Motor Company. Even so, he kept his *stock* in the company which had become quite valuable. *Stock is a special paper giving part ownership in a business. Stock can be bought or sold on a stock exchange.*

Later, Henry Ford hired a ship and sailed to Europe to try to talk leaders into stopping the war. Unfortunately, no one important would even talk to him. Many people thought he was nuts– but at least he tried!

Stop the Fighting!

Rebecca Shelley, from Battle Creek, was a young woman with a lot of faith. She believed the war could be stopped if important people would meet and talk things out. Shelley was a brave woman. Even though she was only 28 years old, she traveled to New York City and in her quiet but forceful way asked to see the German ambassador.

She wrote a letter to her father in 1915 telling about their meeting. Shelley said the ambassador basically agreed that the war should be stopped, but he only said that off the record. Officially he could not make the statement she wanted. At any rate, she realized diplomats must be very careful and she still considered the interview a success.

Rebecca Shelley (Courtesy Bentley Historical Library, University of Michigan)

The United States Joins the Fight

Finally, on April 6, 1917, Congress declared war on Germany. Rebecca Shelley continued to oppose the war, but Ford changed his mind. He was now convinced only a show of strength could end the fighting.

Michigan Industry Helps

Workers in the auto plants made many different things for the war effort. They built about 30,000 airplane engines. The Fisher Body plant in Detroit turned out over 2,000 planes. Altogether nearly 20 percent of all the American World War I military planes were made in Michigan. The airplane was a new invention then. Most were made of fabric and wood. Women in Grand Rapids worked on fabric parts for airplanes and others made plane parts in Bay City.

Surprisingly, the Ford Motor Company built 60 ships. These were built at the River Rouge plant and sailed down the river. Many Model T trucks and ambulances went overseas with U.S. soldiers. Altogether, Detroit made $750 million in war supplies.

Michigan women are making parts for wings to go on WWI airplanes. (Courtesy Bentley Historical Library, University of Michigan)

Everyone Does Something

Michigan farmers were asked to grow more food than ever before. Large amounts were needed to feed not only our own soldiers but to help feed the French and English too.

Women got important jobs both at home and overseas. They became nurses to help the soldiers. Women worked in factories and on farms. They delivered ice to people in the cities for their iceboxes. They were railroad engineers and streetcar conductors. They did their work well and were proud of what they accomplished, but most of their jobs were considered temporary. Nearly all of the women workers were replaced by men after the war was over. Often women did not want to quit, but they were given little choice.

The idea of going to fight in Europe may have sounded exciting, but Michigan soldiers soon discovered the horrors of war. (Courtesy Michigan State Archives)

German Things Are Not Popular

Quickly, everyone in Michigan became enthusiastic and ready to fight. Even though Germans were the largest ethnic group in Michigan, there was much anti-German feeling. The German language was dropped in schools. The town of Berlin near Grand Rapids changed its name to Marne and the Germania elementary school in Saginaw became the Lincoln elementary school.

Big Camp at Battle Creek

A huge army post was built near Battle Creek. It was called Camp Custer and General Custer's widow even came for the opening. Ten thousand acres of farmland were bought. The people of Battle Creek were amazed by the 4,000 train carloads of materials that arrived for the camp. Eight thousand carpenters were needed to do the work. When it was completed, Camp Custer had over 2,000 buildings. During the war 50,000 soldiers trained there.

World War I soldiers at Camp Custer. (Courtesy Michigan State Archives)

Others trained at Selfridge Field, a new air base near Mt. Clemens. It was Michigan's first military air base. One of the soldiers at Selfridge was Eddie Rickenbacker. He already had a connection with Michigan, because he was a well-known race car driver. Rickenbacker became famous during the war by shooting down 26 enemy planes, more than any other flyer with the U.S. forces. Rickenbacker's family, like many other Americans, came from Germany.

What Are the Facts?

1. Who was Rebecca Shelley and what did she have to do with World War I?
2. What did Henry Ford say about war? Do you think he was right?
3. Give some examples which show how large Camp Custer was.
4. Did Michigan do much to help win WWI? Give your reasons.

Use a Map Today!
On a world map, draw a route from the Great Lakes to France indicating a route soldiers and supplies would take to reach the fighting in World War I.

Chapter 13 Section 2

Rum Runners, Gangsters & the 1920s

It is true! The nation voted to stop the sale of alcoholic beverages in 1920. Then the area in Michigan from Ecorse to Port Huron became a central point for smuggling liquor from Canada to the United States.

Several well-known authors, including Ernest Hemingway, had Michigan connections in the 1920s.

After the War — Changes at Home

In 1916 a new state constitution outlawed making and selling alcoholic beverages. That law went into effect on May 1, 1918, a few months before the war was over. A U.S. law saying the same thing started in 1920. Since the new laws prohibited drinking or selling alcohol, it was called a time of "prohibition."

Prohibition Brings Crime

The Detroit River has a good view of the Canadian liquor company Hiram Walker. With a supply of alcoholic beverages so close to Michigan, it did not take criminals like the Purple Gang long to start bringing Canadian liquor and beer across the border. They used fast speedboats and could make the trip in only a couple of minutes.

Prohibition made the 100-mile Michigan-Canadian border, from Ecorse to Port Huron, a battleground between law officers and smugglers who were called "rum runners." The short distance between shores made this area a favorite crossing. It is believed that 85 percent of all the liquor smuggled into the United States from Canada passed through that area—perhaps as much as 500,000 cases a month.

To try to stop the smugglers, the government used the U.S. Customs Ser-

VOTE "DRY" FOR US

"Dry" is a word used to mean no alcoholic beverages. (Courtesy Michigan State Archives)

vice, the Coast Guard, and others- a total of 250 officers.

Criminal activity and violence usually go hand in hand. In 1925 as many as 53 bodies were recovered from the Detroit River. It had become a convenient dumping place for victims!

During prohibition police raided this illegal still in Jackson County. (Courtesy Michigan State Archives)

Best Sellers From Michigan

While some people smuggled liquor, others spent their time in better ways and read books written by Michigan authors.

Edna Ferber was a woman author born in Kalamazoo. During the 1920s she wrote some of her best-known stories including *So Big, Show Boat*, and *Cimarron*. Ferber's *So Big* was very popular and won a Pulitzer prize.

James Oliver Curwood's exciting adventure stories, similar to those of Jack London, were about the rugged life in Alaska. His writings included *The Alaskan, The Gold Snare,* and *Valley of the Silent Men*. Curwood lived in Owosso and his office was built to look like a castle. Tourists still visit Owosso to see "Curwood's Castle." James Oliver Curwood died suddenly from the flu in 1927.

Edgar A. Guest's short poems usually gave his readers a smile or a chuckle. He was often called the "Poet of the Plain People." For many years a new poem by Guest appeared each day in the *Detroit Free Press*. His poem *Home* begins with the well-known line: "It takes a heap o' livin' in a house t' make it home."

Oliver Curwood's studio in Owosso is known as Curwood's Castle. (Courtesy the Michigan Travel Bureau)

Ty Cobb was a famous base-stealing Detroit Tigers player when Ring Lardner wrote about him in his story, *Tyrus: The Greatest of 'Em All*. Lardner's work had a sort of cynical humor to it. Some other stories written by Lardner about that time were: *Bib Ballads, Gullible's Travels,* and *The Big Town*. Lardner was born in Niles but had moved to Chicago by the time he did most of his writing.

Ernest Hemingway did not live in Michigan. He grew up in Oak Park near the city of Chicago. But he spent much time at his family's summer home at Walloon Lake- not far from Petoskey. He enjoyed his time there and used Michigan settings in several stories. An Upper Peninsula setting was used in his book, *The Big Two-Hearted River*.

What Are the Facts?

1. What was prohibition and when did it start in Michigan?
2. What fact of geography made Michigan a favorite place to smuggle liquor into the United States during the 1920s?
3. What do you think the Michigan poet Edgar Guest meant when he said, "It takes a heap o' livin' in a house t' make it home" ?

Express Yourself:
Go to the web site for Michigan Authors & Illustrators developed by M.A.M.E. This site should be under the Library of Michigan/Access Michigan. Use its geographical index to look for any writers living near your town and write a short report about one of them.

Chapter 13 Section 3

Modernizing Michigan

At one time women could not vote and several Michigan women worked hard to see that this was changed. Did you know the Lone Ranger program first came from Detroit radio station WXYZ?

At Last Women Could Vote

The 1920s saw the people of Michigan become more modern in their thinking. In 1918 the state constitution was changed to give women the right to vote. Michigan was two years ahead of the nation in that respect.

It had been a tough fight to get these changes. Men were often against voting rights for women. Some men thought women could not understand the election issues. Saloon owners were against women voting too. They thought if women voted, they would help pass prohibition- and they were right!

Women had worked hard for a long time to have voting rights, or suffrage. *Suffrage is another name for voting rights*, and the phrase "women's suffrage" was used often. The issue had been up for a statewide vote several times, but it always failed to pass. In 1912 Governor Chase Osborn backed women's suffrage. It came close to passing that time, losing by only 800 votes.

This tent was the headquarters for women's suffrage at the Michigan state fair grounds. They urged men to allow them the right to vote. What do some of the signs say? (Courtesy Michigan   State Archives)

Some of the Leaders

Michiganians Lucinda Stone and Mary Doe worked for women's suffrage in the 1800s. Mary Doe was president of the Michigan Equal Suffrage Association. That group allowed men to join, and Michigan Governor Josiah Begole was once its vice president.

Anna Howard Shaw (Art by george Rasmussen) She once said, "It has been argued women are inferior to men because their brains weigh less.... A man in Boston killed himself by drinking 17 glasses of beer on a bet. He was found to have a larger brain than Daniel Webster!"

Another Michigan woman who led in the fight for equal rights was Anna Howard Shaw. At the high school in her hometown of Big Rapids is a memorial to her. Anna had struggled since the 1880s to help women have equal rights. She once said, "Around me I saw women overworked and underpaid...not because their work was inferior but because they were women... and with all my heart I joined the crusade for equal rights." In 1904 she replaced Susan B. Anthony as president of the National American Women Suffrage Association. Anna Shaw died in 1919. She did not live quite long enough to see her dream of voting rights for all American women come true. In 1920, for the first time, any woman could vote in the presidential election.

Voting rights for women was a great step forward. Since that time, women have not only been actively voting, but running for office. In Michigan they have been on city councils, university boards, the state supreme court, and as lieutenant governor. Today, the League of Women Voters and similar groups continue to help educate voters on the issues.

A Hero Born in Michigan

It was 1927– the first time a person flew across the Atlantic Ocean alone in a plane. That person was Charles Lindbergh and his plane was the *Spirit of St. Louis.* Instantly Lindbergh was a worldwide hero. People in Detroit were especially proud because Lindbergh had been born in the city and his mother was a science teacher at Cass Technical High School.

Once Lindbergh was back in the United States, he flew his plane on a tour around the country. Two of his first stops were at Dearborn and Grand Rapids. While at Dearborn he took Henry Ford for a ride— the first passenger to fly in the famous plane after its return.

Radio—Sound from a Box

In the early 1920s the thrill of a new invention, the radio, was sweeping the country. In 1920, The *Detroit News* bought a puny 20-watt radio transmitter and put it in a corner of the sports department. The small transmitter could be heard about 100 miles away, but only under the best conditions. That was one of the first radio stations in the country.

The *News* station had been assigned the call letters WWJ. They were broadcasting boxing fights and symphony concerts. Another newspaper, the *Detroit Free Press,* started a station of its own in 1922.

Charles Lindbergh. (Courtesy Michigan State Archives)

A girl listening to an early radio about 1921. (Courtesy Michigan State Archives)

WWJ broadcast one of the first football games in 1924 from the University of Michigan. Announcer Ty Tyson made the historic play by play report. Tyson was at the microphone again when the first Detroit Tigers game was broadcast in 1927.

In 1930 a third station, WXYZ, began in Detroit. Unfortunately, it wasn't long before the two owners found they were losing money. While they wondered what they should do, one of them remembered his days in the theater. He knew they always made money with a good western. Soon the station's staff was talking over ideas for a new program based on a hero from the wild west. "I see him as a sort of lone operator.... He could even be a former Texas Ranger." Then someone shouted, "There's his name! The Lone Ranger." From 1932 until 1954, live radio stories about the masked man on his white horse were sent across the nation from Detroit.

Hi Ho Silver!

Other great radio drama came from WXYZ. In 1936, the *Green Hornet* took to the air and in 1939 *Challenge of the Yukon* began. That program later became *Sergeant Preston of the Yukon*.

One radio broadcaster recalled, "Detroit was a hot spot in 1938. Radio stations WWJ, WJR, and WXYZ all had drama shows, and as an actor you could work at two or three of them each week."

Better Roads and Bridges

Michigan was becoming physically modern, too. In 1919 the state borrowed $50 million to build new highways. Over 1,000 miles of new roads were being finished each year.

Soon Michigan would also be connected to Canada and drivers could zip between the two countries. Before 1929 the only way to reach Canada was by ferry across one of the three rivers which separate Michigan from Ontario. Or it was possible to take a train and use the Port Huron railroad tunnel.

In 1927 work on a bridge between Detroit and Windsor was started. The bridge's two steel towers soared 263 feet above the Detroit River. The bridge was finished in a little over two years. It opened in 1929 and was the longest suspension bridge in the world at that time. It was named the Ambassador Bridge for the goodwill between the two countries. Now, about 5 million cars go across the bridge each year and Detroit is the busiest crossing place between the United States and Canada.

First International Car Tunnel

The Ambassador Bridge does not handle all of the traffic across the 1,850 foot-wide Detroit River. Soon after work started on the bridge, a tunnel was being bored under the river by another company. The Detroit-Windsor Tunnel opened in 1930 and was the world's first automobile tunnel between two countries. The tunnel is still being used and carries about as many cars and trucks as the Ambassador Bridge.

Other bridges from Michigan to Canada were built later. The 8,021 foot Blue Water Bridge from Port Huron, Michigan, to Sarnia, Ontario, was finished in 1938. The International bridge which begins at Sault Ste. Marie and passes over the St. Mary's River was not completed until the 1960s.

The original Blue Water Bridge between Port Huron and Sarnia, Ontario. (Courtesy East Michigan Tourist Association)

What Are the Facts?

1. Give two reasons why some men did not want women to vote. Did Michigan allow women to have voting rights before the United States Constitution was changed?

2. Name two women and two men from Michigan who backed women's suffrage.

3. What kind of businesses started the first radio stations in Michigan?

4. Name two famous radio programs which were made in Michigan during the 1930s.

5. Name the two countries and two cities the Ambassador Bridge connects.

Use a Map Today!

On a map of Michigan, label all of the places where it is possible to cross from Michigan to Ontario. Use the information on a current state highway map to list the toll for a car to cross over at each place.

1914	World War I begins in Europe	**KEY ⚘ DATES**
1915	Ford Peace Ship sails	
1917	(April) United States enters war	
	(Oct.) Camp Custer opens	
1918	Flu epidemic strikes	
	(May) Michigan's prohibition law goes into effect	
	(Nov.) World War I ends	
	Women allowed to vote in Michigan elections	
1919	Michigan borrows $50 million to build roads	
1920	(Aug.) First radio news broadcast	
1924	*So Big,* a novel by Kalamazoo's Edna Ferber, awarded Pulitzer prize	
1927	Owosso author James Oliver Curwood dies	
	Lindbergh flies across Atlantic	
1929	Stock market crash	
1932	Detroit radio station develops *Lone Ranger* program	

Consider the Big Picture

In 1914 World War I began in Europe. Some Michigan people tried to stop this war but they did not succeed.

Fighting against Germany troubled many Michigan people because their families once came from there.

Once the war was over in 1918, Michigan led the way in allowing women to vote and banning alcoholic beverages.

During these years people from Michigan were proud that Charles Lindbergh was born here, that Ernest Hemingway spent time here, and that well-known radio programs like the *Lone Ranger* came from Michigan.

Building Your Michigan Word Power

On a sheet of paper write the three words given and match each word with the person(s) most likely to be concerned about it: prohibition, stock, suffrage. There is more than one person for each word.

a successful businesswoman from the 1990s	a saloon owner in 1916
a U.S. customs agent from the 1930s	Anna Howard Shaw
a successful businesswoman from the 1880s	an investor
a member of the Purple Gang	a broker

Talking About It   Get together in a small group and talk about-

Henry Ford and Rebecca Shelley knew war was a terrible thing. They tried hard to stop WW I. Do you think it made any sense for them to do this? Today people often say the United States should bomb some terrorist group or nation where we are having problems. Has our viewpoint about war changed?

During the years of prohibition there was much smuggling and crime along the Michigan border with Canada. Once prohibition ended, these problems stopped. Do you think drugs should be legalized to stop crimes related to drug use?

Put It To Use

Imagine you are Anna Howard Shaw. Make an outline for a speech to promote voting rights for women. Will there be men listening to you? What can you say to convince them?

Imagine you are a author. Write down six ideas for books which take place in Michigan.

Bleak Times &
Another War -

1930s & 1940s

Chapter 14 Section 1

Michigan Bends Under the Depression

Had a bad day? Think about this. In 1929 a severe business slowdown hit the country. Car sales went way down. Michigan businesses could not keep all their workers. Many people lost their jobs. To make things much worse, nearly 200 Michigan banks closed and their customers lost much of their savings!

The Good Times End With a Crash

During the late 1920s, the stock market had gone up and up. Millions of people had bought stocks even though the prices were much higher than they had ever been. Investors thought stocks would go up forever. But in October 1929 they suddenly went down! People said the stock market had crashed.

The stock market crash also affected banks. Many of them were involved in the stock market too. When people went to the banks to withdraw their savings they were often told the bank could not pay. Many banks could not come up with enough cash and they had to close. By 1932 nearly 200 Michigan banks had gone out of business. Many people lost all of their savings - savings they would need because they had also lost their jobs.

EIGHT-DAY HOLIDAY FOR ALL BANKS IN MICHIGAN

330 YEAR. NO. 137   DETROIT, MICHIGAN, TUESDAY, FEBRUARY 14, 1933   24 PAGES   THREE CENTS

This newspaper headline gives an idea of the serious trouble with banks in the 1930s

Less Business and Fewer Jobs

The stock market crash and the bank closings were a shock to everyone. People simply did not have money to buy things. It was as if someone had turned off the switch to the economy. Business sales fell rapidly. Michigan business was tied closely to the automobile industry. In Genesee county half of the working people had jobs with General Motors. There were almost 4.5 million cars sold in the country in 1929. The next year there were less than 3 million sold. The year after that, sales fell to less than 2 million.

It was not possible for companies to keep everyone working after such a big decline in sales. As a result, many employees lost their jobs. The Ford Rouge plant had 98,337 workers in 1929. By 1933 there were only 28,915.

The need for Michigan's raw materials fell sharply. The production of Michigan copper was cut in half after 1930. In 1932 shipments of Michigan iron ore fell to less than one-tenth of the previous year. Everyone cut back and no one bought anything that was not absolutely essential. In Lansing only one-third of the workers who had jobs in 1929 continued to work in 1930. It was not just a business slowdown. It wasn't just a recession. It was a depression—the *Great Depression*! It was the beginning of *a tremendous business slowdown which lasted nearly 10 years.*

There had been other business slowdowns before. Never before were so many people living in the cities and they didn't have farms to grow food.

In the depression years a group of unemployed workers rode to Lansing carrying a banner with the words "the army of the unemployed." They wanted people to help them fight starvation. (Courtesy Michigan State Archives)

People Could Not Pay Loans & Taxes

As the depression continued, people ran out of money to pay loans on their homes and farms. Banks took the property back and sold it. There was also the problem of property taxes. If property owners couldn't pay the taxes, the government sold the property to the highest bidder. In 1933 the U.S. Census Bureau estimated Michigan had the highest rate of unpaid property taxes of any state in the nation. Those taxes paid the costs of local government and schools. The cities and schools became desperate due to the lack of property tax income. Grand Rapids and Detroit ran out of money to pay teachers and city workers.

What Could be Done?

In the first three years of the depression, it was difficult to believe the situation was as bad as it was. The general view of government in the 1920s was that government should not interfere in business problems. Michigan Governor Wilbur Brucker told President Hoover, "The people of Michigan will take care of their own problems." But by 1933, 640,000 of Michigan's 4,900,000 people were on welfare.

A class during the Depression years which helped women learn how to sew so they could make clothes for themselves and their families. (Courtesy Michigan State Archives)

Democrats Win

In November 1932 the people of Michigan were tired of the depression. The government seemed to have no solutions so they elected a democratic governor, William Comstock. He was only the third Democratic governor of Michigan since the Civil War. In that same election they voted for Franklin Roosevelt for president. That was the first time since 1852 that a Democrat running for president had received Michigan's vote!

Governor Comstock began a state sales tax to raise money. Three cents were collected on each dollar of sales. Though because of the tough times, the new tax was very unpopular.

Special Programs- WPA & CCC

Once Roosevelt was in office, the federal government started a number of programs to help the jobless. The new idea was to create jobs and pay the workers with federal money. The *Works Progress Administration, or WPA, hired people to do what they could do best. It hired writers to write books and articles. It hired artists to paint and draw.* Many Michigan post offices had paintings done inside their lobbies by WPA artists. Some of these murals can still be seen in the post offices of Caro, Frankfort, Howell, Iron Mountain, Marquette, Paw Paw, and Plymouth. Other WPA projects included hiring carpenters to build public buildings and workers to repair roads and highways. In 1938, Michigan had over 200,000 people in WPA jobs. Another Roosevelt program which had much impact on Michigan was the *Civilian Conservation Corps, or CCC.* That program began in 1933 and lasted until 1942. *The CCC was designed to give thousands of unemployed young men something productive to do.* Nearly 100,000 worked in the Michigan CCC camps while the program was in operation.

The CCC provided jobs for many young men in the 1930s. The men in the picture are having a lunch break in the field. (Courtesy Michigan State Archives)

Young men, most of them between 17 and 28 years old, could join for one year. They were supposed to be from families who were on welfare. Each was paid $30.00 a month, but $25.00 of that went to his family. At that time, privates in the U.S. Army only made $18.00 a month. Besides their pay, the members of the CCC had a clean place to sleep, hot meals, clothes to wear, and the opportunity to join educational programs.

They lived in camps in the northern part of the state. It was not fun and games for these fellows. The camps were usually placed under the direction of an army officer and run much like an army camp. In spite of all the hard work, most of those who joined felt lucky to be a part of the CCC program.

Men in the CCC fought forest fires, built trails, roads, campgrounds, parks, and planted trees— almost 500 million of them! Some of the pine forests we see in northern Michigan today were planted by the CCC on cut-over land. This land had been left bare of trees by the loggers.

People In The News!
Senator from Michigan Gives Millions to Help Children!

James Couzens, the former hard working manager from the Ford Motor Company, amazed everyone by giving $10 million to help needy children. Couzens started life with very little and made his millions as a part owner of the Ford Company. In 1922 he became a U.S. Senator.

During the depression, President Hoover was against spending any money to help those out of work. Senator Couzens made a wise speech saying: "We spend hundreds of millions of dollars on the army and navy in an attempt to guarantee security from outside attack. Why is it any less logical or sensible to spend the taxpayers' own money on our people, to maintain security within the country?" James Couzens kept his job in the United States Senate until he died in 1936.

James Couzens at his desk. (Courtesy Michigan State Archives)

$10,000,000 to charity!

Joe Louis- World Heavyweight Champ-1937

It was said "Joe had more than fighting greatness—he was great as a man, a national hero, and as a citizen of these United States." He came with his family to Michigan in 1926 when he was 12. His teenage years were spent in Detroit, and he learned his boxing skills there. Even after he became famous, his connection to Michigan was strong. He lived in Detroit part of each year. He gave to local charities and he worked with young people.

**Joe Louis, the famous boxer from Michigan, talking to a group of children.
(Courtesy Michigan State Archives)**

In 1937 Joe Louis won the world's heavyweight boxing championship beating a German boxer backed by the Nazi government. He followed the advice of his trainer to always fight clean and on the level. Louis successfully defended his title 25 times between 1937 and 1948. In 1978 Detroit named its new sports arena in his honor. Louis was a beacon of hope for all Americans. He died April 11, 1981, and was buried in Arlington Cemetery near Washington, D.C.

Harbor Beach, Mich- Hometown Boy on Supreme Court!

The city and state celebrates! Frank Murphy's grandparents came from Ireland. He was born in Harbor Beach, Michigan, in 1890. Murphy studied law at the University of Michigan. After graduation, he joined the army and went to France for a short time during World War I.

Murphy was first noticed by the public while he was a judge. Murphy worked to help elect Franklin Roosevelt president in 1932. In 1936 President Roosevelt urged Murphy to run for governor of Michigan. Roosevelt felt if Murphy were on the ballot, it would help Roosevelt's own chances.

While he was governor, Murphy started *civil service* for state employees. *Civil service gives government jobs based on ability and testing.* Before civil service, government workers were given their jobs because of the political party they supported. Even though he was popular, Frank Murphy lost reelection in 1938.

Frank Murphy. (Courtesy Michigan State Archives)

After the defeat, the President appointed him U.S. Attorney General. After about a year in that office, he became a member of the U.S. Supreme Court. He held that very important position until he died in 1949.

In summary, the 1930s got off to a bad start. Then the government started programs to help the needy and people began to work together. Times were still hard but there was more hope for the future.

What Are the Facts?

1. Why were many young men excited about being in the CCC even though they had to do a lot of hard work?
2. Give one example of a project done by the WPA and one by the CCC which can still be seen in Michigan today.
3. List what James Couzens did to help needy people during the Depression.
4. Tell something about the life of Frank Murphy.

Graphs tell the story!
Make three graphs which help explain how the big slowdown in car sales during the Depression hurt Michigan's workers.

Chapter 14 Section 2

Unions: A New Friend at the Factory

Workers needed a lot of help in the 1930s. The work has hard and the pay low. The United Auto Workers union got its start in 1936 with a big "sit down" strike. Read on to find out more.

The Depression & Troubled Workers

The 1930s were hard times for workers. It was tough for businesses to make any profit, so they put pressure on their employees to do more. A worker at a car factory told of a "speed-up." His job was to grind off the rough edges of car bodies after they were welded together. In 1928 he did eight bodies a day and was paid $1.00 an hour. By 1932 he did 32 car bodies a day and his wage fell to 35 cents an hour!

Many workers thought *unions* could help them with their problems. *Unions are groups of laborers formed to improve working conditions and wages. They bargain as a unit with the management of the company where the members work.* Some joined the unions, but many were afraid to join. The idea of unions was not popular with all the people, especially those who did not work in factories.

Working conditions in most factories were dirty, cold, and noisy during the 1920s and 1930s. (Courtesy Michigan State Archives)

Unions Grain Strength

There were labor unions in Michigan before the 1930s, but they were not very effective. They did not usually represent all of the workers at a factory or business. Michigan had a tradition of hiring workers even if they did not belong to a union.

The years 1936 and 1937 were turning points for unions in Michigan. The United Auto Workers, or UAW, became a powerful union in the auto industry. Many people worked hard to make that happen, but three brothers were key leaders in the movement. They were Walter, Roy, and Victor Reuther (RU ther).

The Reuther Brothers

The Reuther family had a long history of being politically active. They moved to the United States from Germany - leaving in the 1880s when life there was becoming more centered on the military. Their father believed in doing things to help people. Walter Reuther moved to Michigan in 1927 so he could earn more money. His wage in West Virginia was only 42 cents an hour and at Ford Motor he earned $1.05 an hour. Such good wages attracted many other people to come to Michigan too.

Soon the Reuther brothers became involved in union activities. Walter and Victor led a strike in 1936. It was a tough strike,

Walter Reuther

but successful. The union won a minimum wage, which was the same for both men and women, and a slower pace for the assembly line. The UAW also represented both skilled and unskilled workers. This approach of including skilled and unskilled workers helped the UAW become more effective.

It became an important strategy for the union to find a plant which made an important car part that was in short supply. Then the union would try to get a strike started in that plant. They knew that would pressure the management to talk with them and not stall for time. A long strike was hard for the union members because they had no income while the strike was going on.

The Great Sit-Down Strike

A major strike took place at the end of 1936 at the General Motors Fisher Body plants in Flint. There had been worker unrest at Fisher Body for some time. Some of the employees noticed that important equipment was being moved out of the factory. General Motors was planning ahead.

They wanted to keep production going elsewhere if a strike took place in Flint.

Suddenly on December 30, 1936, workers stopped and sat down in the plant. They wouldn't leave to go home and they blocked the doors to prevent equipment from being taken out. The workers said they were tired of speed-ups, low wages, poor working conditions and little job security.

The sit-down strike was a fairly new idea. In that way the strikers were protected from a police attack and it stopped the company from keeping the plant running. The sit-down also increased the power of the union because if some workers had been able to do their jobs, they might have felt they had to, and the factory might have stayed open.

This is what the workers in Fisher Body plant #2 chanted during the strike.

> " When the speed-up comes just twiddle your thumbs,
>   Sit down, Sit down.
> When the boss won't talk, don't take a walk,
>   Sit down, Sit down."

Strikers Face Problems

The union had its hands full helping the strikers. Wives of the strikers formed picket lines outside the plants. The union cooked food for the strikers and took it to the plants each day. Sitting in two buildings there were over 1,000 strikers to feed. Sometimes the company guards let the food in and sometimes they did not. The union found warm clothes for the strikers because the company turned off the heat and it was cold outside.

General Motors was becoming desperate. The company wanted to get the strikers out of its buildings. They urged the police to go in after them. On January 11, 1937 the police fired tear gas into the Fisher Body plant #2. The union members were ready. They used inner tubes to make large slingshots on the roof. The slingshots hurled car door hinges down on the police. When the police came closer, the strikers turned on the fire hoses and sprayed them with cold water.

The police backed off to regroup. When they came back, they were sprayed with water and struck by hinges again. That time when the police pulled back, they decided they had suffered enough abuse and began to shoot at the strikers. Thirteen were seriously wounded. The police attacks at plant #2 was called the "Battle of the Running Bulls." Bulls was an old slang word for police.

The Governor Comes

The next day Governor Frank Murphy came to Flint to calm things down. He ordered 3,000 National Guard soldiers to Flint. They arrived with all their battle gear and bayonets on their rifles.

Members of the Michigan National Guard in Flint during the famous sit-down strike of 1937. (Courtesy Michigan State Archives)

Governor Murphy immediately brought leaders from both sides to his office in Lansing. Days of haggling took place. The month of January passed and tension was high in Flint.

The situation was grim for everyone. The governor was receiving a great deal of pressure to use the Guard to go into the factories and get the strikers out. Many people did not agree that strikers should be allowed to break the law and take over factories. And all picketing must stop too. The union sent a message to the governor that they would stay in the buildings and die there if the police or soldiers came after them.

Victory For the Union

As the sit-down strike dragged on day after day, the federal government became worried. National leaders were afraid the strike might become a revolution with much bloodshed. President Roosevelt sent messages to Governor Murphy and others urging them to solve the situation.

On February 11, 1937, after 44 days, General Motors said the company would give in. The United Auto Workers won the right to represent GM workers who wanted to join. Wages were increased too. The strikers were joyous and the city of Flint breathed a sigh of relief.

After the success of the sit-down in Flint, there was an epidemic of sit-down strikes throughout Michigan. At least 130 companies were closed by strikes. Some members of the National Guard even had a sit-down when they weren't paid for their duty in Flint! The courts finally ruled in 1939 that sit-down strikes were illegal.

Ford Fights the Union

The Ford company took a long time to unionize. Henry Ford was very old and Edsel Ford had health problems. A man named Harry Bennett seemed to control most of what the company did. He ruled the company with an iron hand.

In the spring of 1937 there was an event called the "Battle of the Overpass." Seconds after this photo was taken, the Ford guards on the left attacked and beat Walter Reuther and other union members who were handing out leaflets to workers. (Courtesy Michigan State Archives)

Ford continued to resist unions until government pressure was put on the company in the early 1940s. Ford lost an important defense contract with the federal government because relations with its workers were so bad. After a mass walkout of Ford employees in 1941, the company gave in and accepted the UAW.

The United Auto Workers union was then secure in Michigan, and its powerful presence had a great impact on the state. Walter Reuther became president of the UAW in 1946. A great many Michigan workers have joined the UAW and other unions since the 1930s. Michigan has become known as a strong union state.

What Are the Facts?

1. What changing conditions upset industrial workers in the early years of the Great Depression?
2. Name the three brothers who helped build the United Auto Workers union.

3. Who was involved in the "Battle of the Running Bulls" and where did that event take place?
4. What did Michigan Governor Frank Murphy do to keep the peace during the Flint sit-down strike?

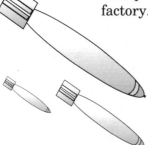

Express yourself:
It is the 1930s. You are a union leader or an executive of an auto company. Write a letter to the editor of your local newspaper giving your views on the situation in your car factory.

Chapter 14 Section 3

At the Home Front- World War II

Bombs falling on Michigan- maybe! The Japanese attack at Pearl Harbor caused the military to worry the Soo Locks might be a target too. During World War II Michigan factories made everything from bombers to penicillin.

Better Jobs, But Worries of War

The grim days of the Great Depression began to fade away like a bad dream. The 1940s brought better business conditions to the state. But another war had started in Europe. Germany had invaded Poland and France. That was certainly a concern, but Michigan factories were pleased with their new orders for war supplies. Some were from England and France and others were from our own government. The new jobs and higher pay offset the worries that the United States might join the war.

Speaking Out

Charles Lindbergh, the famous Michigan-born flyer, spoke out against the U.S. entering the war. So did Senator Vandenberg from Grand Rapids. They felt our country should not worry about Europe, no matter what happened there. Vandenberg worked to keep the country isolated. His view was that the Atlantic and Pacific Oceans would stop any enemy from reaching us.

In spite of what Lindbergh and Vandenberg said, the United States started to get ready in case we had to fight.

Surprise Attack!

On Sunday December 7, 1941, America was jolted when 432 Japanese planes bombed our navy at Pearl Harbor in the Hawaiian Islands. Michigan sailors like Jim Green were there. He was lucky. He survived the attack even though he was in gun turret No. 4 of the battleship *Arizona*. The *Arizona* sank when almost two million pounds of its ammunition blew up and 1,177 of Jim's shipmates lost their lives. With nearly half of our navy destroyed, we had no choice; the United States had to go to war!

The Soo Locks in the Upper Peninsula were considered a very important transportation link. There was an immediate fear that enemy bombers might be able to reach Sault Ste. Marie. So, that area became one of the most heavily guarded places in the nation. Searchlights and radar scanned the sky for approaching planes. American fighter planes were also on standby at northern Michigan airfields.

Excited Detroit draftees ready to head for military bases at the beginning of World War II. (Courtesy Michigan State Archives)

Switching from Cars to Tanks

There was a rush to reorganize factories for war. All kinds of things were soon in limited supply including workers for the factories. Over 600,000 young men and women from Michigan joined the armed forces. The federal government began to *ration* food, gasoline, tires, and many other items. *Ration means to control the use and supply of products.* People could only buy so many gallons of gasoline and so many pounds of sugar or meat each month. The last civilian car was made in February 1942.

Michigan's factories became a national asset. They were used to make all kinds of military supplies. They turned out an amazing number of war related products- everything from parts for the atomic bomb to mint oil used in chewing gum for the soldiers.

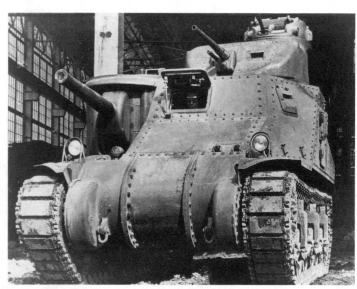

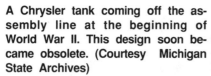

A Chrysler tank coming off the assembly line at the beginning of World War II. This design soon became obsolete. (Courtesy Michigan State Archives)

The shipyards in Bay City made submarine chasers and destroyer escorts. In Midland, Dow Chemical made light-weight magnesium metal for use in airplanes. Kellogg of Battle Creek made K rations (packaged military meals) for soldiers in combat. Thousands of school children gathered milkweed pods for life jackets which were made in Petoskey. Saginaw Steering Gear made over three hundred thousand machine guns and in Kalamazoo the Upjohn company made medicine and the new drug penicillin for soldiers wounded in battle.

The Kalamazoo Stove Company switched from making stoves to armor plate. The Packard company made engines for the navy's high-speed PT boats. Ludington made chemicals. Gliders used for the invasion of France were made in Grand Rapids and Iron Mountain. Most of the state's war production took place in the Lower Peninsula, but the Upper Peninsula increased output of its valuable copper and iron ore too.

Michigan was among the top states in production of war materials. The state earned the title, *Arsenal of Democracy*. Over a period of six years, the auto industry sold $50 billion of war equipment. Out of those sales, 39 percent was for airplanes and aircraft parts; 30 percent was for military cars and trucks, and 13 percent was for tanks.

This photo shows one of the new displays in the Michigan Historical Museum in Lansing.

The display includes materials made in Michigan to help win the war. Michigan car factories made jeeps, and even airplanes like the B-24 bomber and airplane engines. The four-engine bombers shown here are being made at Willow Run.

Photo by Duaine Brenner, courtesy of the Michigan Department of State.

Three Big War Factories

Michigan's industrial know-how was used to build three spectacular operations. They were the Chrysler Tank Arsenal in Warren, the Fisher Body tank factory in Grand Blanc, and the biggest of all, the Willow Run bomber plant near Ypsilanti. Chrysler made over 25,000 tanks during the war. Another 16,300 tanks were built at the Grand Blanc plant.

Willow Run was built in the middle of farms and fields on the edge of Ypsilanti. The federal government spent $100 million on the building and the Ford Motor Company ran the operation.

When the Willow Run plant was finished, it was one of the largest factories in the world. Its assembly line was more than a mile long. Eventually 42,000 people worked at the plant and about one-third were women. Next to the factory a large air field was built. Willow Run began to make B-24 bombers in September 1942. By the time the war ended the plant had turned out over 8,000 B-24s and almost reached the goal of one plane an hour. Part of a Michigan-made B-24 from World War II has become an important display at the impressive state history museum in Lansing.

Problems on the Home Front

Working during the war was not easy. Gasoline was rationed and drivers could only have four gallons a week. To force drivers to save gas, the government set the speed limit at 35 miles an hour!

Michigan's war factories needed thousands upon thousands of workers. Sometimes as many as 500 people arrived each day at Ypsilanti to find a job at Willow Run. They had to find a place to live and that wasn't easy. Often the new workers built shacks covered with tar paper.

During the war, Michigan's population shifted toward the areas around big cities. Macomb County grew 32 percent and Washtenaw County 21 percent. On the other hand, several northern counties lost people. Baraga, Crawford, Kalkaska, and Keweenaw counties shrank by about 30 percent or more.

A reporter for *Life* magazine wrote in 1942 **"Detroit is dynamite"** and it "can blow up Hitler or it can blow up the U.S." That meant relations between blacks and whites were tense. On a warm Sunday afternoon, June 20, 1943, about 100,000 people had gone to Belle Isle to relax. That evening large crowds jammed the bridge pouring back to Detroit. Fighting broke out between the two races.

A car burning during the 1943 Detroit riot. (Courtesy Michigan State Archives)

A very major riot started which continued on Monday while officials from the government argued over what to do. Finally, at 9:30 P.M. truckloads of military police roared into downtown Detroit and cleared 10,000 rioters out of Cadillac square- without firing a shot. The rioters knew the soldiers meant business and by midnight the streets were clear and quiet.

The riot was a tragedy. Thirty-four were killed and 675 more were hurt in the fighting. Over 100 fires were set and many buildings badly damaged. The 1943 Detroit riot showed the terrible things that happen when different groups do not try to live peacefully with each other.

Tuskegee Airmen

In spite of the problems at the home front, the war allowed minorities to show what they were capable of doing. About 200 black men from Michigan trained at the Tuskegee Institute in Alabama so they could be pilots. Among the group was Coleman Young who later became mayor of Detroit. The Tuskegee airmen flew fighter planes and later bombers. One of the units was stationed at Michigan's Selfridge Field for a short time in 1944. The fighter pilots saw action with the enemy in Europe and even shot down one of the dreaded German jet fighter planes.

Women at Work

About one-third of the workers in the factories were women. At first employers did not like the idea of hiring women, but they desperately needed help and they just couldn't find enough men. Those in charge soon found out that women usually did better work and were sick less than men! During the war women earned more money than ever before. For the first time many of them had the chance to quit being waitresses and have jobs where their talents and abilities really counted.

She Can Fly Bombers Too!

Women did more to help win the war than make the bombers; some flew them too! Faye Wolf of Grand Rapids joined the Women Air Force Service Pilots (WASP). The women pilots flew new planes from the factories like Willow Run to air force bases in the United States and Europe. They took the place of regular air force pilots who were needed in combat. Even though no enemy planes shot at the women pilots, the work was dangerous. Some women were killed in training accidents and others crashed because of mechanical trouble.

Danger Falls from the Sky!

When the war began, people thought anything might happen; but as time passed, they came to feel Michigan was safe from enemy attack. No one believed the Japanese or Germans would be able to bomb Grand Rapids or Detroit. But they were wrong! The Japanese began a fantastic plan to send bombs to the United States carried by balloons. The balloons were released in Japan and floated on wind currents which took them along the line of 45° north latitude. Each balloon carried several small bombs designed to start fires and scare people. The balloons had clocks which dropped the bombs at the time estimated they would be over the United States.

World War II Japanese balloon bomb which came as far east as Michigan

Civilians found two of these bombs in Michigan. One landed near Grand Rapids and the other near Detroit. It is possible the Japanese bombs caused some forest fires in the Upper Peninsula. Apparently no other damage was done in Michigan, but in some places people were killed by these bombs. The discovery of the Japanese balloon bombs was kept very secret by the military.

Women from Michigan flew fighters and bombers from the factories to air bases around the world. These pilots are members of the WASPS. (Courtesy USAF Photographic Collection, National Air & Space Museum, Smithsonian Institution)

The United Nations Question

As the war continued, American confidence started to increase. Plans were started for what would happen after it was over. In the summer of 1943, Senator Arthur Vandenberg opened an important meeting of Republican party leaders on Mackinac Island.

214

The purpose of the meeting was to decide if the Republicans would help form a United Nations organization. Once Senator Vandenberg was very much against United States involvement in events overseas. The attack at Pearl Harbor changed his mind. He realized that in a time of long-range airplanes, the country was not safe from enemy attack and the best solution was to stop trouble before it got out-of-hand. However, there were many Republicans who did not see things that way.

After much argument, the Republicans decided they would support the formation of the United Nations. Arthur Vandenberg promoted the idea that both political parties needed to work together on foreign policy. After the war, he was a leader in forming the United Nations.

Senator Vandenberg getting ready to board an airplane in Grand Rapids. (Courtesy Grand Rapids Public Library-Michigan Room)

Peace Returns

By 1945 the fighting around the world was coming to a close. The first new car the nation had seen in three years rolled off the Ford assembly line in July 1945. Germany and then Japan surrendered. Hundreds of thousands of people jammed the streets of every Michigan city to celebrate when they heard the war was over.

People everywhere wanted to begin living normal lives once more. They were ready to get married, start families, and buy all of the things they couldn't while the war was on. The demand for new cars was tremendous. It was the beginning of a long boom in Michigan's economy which lasted for nearly 20 years.

What Are the Facts?

1. What was the nickname given to Michigan during World War II? What was the reason for the nickname?
2. Name four important war-related products made in Michigan during World War II.
3. What sort of things did people in the Upper Peninsula make or produce to help with the war effort?
4. What war work was done at Willow Run?
5. Use examples from this section to explain how World War II gave women and minorities a chance to show what they could do.

Use a map today!
On a world map, draw a route which women flyers could use to deliver B-24 bombers from Willow Run to England. Along the way make refueling stops at Quebec City, Gander Newfoundland, and Reykjavik Iceland.

Digging Deeper
What is the connection between building carriages in Michigan in the 1890s and building of bombers here during World War II?

Evaluate the United States involvement in WWII in light of core democratic values and the resulting costs and benefits viewed from different perspectives.

KEY ❁ DATES

1929	One of every six U.S. jobs related to car production
1930	Frank Murphy elected mayor of Detroit
1932	43% of Michigan workers unemployed
	(March) 3,000 unemployed lead a hunger march to Ford's Dearborn plant
1933	Governor closes Michigan banks for a time
	CCC starts
1934	State sales tax starts as source of revenue
1935	WPA program begins
1936	Frank Murphy elected governor
	(Sept.) UAW-CIO union organized
	(Dec.) Sit-down strike at Flint GM plant
1937	Joe Louis wins heavy-weight boxing championship
1939	Germany invades Poland. World War II begins
1940	Germany attacks France
1941	Michigan factories make war goods. Chrysler delivers first tank
	U.S. bases at Pearl Harbor bombed by Japan
1942	(Sept.) First B-24 made at Willow Run
1943	Riot in Detroit
1945	Senator Arthur H. Vandenberg signs UN Charter
	(August) World War II ends

Consider the Big Picture

The nation started to have major economic troubles in 1929. Many businesses closed and people lost their jobs. Things got worse when banks failed and people lost their savings too.

Businesses pushed their workers hard in a struggle to keep going. This led to strong labor unions and several strikes.

World War II began suddenly for the United States, but soon Michigan was making record amounts of equipment and supplies. So much was made here we got the nickname "Arsenal of Democracy."

Women joined the work force in record numbers during the war. They also helped by flying planes from the factories to the front lines.

Building Your Michigan Word Power

Number a sheet of paper from 1 to 5 and beside each number unscramble the Michigan related words or phrases from this chapter.

     1. rcosnevaiont vliaciin spcor,   2. resiodepns treag,   3. nunio,
             4. modcreacy alarsen fo,   5. dertiona

Talking About It

Get together in a small group and talk about-

Compare and contrast the problems companies had to cut costs and keep businesses going with the problems workers had with speed ups, lower wages, and lay offs.

Would it be better or worse for Michigan if the state's business was not tied so closely with making cars?

Put yourself in the shoes of a state police officer talking to someone who has found a Japanese balloon bomb in Michigan. What would you tell that person? Is it ever right for the government to mislead people or cover up an event like this?

Put It To Use

In World War II many items were rationed so there would be plenty for military use. Make a list of things which might be rationed if there were a long war today.

Suppose you want to form a union at a place where you work. Do some research on unions and how they start. What will you need to do in your situation? What do you think will be the reaction of your co-workers? What problems will you wish to solve with your employer?

15

On the Way to Today's Michigan

Chapter 15 Section 1

Colleges, Homes & Highways• 1945-1950s

After the war, the return of a large number of people from the military affected Michigan. Colleges grew rapidly. There were many new homes built in the suburbs. Then came shopping malls, interstate highways, and a really long bridge.....

Coming Home !

Over 600,000 Michigan servicemen and women were scattered all around the world when World War II ended. As they saw the smoking ruins of war torn Europe or Asia, they wondered what they would do when they got back home. What jobs did they want? Would there even be any jobs to have? Should they start college? Could they find a place to live or would they need to stay with their parents?

With so many young people returning to the United States, the federal government worked hard to have a smooth change to peacetime. Congress passed the law known as the *G.I. Bill of Rights. It gave helpful benefits to veterans— those who had been in the military. The bill included money to go to college, loans to buy homes, and even start businesses.*

Students rushed to study at Michigan's colleges and universities. Take Michigan State College as an example. When the war began, there were 6,356 students. In 1946- 8,500 veterans swamped the college and 9,000 more enrolled the next year. The college scurried to find classrooms and housing.

Dewey for President

The 1948 national election was an exciting time for many Michigan college students and others. That was the first time many veterans had the chance to vote for president. They had a special interest in the 1948 election because the Republican nominee was Thomas E. Dewey. Dewey grew up in Owosso, Michigan and was a graduate of the University of Michigan. Later, Dewey moved to New York state and had twice been elected governor there. Almost everyone thought Dewey would beat President Harry Truman. But Truman surprised many and was reelected.

Thomas Dewey- the man from Owosso who ran for president against Harry Truman in 1948. (Courtesy Bentley Historical Library, University of Michigan)

Soapy Williams

In 1948 Michigan was a strong Republican state and had been so for nearly 90 years. People said Democrats were as rare in Michigan as alligators. In spite of that, a young lawyer named G. Mennen Williams ran for governor as a Democrat. Labor unions supported Williams and he won the election.

Hesper Jackson stands on the left as he talks with Governor G. Mennen Williams. (Courtesy Michigan State Archives)

Williams ran for and won the position of governor six times. That is more times than any other person has been elected governor in Michigan. A later governor, William Milliken, actually held the office for more years because he had four-year terms instead of the two-year terms Williams had.

Governor Williams began a trend toward the control of Michigan's government by the Democratic party. Democrats continue to be an important force in Michigan politics today.

A Nobel Prize Winner

The division of Palestine to form the new state of Israel was a big event in the postwar news. This led to the first tough problem handled by the United Nations.

Michigan-born Ralph Bunche (bunch) was a member of the UN team sent to that area. He helped solve the difficulties between the Arab and Jewish people. As settlements were being worked out in 1948, one of the team members was assassinated. Bunche then became the leading negotiator. For his work with that problem, he was awarded the Nobel Peace Prize in 1950. Bunche was the first African American to receive that award and to hold a top job at the U.S. State Department. The grandson of an American slave, Ralph Bunche was born in Detroit.

Ralph Bunche- Nobel peace prize winner. (Courtesy Bentley Historical Library, University of Michigan)

Growth of the Suburbs

After the war ended, there was a rush to get married and start families. Next, the young couples wanted to find places of their own and they built thousands of new homes.

Most new homes were built in the *suburbs* around the larger cities. *A suburb is a smaller community at the edge of a larger city.* The demand for new houses away from downtown was caused partly by the location of new factories which were also in the suburbs. Between 1947 and 1955, Ford, Chrysler, and General Motors built 20 new factories in the Detroit area. None were within the city limits.

The whole state was growing during the 1950s. By 1960 the population had jumped by almost 23 percent. This made Michigan the third fastest growing state in the country! Only California and Florida were growing faster at that time.

Building Highways

New homes and businesses fanned out from cities. People had to drive a car to shop, go to church, or get to work. Streets were jammed with cars during rush hours. To try to solve this problem, expressways with several lanes going in each direction were built. In 1950 the first expressway in Detroit was opened. This was the John Lodge.

In 1956 the federal government started a major program to build interstate highways between all large cities. Interstate roads are labeled with the prefix "I."

Michigan's most important interstates are I-94, I-96 and I-75. I-94 goes from Detroit to Chicago. Interstate 96 goes from Detroit to Muskegon.

Interstate 75 is Michigan's main tourist highway. Travelers going north on vacation from the Detroit area can reach the Mackinac Bridge and Sault Ste. Marie using I-75. Michigan now has about 1,240 miles of interstate roadways.

Michigan's Most Important Interstates

Roadblock Between the Peninsulas

Although the new highways were a great improvement, motorists still needed a solution for the roadblock they found at the Straits of Mackinac. There was no way to drive from one side to the other. Nearly five miles of water lay in their path. A bridge was needed, but such a long bridge seemed a fantasy.

Today Michigan's two peninsulas *are* connected by the mighty Mackinac Bridge. The bridge crosses the point where the great inland seas of Lake Huron and Lake Michigan meet. It is hard for people to think of such a bridge as an extremely risky idea. Could such a long bridge be built? Would the rock under the water hold up the bridge? How could the costs be paid? Those were big questions which had to be answered. Besides, since 1923 the state of Michigan had operated five ferries which carried cars across the Straits of Mackinac. Wasn't that good enough?

There were, however, several problems with the ferry system. It took about an hour to get a car on board and across the Straits. That was when there was no waiting. Each year during deer hunting season long lines formed in Mackinaw City. So many hunters wanted to go to the Upper Peninsula that lines could be 20 miles long and it might take 24 hours before drivers could get across!

Bridge Ideas Take Shape

After years of waiting, things began to come together in 1953. The Korean War was over and material needed for such a large construction project would soon be available. Bonds would be sold to big banks and insurance companies to pay for the project. They would get interest payments paid from the money charged to cross the bridge. Building the bridge would not cost the state government any money except for upkeep and repairs.

Before the Mackinac Bridge was built at the Straits of Mackinac, there were some terrific traffic tie-ups. (Courtesy Michigan State Archives)

Dr. David Steinman (STINE man) designed the bridge. He was an expert in understanding how wind affects bridges. *The main part of the bridge was going to be held, or suspended, from two heavy cables; so it was called a suspension bridge.* One of Dr. Steinman's ideas was to leave the inside two lanes unpaved. Those lanes would only be covered with a metal grate. Cars could still drive over them, but the wind could pass through the openings and keep the bridge from swaying.

Over 2,000 construction workers moved to the Straits and began the huge project in 1954. Much of the work was quite dangerous. Most of the men worked while hanging from the two main cables high above the water. During the time the bridge was being built, five workers were killed in accidents. The Mackinac Bridge opened November 1, 1957.

Nearly 2 million cars and trucks cross the bridge each year! The bridge has made it much easier for people and products to reach one peninsula from the other.

The Mackinac Bridge under construction on a winter day. (Courtesy Grand Rapids Public Library- Michigan Room)

What Are the Facts?

1. What was the name of the man born in Owosso who ran for President in 1948? Did most people think he had a good chance to win the election?
2. Who has been elected governor of Michigan the most times?
3. Who was the first African American to win a Nobel Peace Prize? What outstanding work did that person do to win the prize?
4. How did people travel between Michigan's two peninsulas before the Mackinac Bridge was finished? What problems did that method have?

Use a Map Today!
Using a road map of Michigan, find and list all of the interstate highways. Are there patterns in the numbering system? Why are some numbers even and others odd?

Chapter 15 Section 2

New Directions and New Stresses-

African Americans struggled for equal rights. Michigan military men and women went to Vietnam while others worked in the space program- astronauts from Michigan!

Changes Come Quickly

There have always been times of change, but in the 1960s changes seemed to come faster and to be more radical. It was a time of major shake-ups in society. Ethnic minorities and women fought for their *civil rights. Civil rights are the rights to be given fair and equal treatment no matter who a person is. Society was not allowing everyone to have the core democratic values.* Michigan made a new state constitution in 1961. In the middle of it all was the Vietnam War which often caused a split between older and younger people.

"Mother of the Civil Rights Movement"

From the mid-1950s to the 1960s was an awakening time about equal rights for African Americans. African Americans all over the country had been treated unfairly. Rosa Parks, an African American woman, was coming home from work in Montgomery, Alabama. She got on a city bus and sat down, weary after a long tiring day. When white riders boarded the bus, the driver told her to leave her seat and stand in the back. She wouldn't do it and she was arrested for her refusal. Rosa Parks' action earned her the title of "Mother of the Civil Rights Movement" because she was one of the first women involved in that struggle.

In 1957, less than two years after the bus incident, Rosa Parks moved to Detroit. Her friends and relatives were worried about her safety if she stayed in Montgomery. Rosa has remained in Detroit, and a street has been named in her honor.

Rosa Parks. (Art by George Rasmussen)

Malcolm X

Different African American people had different ideas about how to change things. Many felt nonviolent protests were the best way, but others believed that anything should be used if it got the job done. Malcolm Little, who had changed his name to Malcolm X, fit into the second group. He believed in militant methods. He grew up in Lansing, Michigan. During his years in Lansing his family was treated badly by some white people. They even burned his family's home. Malcolm X became a leader in the Black Muslim movement but in 1965 he was shot and killed.

Dr. Martin Luther King Visits Michigan

1963 was an exciting year for Detroiters when Dr. King came to lead a civil rights march. On June 23rd he joined about 125,000 people to walk down Woodward Avenue. This was the largest civil rights march in the nation up to that time. At the end of the march he made a speech saying, "Now is the time to lift our nation from the quicksands of racial injustice.... Now is the time to get rid of segregation and discrimination." Two months later Dr. King was in Washington D.C. leading an even larger march and making his world-famous "I Have a Dream" speech.

It Started with a Raid- the Riot of 1967

In Detroit African Americans and whites were trying to work together, but there were many problems. Even so, Detroit was thought to be a good city. Then on Saturday night July 23, 1967 police raided a crowded illegal bar in an African American neighborhood. A large crowd gathered outside while police waited to take everyone away. As the last police car left, the crowd threw bottles and bricks. A riot had begun!

Soon thousands of people took to the streets. Many broke into stores and stole. The looters were both African American and white. Rioters were setting fires throughout the city; then snipers shot at firemen as they tried to put

224

them out. Nine days later the situation finally quieted down. Forty-three people had been killed, 700 injured and 7,000 arrested. Some entire city blocks had been burned as a result of the 1,680 fires which were set.

These burned-out buildings are silent reminders of the violence and destruction from the 1967 riot in Detroit. (Courtesy Michigan State Archives)

Success from Songs

In spite of the problems in Detroit, it was the birthplace of Motown Industries, one of the most successful African American businesses in the United States. Motown is a contraction of the words "motor town," a nickname for Detroit. Motown was begun as a record company by Berry Gordy in 1959.

Good things started to happen for Motown with the release of Smokey Robinson's 1960 gold record, "Shop Around." Other top songs included "I Heard It Through the Grape Vine" by Marvin Gaye. The business started by Gordy grew and soon had annual sales of $50 million.

Some of the top Motown talent included Stevie Wonder and the Supremes (Diana Ross, Mary Wilson, & Florence Ballard).

Not all famous Detroit singers worked with Motown. Aretha Franklin recorded with Atlantic Records. Some of Aretha's greatest hits were gospel-blues. (Courtesy Metropolitan Detroit Convention & Visitors Bureau)

In 1972 Berry Gordy decided to go into the movie business too. He then moved the Motown operation to Los Angeles. Today the original Motown building is the Motown Historical Museum. It is a showcase for the golden years of music produced in Detroit.

War in Asia—Vietnam

Meanwhile, events in southeast Asia were creeping up on the United States. Eventually 367,000 men and women from Michigan were sent to Vietnam. The fighting there began to affect the state in many ways. Communities were shocked by the deaths of soldiers from their towns— young men and women they had known.

By the late 1960s there was widespread belief that the United States was not handling the war properly. College students were upset at the thought of fighting in a war in which they did not believe. Students at the University of Michigan in Ann Arbor were particularly active against the war.

A Vietnam War protest by students at Michigan State University. (Courtesy Michigan State University Archives and Historical Collections)

Michiganians in the Space Program

In the 1960s Americans were eager to explore outer space. The excitement was no greater anywhere than in Michigan. No spaceships were ever launched here but several Michigan people who were a part of the space program became *astronauts*.

Roger Chaffee from Grand Rapids was one of the first. In 1967 he was one of three astronauts in a test launch when the space capsule suddenly caught fire. Before anyone could help the astronauts, they were killed by the flames! Jack Lousma was another astronaut from Grand Rapids. Lousma spent 60 days aboard the Skylab 2 in 1973.

The city of Jackson has a connection with several astronauts and there is a space museum at Jackson Community College. James McDivitt from Jackson piloted the Gemini spacecraft. Al Worden commanded the 1971 Apollo 15 flight to the moon.

James McDivitt (Courtesy NASA)

Brewster Shaw is from Cass City in the "thumb" area. Shaw flew in the space shuttle *Columbia* in 1983 and commanded the shuttle *Atlantis* in 1985. He helped with design changes for the space shuttle after the explosion of the *Challenger*. Jerry Linenger from Eastpointe spent five months aboard the Russian Mir spacecraft in 1997. Some of this time in space was very tense because the Mir had serious problems while he was there.

Beautiful Buildings Designed in Michigan

Besides those exploring outer space, another Michiganian was becoming famous for his work. A young architect named Minoru Yamasaki (min or oo yam ah sock ee) moved to Michigan in 1945. He worked in Detroit and began to design airy, attractive buildings. Yamasaki's greatest achievement was the design of the World Trade Center in New York City. In 1976, when that building was completed, it was the tallest building in the world! Even though the World Trade Center was destroyed by terrorists on September 11, 2001, Yamasaki left behind a treasure of creative designs in the other buildings he planned.

What Are the Facts?

1. Why is Rosa Parks known as the "Mother of the Civil Rights Movement" ?
2. Who started the Motown Record Company? Name three musicians who recorded with Motown.
3. How many men and women from Michigan served in the Vietnam War? List one way the Vietnam War affected Michigan. (continued...)

4. Name the Michigan astronaut who orbited the moon. Which one was at the first U.S. space walk? Give the name of the Michigan astronaut who died in a practice launch of the Apollo spacecraft.

Express Yourself:
Do some research and list the titles of four popular Motown songs. With each title write a line from the lyrics for that song.

Chapter 15 Section 3

Business Twists & Turns: 1970s, 80s, & 90s

Those were the years when: The Chrysler company almost went broke. Stiff competition from foreign car makers began. Several businesses left Michigan. President Nixon resigned making Gerald Ford from Grand Rapids the nation's first President who was not elected.

Oil Crisis Hits Auto Industry!

In 1973 the Arab oil-producing nations stopped shipments to the U.S. in protest of America's support for Israel. Without Arab oil, gasoline became scarce and expensive. Long lines waited at gas stations for fuel. Suddenly everyone wanted to buy small fuel-efficient cars; and Michigan wasn't making those.

A Michiganian Becomes President

As if enough events weren't taking place, President Nixon was involved with the Watergate scandal and had to resign. This made Vice President Gerald Ford the head of our country in 1974. Ford was the first person from Michigan to be President.

Competition From Imports

Since Michigan's economy was so closely tied with the auto industry, the slowdown in sales hurt our economy. People bought Toyotas from Japan and Volkswagens from Germany. Before the oil crisis, the Japanese only sold 180,000 cars a year in the United States. By 1979 the amount was 10 times greater and still growing.

1980 was a turning point for our car makers. For the first time in 80 years another country made more cars than the United States. Japan became the leader.

In 1980 the three largest U.S. automakers were General Motors, Ford, and Chrysler. That year those three companies lost $4.6 billion. The number of cars and trucks made in Michigan kept falling. In 1976 the state turned out nearly 4 million vehicles; by 1980, however, it was less than 2 million.

Since then the situation has improved, but changes in the auto industry still bring major consequences for the entire state. The lives of thousands of employees and their families are affected by what happens.

Michigan and the World

Foreign companies are having an important impact on Michigan and on the state's future. There are 400 foreign-owned companies in the state. Mazda built a giant plant at Flat Rock. Germany's Daimler auto maker bought Chrysler. Kalamazoo's Upjohn was bought by a Swedish drug company and baby food maker Gerber was purchased by a Swiss firm.

Chrysler is the largest company that has been taken over. Chrysler is among the top three manufacturing companies in Wayne, Oakland and Macomb counties, so this change may have a big impact. Years ago, Chrysler also did much defense work for our government. The largest manufacturing companies in at least five Michigan counties are based in other countries.

These foreign companies provide jobs to over 150,000 Michigan workers. Often you can't tell just by the company's name that it is foreign-owned. Some are Canadian and British. A few are French, but Japan has the most. Is this a concern or do foreign companies provide jobs we would not have otherwise? Companies from other countries may have different ways of doing things. They may not worry about closing factories in Michigan because it is far away from their headquarters.

Industry— An Important Part of the State

Michigan's industry is important and significant. Twelve of the nation's largest companies are based in Michigan and two of them, General Motors and Ford, are considered to be the two largest industrial companies in the United States. The total value of the products produced and services performed places Michigan ninth among all the states. Only eight other states produce more.

25th in the world!

A worldwide comparison of the value of Michigan's products and services ranks it 25th. That means if Michigan were a separate country instead of a state, only 24 countries produce more. Michigan is ranked 4th among all 50 states in exports.

Products exported out of the country are becoming more important to Michigan. We export over $50 billion in goods and services. Nearly half of Michigan's exports go to Canada, our next door neighbor. Mexico and Japan are also big customers.

In the future, even more than in the past, Michigan workers will be affected by events happening far away. Changes in the supply of oil, decisions of foreign companies, new ideas in technology, and even terrorism will be some of the things which control what happens in Michigan. After the attack on America in September of 2001, long lines of trucks waited to cross the Canadian/U.S. border, seriously slowing the supply of imports and exports.

A modern assembly line shows most of the welding work done by robots. (Courtesy Ford Motor Company)

What Are the Facts?

1. Which worldwide event caused a turning point for U.S. auto companies? Why were they affected?
2. Give two examples which show how important the auto industry is to Michigan.
3. How does the value of Michigan's industry and services compare to the value of industry and services from other states and countries?

Use a Map Today!
   Use the internet to find out how many cars are made each year in the United States, Japan, Germany. You may want to find a site with an almanac to help you. To compare these numbers, use a world map and draw a bar as you would find in a bar graph on each country to show its car production.

Digging Deeper:
   Explain how economic connections between Michigan and Canada have changed since 1994. How do these changes affect Michigan's exports and imports?

Chapter 15 Section 4

Michigan- Thinking About the Future

What problems and issues do we face today?
How will Michigan change during your lifetime?
What will concern us in the future?

Issues

What is the most difficult issue our state faces? It is hard to say, but many people will have ideas and here are some to think about.

Education

If you ask the teachers in our public schools, they may say it is funding for education. They may say too many students are leaving traditional public schools. That means much less money for their school budgets.

Why are some students leaving the regular public schools? Believe it or not, it has to do with making schools more competitive. Over the last 50 years the world has opened up to more international trade. Goods can be made anywhere and whoever has the smartest and most productive workforce will have the most jobs.

Often students from other countries who visit our schools say they are much too easy. Politicians know this and they are concerned you are not learning enough to be competitive. Many of them believe schools need to be more like other services in our free market economy. They think competition will improve education. If this is true, two main things are needed:

1.) Schools must be measured to see which ones are best.

2.) Students must be free to change schools and go to the ones they believe are the best.

State and national tests, like the MEAP tests here in Michigan, are used to measure schools. The process of testing is called academic accountability. Testing has put schools under great pressure. Schools can lose their accreditation if their test scores are too low. Under Governor John Engler, control of the Detroit Public Schools was taken away from the elected school board. The governor said the test scores were too low and many students were not graduating.

Some educators say there are problems with so much testing. Testing takes much time. Should the time spent testing be spent learning instead?

231

Are the tested concepts things all students need to know? Are there questions which are easier for students of one race? The test writers will say the tests are very good and give valuable results, but people may disagree.

How do students get more options in education? Michigan changed its laws to allow people to choose which public school to attend. If you live in Farmington, you might go to a school in Farmington Hills or another nearby town.

Another way to have more options is to have new public schools. So, state government passed laws for a new kind of public school. This is the public school academy, usually called a charter school. Michigan's first charter school opened in 1994.

A charter school competes for students with the other public schools. Sometimes charter schools focus on a special subject like music, but most do not. Anyone can go to a charter school if there is not a waiting list. Many charter schools are popular and hard to get into. Why is this?

Charter schools start fresh with a new group of students, teachers, and administrators. They often take a new look at what to teach and how to teach it. Many times these schools are attractive to the parents who are most involved with their children's education and these same students often do better in school because their parents are involved. Thus, better students may move to the charter school.

Some leaders desire even greater competition in education. They want to further increase the role of private and religious schools. They say it is unfair for parents who want to use these schools because those

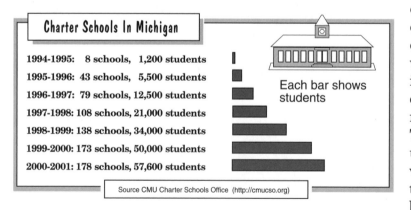

Charter Schools In Michigan

1994-1995: 8 schools, 1,200 students
1995-1996: 43 schools, 5,500 students
1996-1997: 79 schools, 12,500 students
1997-1998: 108 schools, 21,000 students
1998-1999: 138 schools, 34,000 students
1999-2000: 173 schools, 50,000 students
2000-2001: 178 schools, 57,600 students

Each bar shows students

Source CMU Charter Schools Office (http://cmucso.org)

parents must pay BOTH the expensive tuition for the private school and the taxes used to run the public schools. Many parents cannot afford the cost of sending their children to private schools.

To help solve this situation, some politicians and parents support the idea of vouchers. Used in this way, the word voucher means something like a bank check. A voucher is a way to let a family's tax money go to the school they choose. The school may be a private school or a religious school. Can you see any problem with this?

In 1970 Michigan voters amended Article 8 of the state constitution making it illegal to use state money to support nonpublic schools including religious schools. Many people felt using state money for religious schools crossed the line between separation of church and state. This is one reason vouchers are controversial.

6,500

Competition may or may not help you learn more, but it does affect public schools. State government provides over $6,500 for each student going to a public school. If a school loses just 10 students to a charter or private school, there is a big hole in their budget. Cuts must be made and the more cuts made, the less attractive the school becomes. Even more students may decide to go elsewhere. This situation leaves public schools in a tough position. They must improve to keep their students, but often with less money each year!

Another problem at schools– your school– is more violence. Is it because our movies and televisions show more violence? Is it because rap musicians know they can make big money by shocking people and one way to shock is with violent words  in their songs? Is it because some schools are so large students do not know each other? Maybe we have more crime because many people are very self-centered and think little about others. Should each school have metal detectors at the doors? Would school uniforms reduce violence in schools?

School uniforms are a hot topic in schools today. Many students hate them, yet parents, teachers, and administration support them. Why? Adults often see uniforms as a way to promote school safety and decrease discipline problems. For the schools which have uniforms, there are positive effects. Those schools have seen a reduction in violent behavior, vandalism, and possession of weapons. There has been a decrease in student drug use and the elimination of gang clothing. School spirit increases and there can be greater pride in the school's appearance. Schools with uniforms even seem to have higher test scores. Another change is reduced peer pressure to wear the latest fashions.

More school administrators think using uniforms helps students behave better. They can't wear really expensive clothes or shoes which might lead to someone trying to take them. Uniforms may help students be more orderly and to concentrate on learning.

Lots of students think uniforms keep them from expressing themselves. Are you losing some rights by the requirements to wear uniforms? Some parents say they do not want to pay for the cost of the uniforms. So far, most Michigan schools do not require uniforms, but at least one county in Florida requires uniforms for most of its schools!

Jobs

Many factors can affect the number of jobs in a state. First, it needs productive, growing businesses. Next, it needs to offer those things businesses must have to operate well. Some of these things are: trained workers, cooperative government, electric power and transportation.

The first Michiganians survived by hunting and fishing. Finding food was almost a full-time occupation. Then came fur trading. For more than 200 years most Michigan jobs were tied to using nature. Whether it was catching animals for their fur, fishing the Great Lakes, running a pioneer farm, or cutting trees for lumber. Other jobs came from mining copper, iron and other resources from the ground. These jobs all used what nature provided.

The next phase of work in our state was manufacturing. This took a big leap forward in the 1880s and 1890s. At first it was making wood stoves and railroad cars. Next came automobiles. We are now in a new phase which focuses on using information from computers and providing services.

Three Phases of Michigan Business

1. Using what nature provided. trading furs, farming, logging, mining

2. Making products- manufacturing. stoves, cars, medicine, etc.

3. The information age. the internet, computer aided design, etc.

To keep good jobs here, we must offer what businesses need to be successful. Training is important. Michigan will need people trained in computer science and other new fields like biotechnology. The growing use of high technology means a good education is important for a good salary.

Businesses tend to move to places where government works with them. If businesses find state or local government passing laws which make it hard for them, they think about leaving. In the past, business leaders have been critical of some of Michigan's laws.

Some states already have power shortages. Will Michigan be next? Any state without enough electrical power will have trouble keeping businesses and jobs for its people. If we build more power plants, should they use coal as fuel which increases pollution and acid rain? On the other hand, should we have more nuclear power which brings other risks? Michigan has three nuclear power plants, but no new ones have been built since 1986. Even though we have only three nuclear plants, they make over 20 percent of our electricity.

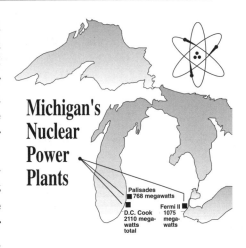

Michigan's Nuclear Power Plants

Palisades
■ 768 megawatts

D.C. Cook
■ 2110 mega-watts total

Fermi II
1075 mega-watts ■

In the past, those interested in protecting the environment were against nuclear power. During the 1980s there were so many protests when a nuclear power plant was being built in Midland, the project was stopped. Now some people think nuclear power might actually be cleaner and more environmentally friendly than power plants burning coal.

Today Michigan businesses are involved with more international trade than ever before. As an example, when a new power plant was built near Zeeland, its generators came from Korea and they were shipped here on a Dutch ship. An office desk made in Michigan may use wood from Brazil and steel from Germany. It then may be exported to Mexico!

International trade has been increasing for some time. After the passage of the North American Free Trade Agreement (NAFTA) in 1994, more Michigan companies have parts made in Canada or Mexico. Truck traffic to Canada has increased considerably. NAFTA allows products made anywhere in North America to be sold in another North American country without special government taxes on the products. In the past, many countries felt it was important to protect their workers by taxing imports.

A number of economists believe free trade without import taxes is better for almost everyone in the long run. This is why the federal government passed NAFTA. But Michigan may lose some jobs where it is not competitive. Can we gain jobs in other areas?

Transportation

Ever since the time of fur trading, transportation has been important to earning a living in the Great Lakes state. Businesses need transportation to move their supplies and products. As our cities spread out, more and more people are trying to use the same roads and highways. Will we face transportation problems which get worse each year?

Michigan has over 9,700 miles in its state highway system and many more miles of county and local roads. Michigan has four main interstates which are I-69 (length 210 miles), I-75 (length 395 miles), I-94 (length 275 miles) and I-96 (length 192 miles). Now I-69 and I-94 are called NAFTA highways since they connect Canadian border crossings and are used by many trucks carrying products in both directions.

If you have been traveling in Michigan, you may wonder where all of the cars and trucks come from. It is not just your imagination, there are lots of people on the roads. One reason is more people now live farther from work. Some of your teachers may drive 20 or 30 miles each day. More products are shipped by truck. Between 1984 and 1999 travel has increased by 41 percent. Some of our highways have tremendous traffic. Parts of I-75 in Detroit average over 190,000 vehicles each day! Overcrowding on our highways leads to "road rage". The number of traffic crashes and accidents has increased steadily.

Some of our major highways were started in the 1950s and 1960s, so many need repairs now. It is very expensive to build new highways and to keep the ones we have repaired. The Michigan Department of Transportation (MDOT) is in charge of much of this work. It is not unusual for the department to spend over one billion dollars a year doing this work. Most of the cost of maintaining the roads comes from the state and federal gas taxes.

Traffic Crashes in Michigan

Source: Michigan Department of Transportation @ www.mdot.state.mi.us/planning/facts.htm

To keep all of these cars and trucks moving, we use a huge amount of fuel– over 5.6 billion gallons a year in Michigan! Any fuel shortage can affect our transportation system.

In the future it may happen that fewer people will need to use the highways. They may use a computer in their home and not travel to an office. Twenty years from now it may be far more important to have high-speed internet access than a good highway. Instead of postal trucks bringing large catalogs to your home, you may view them on the internet!

236

The Environment- Our Great Lakes

If you ask those especially interested in the environment, they may say they are concerned about drilling oil and gas wells in the Great Lakes. They may also mention the possibility of Great Lakes water being sold or drained away to be used in other parts of the country. Maybe the invasion of plants or animals from other places into the Great Lakes worries them. Zebra mussels have traveled to the Great Lakes from the water in the ballast tanks of foreign ships. They have caused a number of problems already.

When you glance at a globe you can see much of our world is covered with water. But when you stand at the edge of one of the Great Lakes, you are looking at some special water. This is fresh water which we can drink and use for irrigation, not the salt water of the ocean which cannot be used for those things. The Great Lakes, which Michigan shares with other states and with Canada, is the world's largest source of fresh water– over 4,400 cubic miles of fresh water!

Should water from the Great Lakes be sold to other states or countries?

If your family is one of Michigan's more than 830,200 boat owners, you have probably noticed something alarming. The water level of the Great Lakes has fallen about 40 inches in recent years! Of course water levels in any lake change with the seasons, but the Great Lakes appear to be in a down trend. The level may fall as much as six feet in the next 160 years.

The Great Lakes still hold lots of water and some people want to share it. In 1998 a Canadian company received a permit to take 2.6 million gallons a day from Lake Superior and ship it to Asia. It would be sold as fancy bottled water. Enough political leaders raised an outcry and the plan was stopped. But another company has a permit to take water from an Alaskan lake for the same purpose. Is there a difference?

Under the NAFTA treaty, natural resources can be sold to anyone in the world without restrictions. Great Lakes water might be considered to fall under these rules. If it does, what will happen? Certainly it will be hard to control how much leaves the Great Lakes!

Parts of the United States are in real need of water for their cities and for their farms. What if those places build pipelines to take water from the Great Lakes? The water will be put to good use, so are people in the Great

Lakes region just being selfish if they try to stop the water from being taken away? We do live in a free market economy. Do people in other states complain when we buy their coal?

The Great Lakes are also in danger from new creatures brought here by ships. Most scientists believe this is how the sea lamprey, zebra mussel and round goby fish from the Black Sea all found their way into the Great Lakes. These creatures may have attached themselves to the bottoms of ships or been in their ballast water. Ballast water is used to help balance the ship when cargo is loaded or unloaded. For example, a ship entering Lake Superior for a load of iron ore may

sea lamprey

dump a large volume of ballast water just before loading the iron. In 2001 the Michigan legislature passed a law requiring ship owners to give the state copies of their ballast water practices. However, the law does not do much to punish those who are not up to standard or those who forget to provide the information.

New creatures introduced in the Lakes are always a danger because they may have explosive growth if there are no predators. Their presence may also threaten the existence of fish who are naturally found in the Great Lakes.

Another potential threat to the Lakes is drilling for any oil that might

be underneath them. Some people think modern oil drilling is safe enough so no major spill could take place. The drilling will be done at least 1,500 feet from the water's edge, but it still can mean pipelines, pumps and storage tanks along the shoreline. There are already seven wells working in Bay and Manistee counties this way. Some have been in operation as long as 20 years, but do you think tourists will like more?

What Are the Facts?

1. The MEAP tests are used to evaluate schools and to try to bring which economic concept into the education system?

2. If a politician talks about being against using vouchers in education, what does he or she mean?

3. How many nuclear power plants does our state have and what percentage of our electricity do they make?

4. How does the NAFTA treaty affect Michigan jobs and how might it affect the Great Lakes water?

5. Use the internet to find the current budget for the Michigan Department of Transportation.

6. Name three creatures which have come to the Great Lakes in or on ships from other places. Do our current laws severely punish ship owners who bring in new creatures?

Express Yourself!

You have the opportunity to talk to a Michigan legislator who is in favor of selling water from the Great Lakes to be used in other states or countries. Write five questions you want to ask this legislator.

Digging Deeper:

If your school decides to require students to wear uniforms, which core democratic values might you have to give up?

KEY ❀ DATES

1947	First commercial TV broadcast at WWJ in Detroit
1948	Thomas Dewey runs for U.S. President
	G. Mennen Williams elected governor. Served six terms
1950	Ralph Bunche wins Nobel prize
1954	Nation's first shopping mall at Northland starts a national trend
1955	Rosa Park arrested over right to a bus seat in Alabama
1956	State begins building interstate highways
1957	Mackinac Bridge opens in November
1963	Voters approve a new state constitution
	Dr. King leads 125,000 people in Detroit march
1965	President Johnson orders U.S. combat troops to South Vietnam
	James McDivitt is first Michiganian in space
1973	Arab countries cut off oil to U.S.
1974	Auto production slump
1977	Renaissance Center is built in Detroit
1980	Japan makes more cars than U.S. for first time
1993	Coleman Young retires after being mayor of Detroit for 20 years
1994	North American Free Trade Agreement (NAFTA)- trade with Canada grows
1995	Last copper mine in Michigan closes, over 1,000 people lose jobs
1997	New Museum of African-American History opens in Detroit
1998	Chrysler bought by Daimler company of Germany
1999	General Motors begins move of headquarters to Renaissance Center
2000	Comerica Park opens- new home for Detroit Tigers team
	General Motors announces the phase out of Oldsmobile- started in 1899
2001	Detroit celebrates its 300th birthday!
	Detroit Metro Airport's 2 million square foot Midfield terminal opens
2002	Ford Field football stadium opens for the Detroit Lions

Consider the Big Picture

Once World War II ended in 1945, Michigan grew quickly. We had many new highways and people moved to the suburbs. There were new jobs in factories making products which had not been available for several years.

The Mackinac Bridge was finished in 1957. For the first time people could drive directly between Michigan's two peninsulas.

There were new stresses and changes in the 1960s. African Americans pushed for their civil rights. College students protested the war in Vietnam.

Michigan's key business, the auto industry, faced big problems in the 1970s and 1980s. It is still very important, but not quite as much as before.

Today Michigan has much more international business. There are more exports and imports. The NAFTA treaty and modern communications are two reasons for this. In recent years some major Michigan businesses were bought by foreign companies.

Many changes are taking place in education as political leaders try to introduce competition among our schools.

The Great Lakes are the world's largest single supply of fresh water. How can we best protect them for future generations?

Talking About It   Get together in a small group and talk about-

Does it do much good for groups to start a riot as happened in Detroit in 1967? Does this ever help their cause? What are the results of a riot for a city and its people?

What actions can Michigan's government take to help keep and bring new jobs to the state?

How would a long term shortage of gasoline affect Michigan?

Put It To Use

Make a time line about an aspect of Michigan's recent history. Some ideas are: the development of the Motown music industry, Michiganians as astronauts, civil rights milestones as they relate to Michigan, changes in Michigan highways and transportation, developments in the car industry, etc.

Here are the meanings of words which relate to Michigan history. These words and terms are *italicized* in the text. Knowing these words will help you understand what you are reading. Some words may have other meanings, but the meanings given here are those used in this book.

A.D.- The Latin words anno Domini which mean "year of our Lord." This is the time period we are living in now. It is measured in years from Christ's birth. The year 1999 is 1,999 years after Christ's birth.

abolitionists- (AB oh LISH un ists) people who wanted to abolish or end slavery.

acid rain- weak sulfuric acid formed by rain. This acid is made when traces of sulfur are burned in coal and oil. Acid rain injuries young fish and can damage trees and plants.

acre- (Aker) a measure of land which is a square about 209 feet on each side.

ague- (AY g'you) a disease caused by parasites in the blood which people got from mosquito bites. A type of malaria.

Anishinabe- (ah nish in A bey*) an Ojibwa word meaning first man or original man. * There are several ways to say Native American words. Some people drop vowel sounds at the beginning of words. Here the last "a" is said very long. This is our best understanding of the pronunciation from *A Dictionary of the Ojibway Language* by Frederic Baraga. Baraga spent many years living and working with Native Americans.

archaeologist- (ar key AL uh jist) a scientist who studies about past human life using bones, pottery, fossils, and other clues.

Arsenal of Democracy- (ARS en al) name given to Michigan because it was among the top states in making equipment such as airplanes and tanks for World War II.

assembly line- a system used in factories where the work travels to the worker and each worker does only a small step before it goes on to the next person. This makes assembly quite fast and cuts costs.

astronauts- (AS tro not) those who fly in spacecraft and explore outer space.

base line- an imaginary line going east and west across the Lower Peninsula used to layout the townships in Michigan.

brine- underground water which has much salt along with other dissolved chemicals. The water can be evaporated and the salt used. Sometimes the other chemicals are valuable too.

bulk cargoes- freight or goods which can be poured loose into a ship's hold like wheat, iron ore, or limestone. Great Lakes freighters are specially designed for this kind of freight.

canal- (KAN al) man-made river used for small boats.

cavalry- (KAV al ree) the part of the army which rides on horseback.

cholera- (KOL er a) an often fatal disease which causes a rapid loss of body fluids.

civil rights- (SIV el) the basic rights people have so that each person is treated equally and fairly, no matter who they are.

civil service- a system which hires government workers based on ability and testing.

Civil War- a war between two or more parts of the same country. The United States had a civil war between the northern states which were against slavery and the southern states which were for slavery between 1861 and 1865. The war started when the southern states tried to leave and form their own country.

Civilian Conservation Corps (CCC)- (corps sounds like KOR) a government-run program during the Great Depression which gave jobs to thousands of unemployed young men. They usually lived in camps and did outdoor work such as building roads or planting trees.

coral- (KORal) the rock-like skeletons of various salt water forms of life which live in large groups.

county- the largest unit of local government within a state. Counties contain cities, villages, and townships. Most counties in Michigan are square boxes as shown on maps.

coureur de bois- (koo ER deh BWAH) illegal fur trader. It means "woods runner".

cutover country- land where the trees had been cut for lumber leaving only stumps, piles of brush, and wood waste behind.

Democratic Party- a political party of the United States which began about 1825. Today this party is usually thought of as being the more liberal party. Their ideas are supposed to help the average person and are often less friendly toward business.

erosion- (ih ROW zhen) the wearing away of soil or rock by wind or water.

ethnic groups- those based on race or place of origin. Each group has similar customs and beliefs. Afro-Americans, Arab Americans, English and Finnish are four examples.

exports- items made or grown in the United States which are taken to other countries to be sold.

G.I. Bill of Rights- G.I. stands for government issue. A law passed near the end of World War II to help former soldiers and sailors with college expenses, starting businesses, and the change to civilian life.

geologist- (jee OL oh jist) a scientist who studies rocks and the formation of the earth.

gill net- a net suspended in the water which allows the heads of fish to pass through, but catches them on their gills as they try to escape.

glacier- (GLAY sher) a very thick ice sheet which slowly covers a wide area of land because more snow falls in the winter than can melt in the summer.

Great Depression- (dee PRESH en) the years from 1929 until about 1939 when there was a great business slowdown; banks closed; companies went out of business, and many people could not get jobs.

griffon- a make-believe animal with the body of a lion and wings of an eagle. A carved griffon was placed on the bow of LaSalle's ship which was named the *Griffon*.

gristmill- a mill for grinding grain into flour. It was usually powered by a waterwheel.

immigrate- (EM eh grate) move into a foreign country to live there.

imports- products from another country which are shipped to the United States and sold.

Jesuits- (JEZH wits) a highly educated Catholic religious group from Europe.

lacrosse- (le KROSS) a French name for the Indian game of baggataway. An outdoor game using a ball and long sticks with small nets at the bottom. Each team has a goal net used for scoring.

latitude- (LAT eh tude) a measurement of the earth going north and south from the equator. The horizontal imaginary lines which run across a map or globe.

lock- part of a canal where the water level can be raised or lowered to move a ship from a higher or lower lake or river.

longitude- (LON ji tude) a measurement of the earth going east and west from a city in England. The lines which run up and down on a map or globe.

lumber barons- those who made much money in the lumber business and owned the land and sawmills, etc.

massacre-(MAS eh kur) a battle where most of those on one side are killed and there is a complete victory for the winner.

Michilimackinac- (MISH ill eh MAC in aw) the general area of the Straits of Mackinac, and the center of the fur trade in the Great Lakes area for many years.

migrate- (MY grate) movement of an entire group of people from one area to another. Usually such moves are caused by disease, a war, changing climate, a lack of food, or other serious problems.

militia- (mel ISH uh) a group of citizens used as a regular military force only in emergencies.

missionary- (MISH eh NAIR ee) person who is sent to preach or teach others about a religion.

Northwest Ordinance- laws passed by Congress in 1787 to govern the Northwest Territory. Included were the necessary requirements to be met before a state could be formed and other laws about education, slavery, and taking land from the Indians.

ordinance- (OR din anse) a law passed by the U. S. Congress under the Articles of Confederation before 1790.

pasty- (PASS tee) a meat pie including potatoes, turnips, and onions. It was considered the box lunch for Cornish miners.

peninsula- usually a large piece of land nearly surrounded by water.

Petoskey stone- (peh TAH ski) Michigan's state stone. It is a fossil of sea coral which goes back to the time the state was covered by an ocean.

portage- an area on a river where canoes or boats must be carried because the way is blocked by shallow water, fast water, or rocks, etc. Or a short distance of land which has to be crossed between two rivers or lakes.

priest- a minister and religious leader in the Roman Catholic Church.

prime meridian- (prime mer ID ee in) an imaginary line running north and south through the Lower Peninsula and Upper Peninsula used to layout the townships in Michigan. In combination with the *base line* it locates any township and its boundaries.

prohibition- (PRO heh bish en) the period of time when it was against the law (prohibited) to make or drink alcoholic beverages.

province- (PROV inss) a unit of government in Canada which is like a state. Canada has 10 provinces.

quadricycle- (KWAD reh si kal) quad means four. The name given to the first cars because they used four bicycle tires and were like bicycles.

Quakers- (KWAKE ers) a religious group against violence and slavery.

Quebec Act- (KAY bek) laws passed in 1774 by the British government in an attempt to keep the French settlers in Canada and Michigan happy. Among other things, it allowed the use of French laws for business and private property matters and allowed Catholics to practice their religion.

ration- (RASH en) in World War II the government limited the amount of food, gasoline, and other things such as shoes which civilians could buy. They did this so the military would have the supplies needed to fight the war.

rebellion- (ri BEL yen) an uprising or armed attack against those in control such as the government, a king, or the military.

Republican Party- (ri PUB li kan) a political party started in 1854 as an anti-slavery party. Today this party is usually less likely to support overspending and is more friendly to businesses. It is often felt to be the more conservative party.

scalp- the top part of the human head which holds the hair. Indians and European warriors cut scalps from an enemy as a token of victory.

sea lamprey- an eel-like animal which feeds off fish by sucking their blood.

secession - (sea SEH shun) the act of one part of a nation leaving the rest to form a new country.

shanty boys- (SHAN tee) nickname for men who cut down trees for a living. These people are also called lumberjacks or loggers.

siege- (SEEJ) A long attack against a fort or city lasting for many days or weeks.

speculation- (SPEK you lay shen) a risky venture of buying something with the idea of selling it when the price goes up.

squatters- (SKWAT ers) people who did not buy the land where they lived. They just moved there and built a home.

St. Lawrence River- (the St. stands for saint which sounds like SAYNT) the river which drains the Great Lakes into the Atlantic Ocean. It goes between the United States and Canada part of the way and then goes north into Canada until it reaches the ocean.

St. Lawrence Seaway- the name for the waterway which is used for shipping between the Atlantic ocean and the Great Lakes. It includes the St. Lawrence River and the Welland Canal.

stock- a special paper which shows part ownership in a company. Stock can be bought and sold on a stock exchange.

suburbs- (SUB erbs) smaller towns close to or touching the edge of a large city.

suffrage- (SUF rij) the right to vote.

surveyor- (ser VAY er) a person using special instruments to find boundary lines for maps.

suspension bridge- (sus PEN shun) a bridge which is held or suspended from heavy cables attached to two or more towers.

tomahawks- small metal hatchets used in fighting, often by Native Americans.

township- land surveyed so that it is in square blocks, six miles on each side. In Michigan, townships are small units of local government like little counties. All land which is not a part of a city is in a township.

treaty- (TREE tee) a formal agreement to settle a conflict.

tribes- groups of related Native Americans similar to small nations. Each tribe has the same customs and beliefs.

Underground Railroad- a system which was created to help slaves escape from the South. It was not underground and not a railroad. It was called underground because it was secret and a railroad because it was a transportation system.

Union- (YOUn yen) the northern states in the Civil War. Michigan, Ohio, Indiana, Pennsylvania, etc. were all Union states. They were called Union because they wanted the country to stay united and not divide into two parts.

unions- (YOUn yens) workers who join together to negotiate as one voice with company owners. Union members usually want higher pay and better working conditions.

uprising- (UP rize ing) an armed attack against those in control. See rebellion.

voyageurs- (VOY uh zhahs) Frenchmen hired by the fur companies to paddle the canoes carrying supplies, furs, and people.

Whig Party- an early political party which faded away after the Republican Party was formed in 1854.

Works Progress Administration (WPA)- a federal organization which created jobs for the unemployed during the Great Depression. It often put people to work doing things they did best such as writing, painting, or building, etc.

zebra mussel- a tiny water animal with a hard tough shell. It creates problems because it multiplies so fast and can completely cover large areas quickly. It can ruin lakes for fish and other water creatures.

If you want to learn more... This is a list of books you can read to learn more about Michigan. There are also other materials available on most of the subjects, but this list contains many of the best. Also read the *Michigan History* magazine by the Michigan Historical Center in Lansing.

Ashlee, Laura R., *Traveling Through Time*, Lansing, MI., Bureau of History, Michigan Department of State, 1991.

Barry, James P., *Old Forts of the Great Lakes: Sentinels in the Wilderness,* Lansing, MI., Thunder Bay Press, 1994.

Blashfield, Jean F., *Awesome Almanac—Michigan*, Walworth, WI., B & B Publishing, 1993.

Cleland, Charles E., *Rites of Conquest—The History and Culture of Michigan's Native Americans*, Ann Arbor, MI., University of Michigan, 1992.

Clifton, James A., *The Potawatomi*, Philadelphia, PA., Chelsea House, 1987.

Ducey, Jean, *Out of This Nettle*, Grand Rapids, MI., Baker Book House, 1983.

Grimm, Joe, *Michigan Voices*, Detroit, MI., Wayne State University, 1987.

Massie, Larry B., *Michigan Memories*, Allegan Forest, MI., The Priscilla Press, 1994.

May, George S. *Michigan: An Illustrated History of the Great Lakes*. North Ridge, CA: Windsor Publications, 1987.

McConnell, David B., *Forging the Peninsulas*, Hillsdale, MI: Hillsdale Educational Publishers, 1989.

Pyle, Susan Newhof, ed. *A Most Superior Land: Life in the Upper Peninsula of Michigan.* Lansing: Two Peninsula Press, 1987.

Sivertson, Howard, *The Illustrated Voyageur*, Mount Horeb, WI., Midwest Traditions, 1994.

Tanner, Helen Hornbeck, *The Ojibwa*, Philadelphia, PA., Chelsea House, 1991.

Thomas, Steven L., *Michigan Government and You*, Hillsdale, MI, Hillsdale Educational Publishers, 1993.

Towle, Wendy, *The Real McCoy*, New York, N.Y., Scholastic, 1993.

Troester, Rosalie Riegle, ed. *Historic Women of Michigan.* Lansing: Michigan Women's Studies Association, 1987.

Vogel, Virgil J. *Indian Names in Michigan.* Ann Arbor: University of Michigan, 1986.

Wakefield, Larry, *Ghost Towns of Michigan*, West Bloomfield, MI, Northmont Publishing, 1994.

Weddon, Willah, *First Ladies of Michigan*, Lansing, MI., NOG Press, 1994.

Weddon, Willah, *Michigan Governors: Their Life Stories*, Lansing, MI., NOG Press, 1994.

Whelan, Gloria, *Night of the Full Moon*, New York, N.Y., Alfred A. Knopf, 1993.

Whelan, Gloria, *Once on This Island*, New York, N.Y., Harper Collins Publishers, 1995.

249